Re-Understanding Media

Re-

Feminist Extensions
of Marshall McLuhan

Edited by Sarah Sharma and Rianka Singh

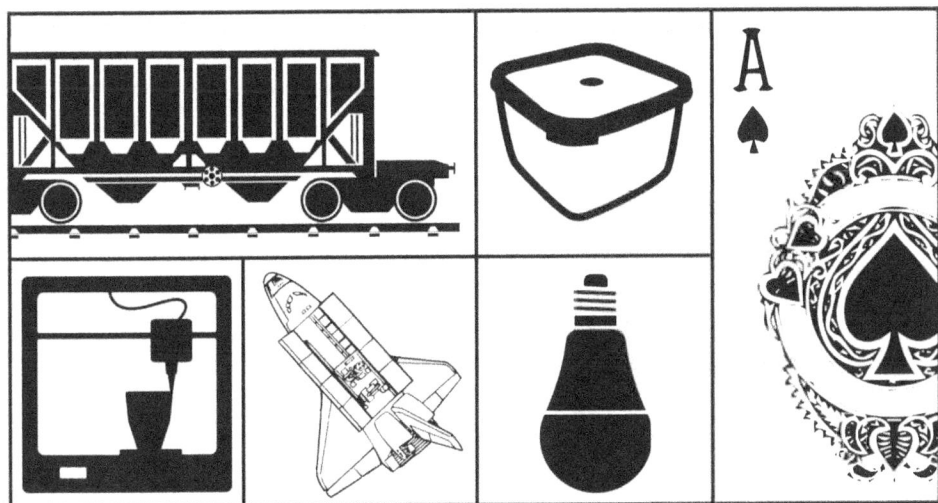

Understanding Media

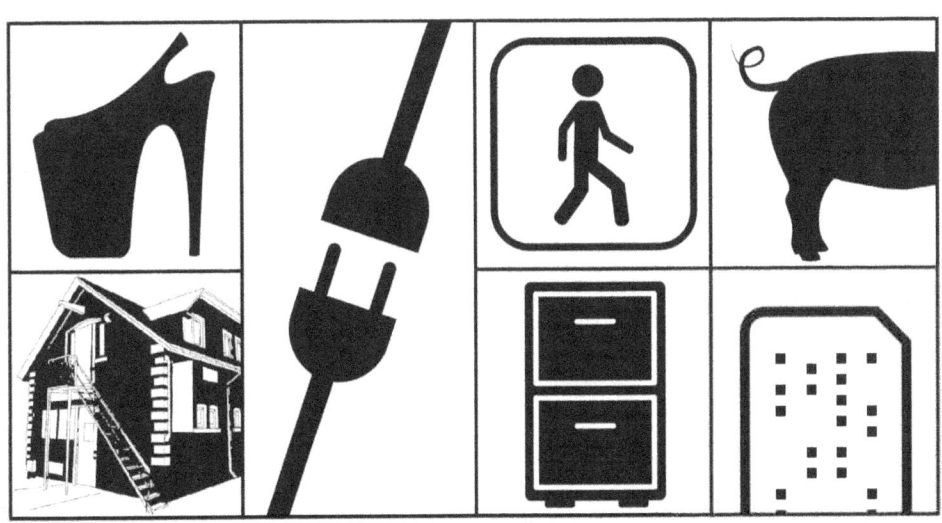

Duke University Press   Durham and London   2022

© 2022 DUKE UNIVERSITY PRESS All rights reserved
Designed by Aimee C. Harrison
Project editor: Annie Lubinsky
Typeset in Warnock Pro and Helvetica Neue LT Std
by Westchester Publishing Services

Library of Congress Cataloging-in-Publication Data
Names: Sharma, Sarah, [date] editor. | Singh, Rianka, [date] editor.
Title: Re-understanding media : feminist extensions of Marshall
McLuhan / Sarah Sharma and Rianka Singh.
Description: Durham : Duke University Press, 2022. | Includes
bibliographical references and index.
Identifiers: LCCN 2021030505 (print) | LCCN 2021030506 (ebook)
ISBN 9781478015253 (hardcover)
ISBN 9781478017875 (paperback)
ISBN 9781478022497 (ebook)
Subjects: LCSH: McLuhan, Marshall, 1911–1980—Criticism and
interpretation. | Feminism and mass media. | Mass media—Social
aspects. | Communication and technology. | Technology and civilization. |
BISAC: SOCIAL SCIENCE / Media Studies | SOCIAL SCIENCE / Feminism &
Feminist Theory
Classification: LCC P96.F46 R486 2022 (print) | LCC P96.F46 (ebook) | DDC
302.23082—dc23/eng/20211105
LC record available at https://lccn.loc.gov/2021030505
LC ebook record available at https://lccn.loc.gov/2021030506

Cover art: Sketch of the Coach House (bottom left square) by
Jana Jifi.

Contents

Preface: The Centre on the Margins vii
SARAH SHARMA

Acknowledgments xiii

Introduction: A Feminist Medium Is the Message 1
SARAH SHARMA

Part I Retrieving McLuhan's Media

1. Transporting Blackness: Black Materialist Media Theory 23
   ARMOND R. TOWNS

2. Sidewalks of Concrete and Code 36
   SHANNON MATTERN

3. Hardwired 51
   NICHOLAS TAYLOR

4. Textile, the Uneasy Medium 68
   GANAELE LANGLOIS

Part II Thinking with McLuhan: An Invitation

5. Dear Incubator 87
   SARA MARTEL

6. Wifesaver: Tupperware and the Unfortunate Spoils of Containment 98
   BROOKE ERIN DUFFY AND JEREMY PACKER

7. "Will Miss File Misfile?" The Filing Cabinet, Automatic Memory, and Gender 119
   CRAIG ROBERTSON

8. Computers Made of Paper, Genders Made of Cards 142
   CAIT MCKINNEY

9. Sky High: Platforms and the Feminist Politics of Visibility 163
   RIANKA SINGH AND SARAH BANET-WEISER

Part III Media after McLuhan

10 Scanning for Black Data:
A Conversation with Nasma Ahmed and Ladan Siad 179
SARAH SHARMA AND RIANKA SINGH

11 3D Printing and Digital Colonialism:
A Conversation with Morehshin Allahyari 192
SARAH SHARMA AND RIANKA SINGH

12 Toward a Media Theory of the Digital Bundle:
A Conversation with Jennifer Wemigwans 208
SARAH SHARMA

Afterword: After McLuhan 225
WENDY HUI KYONG CHUN

Bibliography 233

Contributors 255

Index 259

Preface | **The Centre on the Margins**

SARAH SHARMA

I'm working in my office, which is a tiny coach house on the margins of the University of Toronto campus. It is Marshall McLuhan's former study, now the McLuhan Centre for Culture and Technology, but established in 1963 for McLuhan as the Centre for Culture and Technology (figure P.1).

It's also the site of his historic Monday Night Seminars, where McLuhan held court for his students, the public, and the occasional interested celebrity. These Monday Night Seminars have been ongoing sporadically under the center's various directorships since McLuhan's time. I hear the doorbell ring, followed by the heavy door bursting open. I've always found it quite telling that the media theorist who imagined that the coming electronic age could give way to a world made up only of centers of power without margins was allotted such a small building on the margins of campus to house his center for media study. Its location is also indicative of the marginal status of media studies as an academic discipline during McLuhan's time. In response to the doorbell, I call out an apprehensive "hello" while running down a staircase so narrow that only one body at a time can squeeze through.

There he was again! He was almost always white haired and wide eyed, clutching papers—an essay or an old dissertation, a notepad, and a camera. He would ask me who was in charge of the place. Could he speak to the manager? Could I introduce him to the researchers or the director? Could he walk around and soak up the energy of Marshall McLuhan? He's wondering if maybe he could sit where McLuhan sat for just a little while? He was here to learn about McLuhan. Could I tell him something? He had arrived from down the street, the other side of campus, another town, from the South, and sometimes from across the Atlantic.

P.1 Marshall McLuhan outside the Coach House Institute. Courtesy of Robert Lansdale Photography, University of Toronto Archives.

He would interrupt my classes and meetings. He would appear at the window of the main room with his hands forming goggles over his eyes. He would barge into my lectures asking, "Is there someone here who knows about McLuhan?" Once he walked in and stood in front of me while I was addressing the class and started telling my students he knew McLuhan personally. He would often tell me that McLuhan predicted the digital age. He would tell me how McLuhan's theories are really important because technology today!

I would be polite and nod my head, thanking him for his profound insight. He would write me unsolicited emails and letters and send me copies of his new self-published book, essay, or article typed in Roboto font, and sometimes the audio of a presentation he made on McLuhan. He was entrepreneurial and so had some of his own business cards made—he was also running a center for technology. Where was it? It was online at this address.com. He was running his own McLuhan speaker series. He would ask me for feedback on his writing. Did I have office hours? McLuhan had told him something I should probably know. He was working on algorithms, cell phones, AI, VR, and driverless cars. Did I know that these media are really important and have effects on culture? Did I know that McLuhan predicted these media too?

He was McLuhan's former student, now a McLuhan consultant, and could teach one of my classes if I liked. He'd had the right sort of access to McLuhan that no one else could claim. He would offer unverifiable accounts of what McLuhan was just about to say, before his sudden stroke, regarding the emerging electronic world. He was an appointed McLuhan Fellow from well before my time and could he please get a key to the building. He is a McLuhan interlocutor; here is what he knows. He is McLuhan's Indian guru and therefore we must have a connection too.

McLuhan was his teacher. He was McLuhan's last student. He was McLuhan's very last student. Did I want to know what McLuhan last said to him? In short, this man would walk into the McLuhan Centre searching for evidence of McLuhan and find me instead. The disappointment was palpable, often making its way to his social media tirades about the Centre's new direction and new occupants. I did not have a direct line to McLuhan. If I had not been his apprentice, could not channel his spirit directly, or contact him via Ouija board, what was I doing there? More to the point, what was a feminist technology scholar doing there?

When I was appointed the new director of the McLuhan Centre for Culture and Technology in 2017, the coach house was still infamously known as a clubhouse for McLuhan fans. Like many visitors outside of this orbit, I encountered a difficult space steeped in patriarchal attachment to the great father, replete with essentialist understandings of race and gender along with a disturbing emphasis on global development theories. The Centre also seemed to be plagued by being in constant revival much like its founder. Every few years McLuhan's disciples would predict that he was going to be more important than ever now, again. In an attempt to popularize him, they would elevate his work and legacy while guarding their particular reading of his theories. But fandom, hagiography, endless revivals, and self-serving resuscitations of a revered figure are far from scholarly research and farther still from feminist work.

What I found instead was a space that did not need a revival but rather, a retrieval. Like a hex, I raised a hot pink banner across the coach house for my first year as director (figure P.2). Not only did I want the space to be visible from the street, but I was going to highlight for my first year what I recognized as a possible feminist version of McLuhan's most famous aphorism, that the medium is the message. To me, the crux of his original theory of media and power seemed to be most alive within feminist scholarship on technology. And by critical feminist approaches I mean in particular the work on technology that does not treat difference and identity as if it is an addendum to technology but rather scholarship that understands how technology alters and can determine the social experience of gender, race, sexuality, and other forms of social difference.

Herbert Marshall McLuhan (July 21, 1911–December 31, 1980) was a Canadian English professor and scholar whose musings on the television set and the media theory of Harold Adams Innis propelled him into media study in the 1950s at the University of Toronto. McLuhan's theories of media are understood to be a cornerstone of communications and media

P.2 The coach house dressed in hot pink *MsUnderstanding Media* poster. Photo courtesy Erin MacKeen.

theory, and his works include *The Mechanical Bride* (1951), *The Gutenberg Galaxy* (1962), *Understanding Media* (1964), and *The Medium Is the Massage* (1967). McLuhan is often referred to as the "father of media studies" for turning attention to the medium's message, to the technology, over the content.[1]

Since 2017 I've been paying homage to McLuhan thematically while gathering the critical feminist, race, queer, and Indigenous media scholars, artists, and activists who take up McLuhan's privileging of the medium in novel and politically significant ways. However, they do so without pledging allegiance to its father. And really, they don't need to. Their work shares a common and enduring thread worth highlighting within feminist media studies but also for McLuhan scholars: these thinkers have been doing the critical work of locating how exactly the medium is the message. Their media study shines a light on the ways that inequitable power dynamics are tied to the properties and capacities of technologies that mediate power in social and institutional spaces. Thus, back to our playful themes at the Centre, rather than McLuhan's *Mechanical Bride* we have the *Mechanical Bro*; rather than *Understanding Media*, we can *MsUnderstand Media*, and rather than argue over which medium is hot or cool we might recognize the *HotMessAge* in which we live and think about the technological possibilities for radical and just social change. And rather than pretend we all live in a Global Village, especially during COVID-19 and the antiblack and anti-Indigenous racism that are all plagues to a better social world, we can consider the *The Global SpillAge*. The purpose of the Monday Night Seminar series guided by these plays on McLuhan's key works during my time as director of the McLuhan Centre has been to highlight and elevate the critical voices that had historically been left out of both the building and the discourse. It is also a means to address the common question I'm often confronted with when feminist scholars ask me, "But you don't really like McLuhan, do you?" I am not so much concerned with the man or his legacy as I am with the way in which his media theory has inspired me to think about power and structural differences. Thus the thematics for the Monday Night Seminar programming over the last few years at the McLuhan Centre are meant to turn toward McLuhan, not away from him. They do not seek to repair him. Rather, they are meant to confront the limitations of McLuhan's problematic examples while taking up the broader potential in understanding that the technological is a specific vector of power that demands a feminist understanding. This book gathers a small sample of the scholars that visited and participated at the center's Monday Night Seminar series and other related programming over the last few years. What is collected here is not nearly exhaustive or fully representative of the potential and scope of these conversations, but they speak to some of the conversations that have been taking place in the McLuhan coach house on Monday nights and at the center's other public events since 2017. This book offers a re-understanding of McLuhan's *Understanding Media* for feminist ends. The chapters presented here do so in the hopes of a more critical and engaged approach to McLuhan and *a feminist medium is the message*.

—SARAH SHARMA, director of
the McLuhan Centre for Culture and Technology
January 2021

Notes

1. Marshall McLuhan is often regarded as a central figure within the Toronto School of Communication. This so-called Toronto School includes those theorists at the University of Toronto in the decades from the 1950s to 1980 who focused on the centrality of communications technologies to cultural, social, and institutional change. The Toronto School is often referred to as also including Harold Innis, Edmund Carpenter, Walter Ong, and Eric Havelock. We want to insist here on this page, and along with our other like-minded feminist technology scholars at the University of Toronto, that this Toronto School also includes the first woman professor and, more importantly, feminist in the Department of Metallurgy and Materials Science, Ursula Franklin.

Acknowledgments

We'd like to thank all of those who took up the invitation to explore with us the possibilities for a critical extension of McLuhan's medium is the message at the McLuhan Centre for Culture and Technology between 2016 and 2021: Awo Aboko, Cass Adair, Nasma Ahmed, Mitchell Akiyama, Morehshin Allahyari, Beverly Bain, Anne Balsamo, Sarah Banet-Weiser, Jody Berland, Rena Bivens, Zach Blas, Megan Boler, Alexandra Boutros, Tracey Bowen, Miranda Brady, Jack Bratich, Jayna Brown, Simone Browne, Roberta Buiani, Kenzie Burchell, Nadia Caidi, Terril Calder, Nicole Charles, Florence Chee, Julie Chen, Lily Cho, Wendy Hui Kyong Chun, Nicole Cohen, Beth Coleman, Natalie Coulter, T. L. Cowan, Lauren Cramer, Michael Darroch, Alessandro Delfanti, Greig de Peuter, OmiSoore Dryden, Brooke Erin Duffy, Stefanie Duguay, Zeinab Farkokhi, Emily Flynn-Jones, Yuriko Furuhata, Radhika Gajjala, Gary Genosko, Banu Gokariksel, Baruch Gottlieb, Melissa Gregg, Sarah Hagi, Hazal Halavut, Rachel Hall, Alex Hanna, Cassandra Hartblay, James Hay, Mark Hayward, Alison Hearn, Radha Hegde, Andrew Herman, Garnet Hertz, Faiza Hirji, Mél Hogan, Sun-ha Hong, Ursula Huws, Steven Jackson, Jenna Jacobson, Yasmin Jiwani, Tero Karppi, Patrick Keilty, John H. M. Kelly, Aphra Kerr, Ganaele Langlois, Jessica Lapp, Sophie Lewis, Elisha Lim, Steven Logan, M. E. Luka, Sara Martel, Shannon Mattern, Rhonda McEwen, Karen Dewart McEwen, Cait McKinney, Jaqueline McLeod Rogers, Tara McPherson, Hélène Mialet, Tanner Mirrlees, Michelle Murphy, Lisa Nakamura, Judith Nicholson, David Nieborg, Safiya Noble, Rebecca Noone, Susanna Paasonen, Jeremy Packer, David Parisi, Felan Parker, Barbara Perry, John Durham Peters, Ben Peters, Kamilla Petrick, David Phillips, Whitney Phillips, Praba Pilar, Jennifer Pybus, Scott Richmond, Lilian Radovac, Jas Rault, Carrie Rentschler, Alessandra Renzi, Sarah T. Roberts, Craig Robertson, Shirley Roburn, Chris Russill, Kim Sawchuck, Natasha Dow Schüll, Leslie Regan Shade, Christine Shaw, Ladan Siad, Kumi Silva, Skawennati, Andrea Slane, Avery Slater, Sandy Allaquore

Stone, Joshua Synenko, Victoria Tahmasehi-Birgani, Nicholas Taylor, Phillipe Theophanidis, Elise Thorburn, Lilia Topouzova, Armond Towns, Dori Tunstall, Jennifer Wemigwans, Nick Dyer-Witheford, Bianca Wylie, Liam Cole Young, Geoffrey Winthrop Young, and Jasmine Zine.

At Duke University Press, Elizabeth Ault shepherded this project and gave us latitude in the style and format of chapters so that we could include as many new and emerging experts in and outside of academia as possible. Benjamin Kossak, Annie Lubinsky, and Christopher Robinson were instrumental in the preparation, design, and copyediting of the manuscript. We are also grateful to the anonymous reviewers whose generous and close readings helped us strengthen the book.

Graduate student fellows, faculty, and friends at the McLuhan Centre were pivotal in this book coming together. Thanks to Réka Gál, Grayson Lee, Alex Ross, Lee Wilkins, Stephanie Fisher, Leslie Shade (again), and Erin MacKeen. Sarah would like to thank her trusty writing group in Toronto (Dana Seitler, Tess Takahashi, Selmin Kara) for reading early drafts of the proposal. She also thanks Andrew McLuhan for his friendship and support. Sarah is grateful to her colleagues at the ICCIT and would like to especially acknowledge Anthony Wensley for providing immediate support to her through the ICCIT at the very beginning stages of this project. And finally, Rianka and Sarah would both like to extend the biggest of thanks to Patty Facy for assisting in every facet of this book project from heating the Coach House to keeping all the papers in order.

Introduction

A Feminist Medium Is the Message

SARAH SHARMA

Feminism is not the first thing that springs to mind when considering Marshall McLuhan. The world-renowned Canadian media theorist and so-called father of media studies was not a feminist, and I certainly have no intention of reviving him as one. Nevertheless, I believe that it is necessary to retrieve his work for feminist ends. McLuhan's media theory offers a singular conception of the technological as a structuring form of power—one that offers feminist media studies insight into how a culture's dominant technologies can alter and determine the social experience of race, gender, class, and sexuality. This volume emerges out of a concern for the understandable lack of feminist engagement with McLuhan and the erasure of critical race and feminist media studies perspectives in the scholarly updating of McLuhan for contemporary readers. McLuhan's media theory has much to offer feminist media studies. This is the central claim of this volume. Moreover, the political potential and critical import of McLuhan's media theory depends upon a feminist retrieval. The chapters in this volume consist of a series of original essays, experimental writings, and interviews from emerging and established media studies scholars, artists, activists, and technologists. A key aim of this volume is to employ a feminist approach to

McLuhan's media theory to show how inequitable power dynamics become insinuated as part of the properties and capacities of technologies and machines that mediate power in social and institutional spaces. Together we advance a feminist version of McLuhan's key media studies text, *Understanding Media: The Extensions of Man* (1964) and with it a feminist version of "the medium is the message."[1]

Marshall McLuhan's *Understanding Media* played a significant and highly visible role in developing the academic discipline of media studies—most famously the penchant for understanding the specificity of forms and technologies constituting a twentieth-century electronic culture. McLuhan's well-known dictum that "the medium is the message" paved the way for the academic study of various media such as print, radio, TV, and film. His media theory broadened conceptions of media to include nontraditional media objects such as clothing, clocks, and light bulbs as well as a range of transportation technologies like wheels, bicycles, airplanes, and motorcars. McLuhan shifted the focus from a traditional understanding of media as content delivery method to the formal properties of media/technology. For McLuhan, the message of the medium "is the *change* of pace or scale or pattern that it introduces into human affairs."[2] McLuhan generalized all of human history into three media epochs: oral, print, and electronic. Each media age created a distinct social character or Media Man: tribalized, detribalized, and retribalized. The electronic era would return the phonetic, compartmentalized, linear, fragmented, nationalistic-thinking Print Man to the collaborative, connected, immersive and compassionate tenets of Oral Man. Electric Man would have a new depth of awareness that could catapult him out of the restrictive mental and political confines of print society.

McLuhan's media theory transformed both academic and popular understandings of media. On the scholarly front, McLuhan's theories have continued to be revisited, updated, and applied to new media contexts as well as influencing other strands of media theory internationally, such as German media theory. It was Friedrich Kittler who boldly opened his *Gramophone, Film, Typewriter* stating "media determine our situation" in reference to McLuhan's "medium is the message." His enduring relevance to the contemporary moment is reestablished over and over again.[3] On the popular culture front, he has enjoyed the status of global media studies guru. He is nothing short of a cult figure. After the release of *Understanding Media*, McLuhan was a household name, and the phrase "the medium is the message" became part of popular parlance. Some of his famed appearances include a walk-on speaking role in Woody Allen's *Annie Hall*. He is the subject of a Canadian Heritage Minute, a televisual fictional attempt to capture the moment during his graduate seminar at the University of Toronto which was the first time he realized that the medium was indeed the message. The voice-over relays, "This man changed the way the world thought about communication." McLuhan's Centre for Culture and Technology, housed in an old coach house on the margins of the University of Toronto campus, was established in 1963 and received visits from Yoko Ono, John Lennon, and Canadian Prime Minister Pierre Elliot Trudeau. In the mid-1990s, with the commercialization of the internet, *Wired* magazine anointed McLuhan as their patron saint. On July 21, 2017, on what would have been McLuhan's 106th birthday, Google celebrated McLuhan with his own Google browser doodle. The internet unleashed a torrent of stories about McLuhan as the father of media studies. From the *Hindustan Times* in India to the *Telegraph* in the UK, newspaper stories celebrated the great man who predicted the internet. In June 2018, digital business tycoon Elon Musk tweeted an unattributed author photo of McLuhan without any accompanying text shortly after attaching his Tesla Roadster to his SpaceX Falcon rocket en route to Mars.

The celebration of McLuhan is a difficult one for feminist media studies to contend with. While he ushered in the field of study of media *as* media, his texts are peppered with frequent misogynistic, racist, and nonsensical commentary. His cult status and praise for his scholarly contributions seem too often entangled with those who consider themselves McLuhan experts. His theories are grand and universalizing, referring to epochal shifts in media ages that include a media typology of a singular white male subject. It is well known that McLuhan turned to essentialist and racist categorizations of both African and Indigenous cultures, particularly in describing Western and non-Western literacy.[4] It doesn't help that the scholarly updates of McLuhan for new times occur as if feminist and critical race approaches to technology have never existed. In 2004, Leslie Shade and Barbara Crow argued powerfully that the legacy and scholarship dedicated to McLuhan "does not address, incorporate or attend to gender in its conceptualization nor engage with any of the insights and/or contributions in feminist scholarship on technology."[5] McLuhan's legacy is maintained by a group of global disciples who have taken it upon themselves to declare what McLuhan would say or think today. Anthony Enns argues that the lack of political engagement within McLuhan's work has long been regarded as one of the main reasons his work is rejected and even ridiculed as unserious scholarship.[6] Much of the extension of McLuhan's theories into the digital age interpret his notion that media determine culture as a singular effect upon the same singular universal human subject McLuhan was concerned with. Such a view parallels the dangerous and uncritical view of technology espoused by Elon Musk and is evidenced by the tech-bro culture of Silicon Valley, who remain willfully blind to the realities of the uneven technological futures they are increasingly responsible for.

Feminist Media Theory Is Not a Fan Club

McLuhan's failure to acknowledge the dynamics that bind together bodies, rhythms of life, power relations, and technology should relegate him to the tired domain of great white male legacies. Instead, I have found that his insights inspire a new critical project for feminist media studies. McLuhan himself might not have had his eye on economics, politics, and bodies, but "the medium is the message" is a media theory relevant to feminist and critical approaches. Taking it up as a critical framework is an invitation to more deeply consider social structures and power dynamics that inhere in technology. As Jonathan Sterne has argued about other great male figures within media and communication studies, we can still run with the "the curiosity of scholars" and can do so "without taking their findings as timeless truths."[7] Similarly, John Durham Peters astutely writes, "Just because McLuhan was worried about Dagwoods, effeminate men, and henpecked husbands doesn't mean we need to be. We can take his analysis without taking his attitude."[8] As Janine Marchessault has argued, McLuhan had a quite telling and instructive treatment of gender in *The Mechanical Bride: Folklore of Industrial Man*.[9] For example, Marchessault points out that gender is a significant category in McLuhan's critique of postwar America, but his focus was not just on the objectification of women's bodies in advertisements but on the ways women's bodies were instrumentalized and rationalized to mirror the relationship between finance and engineering.[10] We are also inspired by Anne Balsamo's *Technologies of the Gendered Body*, which takes a cue from McLuhan's focus on the creative possibilities that come from understanding how new "media work us over" but more specifically how media works upon bodies differently.[11] Balsamo reads in McLuhan "a submerged discourse of gender that continues to organize and make intelligible the discourses of the body in late capitalism."[12] Or we can do as Armond Towns does and take his media theory on directly, turning the analysis back on his own texts. Towns argues that McLuhan's treatment of Black people in his media theory is an indication of the white supremacist view of Black people as a medium and ultimate extension of white Western man.[13] The contributors to this volume confront McLuhan's treatment of gender, race, sexuality, and class directly in order to unravel the medium-specific logics, or what we could call the *techno-logics* that produce and maintain social differences.

It is important to note here that the question of McLuhan's gender politics is often addressed in one of three ways. One response is to dismiss him as antifeminist and refuse to read or engage him. A second is to let him off the hook for being a man of his times. How often have feminist scholars had to endure the hideous explanation that racism and sexism were part of the past? Such a view strangely follows the logic of linear history—a view that McLuhan himself would have written off as an excuse that only a Print Man locked in his confining, compartmentalized, and linear mindset of the printed word would espouse.[14] But I digress. There's no Ouija board here to tell us what Marshall McLuhan would say anyway. Nonetheless, a third response to McLuhan and gender locates the role women played in his scholarship. For example, the handwriting of Corinne McLuhan (his wife) has been a subject of intense archival examination.[15] The notes taken by his female assistants have been archived and discussed as the invisible hand of women in his work.[16] His relationships with Jane Jacobs and Jaqueline Tyrwhitt are also offered as an indication that he was sympathetic to women.[17]

While recognizing the earnest efforts of these scholars to find a place for women in his work, *Re-Understanding Media* does not need McLuhan to be a feminist. This book is not concerned with McLuhan and his life and times per se, but rather with his media theory and the possibilities of a feminist "medium is the message." Finding the women in McLuhan's work or listing the women who have written about McLuhan does not indicate feminist engagement. In the former case, it universalizes the category of woman while forgetting that being a woman is not the same as being a feminist. We are not concerned with adding to the hagiography of McLuhan or cleansing his personal reputation. Thus, none of these three responses to gender and McLuhan speaks to this project. Instead we are interested in how his media theory allows for the most critical framework for thinking about technology and power. So even though he did not account for structural differences in his work, he approached technology as a structuring form of power.

When McLuhan's theory is fully engaged, it offers a political understanding of *media beyond content* and of *technology beyond a tool*. To consider the message from a feminist perspective is to consider the multiple relational changes in pace, pattern, and scale a media technology can introduce within a society. A feminist approach to "the medium is the message" rejects the focus on the message as a singular change upon a singular subject and instead locates the multiplicity of unaccounted changes ushered in by the media technology related but not limited to changes in pace, pattern, and scale. This book extends McLuhan into new critical terrain in order to re-understand the forms of subjectivity, social arrangements, rhythms of relations, and specific power dynamics that are entangled, influenced, or even determined by the time-shifting and space-altering logics of a culture's governing technologies and technological systems. This book also extends McLuhan's pivotal broadening of the scope of which technologies are understood to be media.

In *Understanding Media*, McLuhan famously turned to the light bulb to introduce his overall media theory. The message of the light bulb was the radical social and economic transformation that ensued when the definitional and experiential boundaries of day and night shifted, with newly light-filled rooms. But to extend this theory into gender and labor studies, one can consider how the light bulb shifted the gendered labor of the day and ushered in a new politics of night replete with new subaltern publics, transgressive politics, and different modes of policing. The light bulb also made possible the second shift or double day that second-wave feminists have illuminated in their own work.[18] The new social patterns and the structure of social differences that emerged were inexorable to the light bulb. In this example of the light bulb, we might begin to see the political potential of this media theory as pointing media scholars to the media logics at play in forms of systemic inequality and structural difference. McLuhan's media theory insists on both the ontological and epistemological power of media. Through McLuhan we can understand how the medium sets the parameters and possibilities for not only communicative action but political and social change. These chapters reveal the differential techno-logics of power tied to a wide range of media objects by extending a feminist "medium is the message." To understand our environment, we must extend our conception of what is included when we talk about media. Further to this, media like railroads, sidewalks, computer cords, textiles, incubators, Tupperware, filing cabinets, index cards, platform shoes, black data, and 3D printers cannot be properly understood as media without a feminist analysis.

To take up McLuhan's media theory within the purview of feminist media studies—a critical approach to media study oriented to issues of gender, race, sexuality, and social justice—means that one must consider how the terrain of struggle in question is technologically produced. Thus, McLuhan's understanding of technology as a form of power is an understanding of media that precludes questions about representation, ideology, policy, and even political economy. In other words, it is necessary to consider the precise technological conditions of possibility that can have a determining effect and are tied to the terrain of struggle.[19] McLuhan's understanding of technology as a form of power raises new questions about representation, ideology, policy, and even political economy, whether he addressed them directly or not. Feminist and critical race scholars have long been doing the work of examining exactly how the medium is the message—by locating specifically how, where, and to what extent (a) different technologies alter the tempo, scale, and rhythms of life in differential ways for different populations while also paying specific attention to (b) how patriarchy, racism, and other violent forms of power are extended through technology and (c) how technologies extend people's ability to resist patriarchy and racism. But I would add a very crucial caveat here. McLuhan's media theory can add an additional layer to these critical approaches because his theory allows us to consider the technological while still being medium specific and context specific. Work addressing the question about what a medium affords in terms of difference or how inequities are baked into various media technologies is already doing this to a certain extent.[20] This represents some of the most critical work in the field. But we must still address the fact that technologies cannot be understood outside race, class, gender, and sexuality. And we may want to spend some more time on what the notion of baking may foreclose in terms of thinking about techno-logics. Moreover, we must accept that race, class, gender, and sexuality cannot be understood outside of their intersection with the technological. And we must be careful that turning to baking as a metaphor does not then translate into an understanding of difference in terms of singular identity categories accidentally treated as separate ingredients. McLuhan's media theory allows us to avoid this potential misstep. By providing a feminist refocusing of McLuhan, this project gathers the force of feminist materialist perspectives in order to provide a more detailed consideration of how the technological is an important dimension of intersectional experience.[21] We incorporate McLuhan into the project of feminist media studies in order to inspire further thinking and urge scholars to take on the necessary task of locating the medium-specific techno-logics of how power operates in culture.

A Feminist Medium Is the Message

It may seem an odd starting point, but I begin both my graduate and undergraduate feminist technology courses by explaining the relationship between technology and power through the work of Canadian media theorists Harold Adams Innis and Marshall McLuhan. In *The Bias of Communication*, Innis connected the rise and fall of empires to the properties of a given culture's dominating media forms.[22] An empire needed to be able to extend its power across vast distances (space) and also endure over history (time). The crux of Innis's media theory is that power is derived not from the content of the medium but from a technology's space- or time-binding capabilities. While Innis compared stone, clay, and tablets (time-binding) to the properties of parchment and paper (space-binding), the contemporary digital context brings us tweets, webpages, blogs, YouTube channels, Reddit, and 4chan. What we learn from Innis, McLuhan, and other scholars within the so-called Toronto School of Communication, is that our governing technologies portend a techno-logic.[23] The way power works, the shape it takes, will be very specifically tied to the medium in question. Part of our critical work as media scholars, then, is to locate these techno-logics in order to reveal how power is working on bodies, genders, classes, races, and populations to produce difference and inequality. This means paying attention to a relationship between technology and difference where technology is not just a tool wielded by different people differently or where technology is an addendum to a particular identity. It means we must also consider how the technological is a mode of power within systems of social struggle. For example, we must ask how technologies produce race.[24] McLuhan's theories of media challenge the dominant cultural understanding of technologies as tools whose effects depend upon their use. In fact, that technologies are even imagined as tools (neutral in and of themselves) that depend on policy changes, shared forms of control, or perceived as in need of more diverse representation in their development is part of today's dominant techno-logic. What gets built and designed is determined by the requirements of patriarchy, capitalism, and white supremacy. Technologies are understood to be powerful materials designed and harnessed to alter the social world. Technologies can determine the social order in unanticipated ways—in particular, they change social conceptions of time, space, and distance and more fundamentally what it means to be human and in relation to one another.

Many feminist technology scholars have already argued that within a patriarchal society, technologies function to extend patriarchy.[25] In more radical traditions of feminist thought, technology is understood as inherently patriarchal.[26] The connections between misogyny, imperialism, and the technological power grab is not a hard one to make. A cultural history of fathers and their dominance over the television remote control has already been written.[27] More recently, smart home technologies appear at the forefront of domestic abuse cases as the new weapons of gendered domination and control.[28] This includes not only tracking a partner's movements through home surveillance technologies but also controlling environmental conditions against the other's will (heating, lighting, and lock mechanisms). Even a cursory glance at contemporary tech industry culture, often labeled tech-bro culture, yields similar results.[29] In the summer of 2017, former Google employee James Damore made headlines when his company-wide Google Diversity Memo leaked.[30] In it, he argued that biological differences between men and women make diversity-based hiring in the tech sector problematic. Damore was concerned that equal representation was going to be bad for Google's business and the future of software engineering in general.

Media trolls and peons who have become pundits and presidents by virtue of Wi-Fi clearly recognize something about the techno-logics of power and the imperial space-binding power of digital technology. We are not suggesting that McLuhan be forgiven for his misogyny and racist formulations. Instead, if we confront it directly, what we find in McLuhan is a significant link that explains how sexism and racism are always tied to the technological. McLuhan was certainly not oriented toward the political project of feminism or critical race theory, and we do not need him to be. Today, like Innis, we must consider the centrality of how media bind time and space and how the logistical capacity of media is manipulated and directed in ways that oppose a more just world. Digital trolls take advantage of this capacity to spread their vitriol fast and far, exerting power not only through ideological and emotional harm, but also through the capacity to overwhelm others' temporal needs and diminishing others' safe space. The 9/11 terrorists understood, for example, the potential media complex of skyscrapers/airplanes/live television.[31] The attack was devised with the spectacular power of live media coverage in mind and specifically timed to hit the two towers so that the second tower would be broadcast live. This is not about media content as primary but rather about media content determined by the temporality of live media. Trolls and terrorists recognize the destructive potential of each medium's different paces, patterns, and scales, amassing technological power in innocuous ways. Like Elon Musk, they appear to have a pretty good handle on "the medium is the message" as a technological strategy to maintain patriarchy, white ethno-nationalism, and the perpetuation of class inequality.

A critical approach to gender and technology demands a feminist retrieval of "the medium is the message" not only to account for the power of technology but also to imagine the possibilities for new techno-logics. This is an understanding of technology that feminist media studies scholars working at the intersection of gender, critical race studies, disability studies, and technology are already bringing to bear.[32] Nevertheless, as it stands, the set of words "gender and technology" usually refers to women in the tech industry or that technology is a tool that is used differently depending upon one's gender. In each case, technology is treated as an external force that needs to be better managed. More specifically, gendered technology is often understood to refer to access to technological resources and capacities that have been described as the gendered digital divide. The internet is imagined to be an emancipatory technology for marginalized populations. It is also common to talk about gendered technologies as representational objects that become gendered by design and marketed. In other words, objects acquire feminized colors or are adapted or, more precisely, maladapted to women's bodies, such as air conditioning, knee replacement surgery, pacemakers, and NASA space suits. But none of this accounts for technology's depth of involvement in the structuring of difference or in the confining category of *woman*. Race and technology, sexuality and technology, and class and technology are treated similarly. Technology is an externality or an addendum within this framework. The problem is that people fail to account for technology as one of the forces that constructs, produces, cultivates, activates, delineates, categorizes, reproduces, maintains, and changes gender and other cultural categories.

While the key aim of this book is to advance a theory of technology and social difference by way of a feminist version of McLuhan's theory, it also serves as a corrective to the way that McLuhan continues to thrive globally at the expense of so much of the important and critical work that takes place within feminist media studies. The recirculation of McLuhan over and over again and the elision of feminist and critical race approaches occurs not just because it's business as usual for patriarchal hagiographies of great academic men. Nor does this happen just because of the systemic and well-documented poor citational practices of male scholars who fail to cite the scholarly work of nonwhite male scholars. The erasure of feminist influences within the uptake of McLuhan is also because of what is always at stake in McLuhan's theory: technology—the imagined guaranteed domain of masculine prowess, ingenuity, and insight.

The chapters that follow take up McLuhan's invitation to locate the technologics that inhere in different media to determine how power operates in culture, but leave behind McLuhan's universalizing and grand narratives. They do not engage in hairsplitting over McLuhan's inaccurate technical detail. Instead we collectively pause on the more significant contribution of McLuhan—one which asked people to think about how technology serves as the bridge between culture and power. He was by no means an expert on hardware, future software, fiber optics, satellites, or the human senses. His grandiosity betrays him in the same way so many men today consider themselves technologists simply because they are online a lot of the time.

This volume showcases some of the contributions of critical race and feminist media theory to McLuhan, sharpening and revealing the political potential of such an approach. At the same time, the book provides a sustained challenge to the continued dominance of masculinist and universalizing media theories. It offers feminist media studies a feminist materialist approach inspired by McLuhan. It offers a way of thinking about the wider technological possibilities of the apps, devices, forms of popular culture, objects, programs, technological systems, and texts that are in question in our work within feminist media studies and explores what it means to give up some sense of agency in the face of technology and the way we theorize it. It works against the masculinist notion that the power to control media is paramount, a position that is replicated within liberal feminist arguments that technology or media platforms should be seized by women or that power will be redistributed by having better representations of women in media content (see chapter 9).

Structure of the Book

PART I

McLuhan's *Understanding Media* begins by outlining his major theoretical interventions and his case for the study of media as an academic discipline. It is also where he provides the most developed explanation of "the medium is the message," which provides the source of inspiration for this collection of feminist retakes, takes, and offerings for further media study. We have organized the chapters of *Re-Understanding Media* into three parts.

Part I of *Re-Understanding Media* brings a critical and feminist approach, along with an analysis of gender, to the media technologies that McLuhan indirectly addressed in his long list of media objects in *Understanding Media*. These included "Wheel, Bicycle and Airplane," "Roads and Paper Routes," "Games: The Extensions of Man," and "Clothing: Our Extended Skin." In part I of *Re-Understanding Media*, instead of wheel, bicycle, and airplane, roads and paper routes, games and clothing, we bring you Armond Towns's "Transporting Blackness: Black Materialist Media Theory" (chapter 1), Shannon Mattern's "Sidewalks of Concrete and Code" (chapter 2), Nick Taylor's "Hardwired" (chapter 3), and Ganaele Langlois's "Textile, the Uneasy Medium" (chapter 4).

Armond Towns's chapter "Transporting Blackness," takes up McLuhan's key insight that transportation technologies are media. While McLuhan was interested in how transportation technologies, such as roads, wheels, and airplanes, moved people and things while also transforming the people and things that are moved, Towns considers what this means in the context of histories of gendered Black mobility, where it is specifically Black women who were seen as things to be moved. Turning to the complex of media within the Underground Railroad where it was not just roads, wheels, and trains but also attics and cargo boxes where Black women were moved, Towns puts McLuhan in conversation with Hortense Spillers, Katherine McKittrick, and other Black feminist theorists in order to address the limitations of McLuhan's media theory of transportation, clarifying that while these transportation systems are media, they are not suddenly neutral in how they move people.

McLuhan's discussion of roads in his chapter "Roads and Paper Routes" is rooted in his interest in technological acceleration and cultural power. McLuhan's theory of roadways hones in on the speed of information. McLuhan's critical argument is that "any new means of moving information will alter any power structure whatever."[33] McLuhan considered roads to be a medium that gave way to newer electrically mediated ways of transmitting information. Shannon Mattern's chapter "Sidewalks of Concrete and Code" starts with McLuhan's tenet that media are responsible for specific changes in the organization of space. But Mattern steps off the road and onto the sidewalk, where she traces the long media history of sidewalks and shows that this liminal and often unassuming space takes on new meaning with the growing dominance of networked, ambient technologies. She points to how sidewalks have always been a site of contestation, marked by unequal gendered and raced power dynamics tied to access, movement, and the right to space.

In Nick Taylor's chapter "Hardwired," he "follows the wires" that materially connect quotidian media devices. Taylor links the management of the wires in gaming consoles to gendered domestic life and the production of new contemporary techno-masculinities. Taylor imagines how McLuhan would write about wires today, given that they are media that "consist of pure energy without any content."[34] While McLuhan did write on games in "Games: The Extension of Man," this predates video games or mediated card games. Nevertheless, McLuhan's argument that "all games are media of interpersonal communication" allows Taylor to consider the media that give way to games and what they communicate about interpersonal gender communication in the home.[35]

Ganaele Langlois's chapter on Shipibo-Conibo textiles offers a new perspective on how Indigenous textiles become media interfaces. Langlois's chapter builds on McLuhan's key chapter, "Clothing: Our Extended Skin," where he outlines an approach to clothing as an extension of skin and media interface. It is in this chapter that McLuhan's tendency toward misogynistic and racist language appears to be tied up in his understanding of how other bodies are interfaces for white male power (see again chapter 1). For example, McLuhan argues that changing American women's fashion is more tactile and invites touching rather than looking before commenting on how "backward people" sense differently than "highly visual industrial societies."[36] In positioning textile as global media, Langlois's chapter offers a feminist and decolonial intervention on McLuhan's media theory of cloth. The chapter focuses specifically on Indigenous Amazon textiles, which, as the chapter shows, are sites of appropriation and exploitation. She argues that textiles are not only an extension of the skin but also extend the environments in which they are produced.

PART II

The second section of the book includes a series of essays by media scholars whom we requested to engage McLuhan in the work they were already doing—seeing in their intriguing scholarship the potential to integrate McLuhan and the politics of gender in new ways. We invited these scholars to reconsider their media and synthesize McLuhan with the gendered technologics these media portend. These chapters address incubators, Tupperware, spindles, filing cabinets, and index cards.

Sara Martel's chapter positions incubators as life-sustaining media technologies (chapter 5). Martel's creative chapter is a love letter to the incubator that kept her son alive when he was born prematurely. In her letter, Martel positions the incubator as her "machinic coparent," showing how the medium reveals reproduction as technological. Martel's letter, along with the corresponding notes that follow, provides a way of reading the incubator through McLuhan's theories of sensorial experience and medium as environment.

In chapter 6, Brooke Erin Duffy and Jeremy Packer's "Wifesaver: Tupperware and the Unfortunate Spoils of Containment," we see a shift from McLuhan's thinking about media as extension to thinking about media of containment. Packer and Duffy show that Tupperware as medium does not only extend "women's capacity to contain or nurture life," but also exists as a containment medium that reifies existing structures of patriarchy and labor. Tupperware as a feminized industry as well as material objects indexes wider binaries that have historically organized food and domestic labor, including hunter/gatherer, commercial/domestic, production/reproduction, and professional/amateur. Duffy and Packer argue that these same binaries have structured traditional understandings of gendered and raced power. Tupperware is therefore cast as a powerful media object that forces us to ask, "Who contains what, and to what ends?"

In chapter 7, "'Will Miss File Misfile?' The Filing Cabinet, Automatic Memory, and Gender," Craig Robertson also addresses media of containment. Robertson shows how the filing cabinet, a critical information technology, articulates early twentieth-century ideas of efficiency and gender. In storing paper, the filing cabinet and the file clerk figure in this chapter as a media complex that simultaneously introduced a new form of containing information and produced new information about how we should regard gender in relation to work. Robertson argues that the medium for filing has an embedded techno-logic of gendered labor.

Cait McKinney's chapter on index cards questions their absence in McLuhan's *Understanding Media*, considering that they were a prominent new medium or "precomputational device" at the time of his writing. Index cards were an important component of the gendered history of early electronic information management. Chapter 8 focuses on the Knitting Needle Computer, a system that semi-automated the encoding and retrieval of information from the 1960s to the 1980s. McKinney argues that this system offered its users an approachable entry into computing by using gendered tools like knitting needles to encourage women to adopt an emerging information technology.

This section closes with Rianka Singh and Sarah Banet-Weiser's "Sky High: Platforms and the Feminist Politics of Visibility" (chapter 9). In this chapter, Singh and Banet-Weiser bring into question the political utility of digital platforms for feminism. They argue that the recent focus on the digital platform and feminism's relationship to it, with the #MeToo movement as the most obvious example, must acknowledge a feminist relationship to the platform which both precludes and extends beyond the digital. The longer history of the platform that emerges in this chapter shows that the relationship between visibility, women, and platforms is much more complicated than current scholarly and popular treatment of digital platforms assume. They argue that while platforms have indeed long made people visible, such visibility has not always been to the benefit of feminist politics. Those who unduly struggle to survive, namely women, Black, queer, poor, and disabled folks, might experience platform-mediated elevation not as empowering but rather as yet another impediment to survival. The chapter takes inspiration from McLuhan's *Understanding Media* playbook and focuses on nontraditional media platforms in order to consider how the platform defines and delimits the possibilities for feminist action.

PART III

Part III consists of critical questions about media that are explicitly tied to digital technologies and exist as post-McLuhan media objects through a feminist lens. These final three chapters are presented as interviews with artists, technologists, and scholars. Each provides insight on media that have come to significantly alter social and political life in the twenty-first century, and that McLuhan could not have addressed in *Understanding Media*.

"Scanning for Black Data" is an interview with community organizers and technologists Nasma Ahmed and Ladan Siad (chapter 10). This conversation with Ahmed and Siad asks us to consider a technological experience of blackness. While neither Ahmed or Siad see McLuhan as a feminist or a critical race scholar, like McLuhan, they assert the utility of a power analysis of technology. Drawing on concepts of refusal and humanness from Sylvia Wynter, Tina Campt, and Arthur Jafa, Ahmed and Siad put them in conversation with McLuhan to examine how Black life is conditioned by technology.

Media artist Morehshin Allahyari introduces a feminist theory of 3D printing in our interview with her (chapter 11). Allahyari traces how she came to use 3D printers in her artistic practice. She explains how her feminist approach to 3D printing counters the initial hype, adoption, and monetization of the technology by realizing the political potential of 3D fabrication. Al-lahyari shows us with her feminist and decolonial perspective that 3D printers do not just reproduce and replicate, but rather offer a point of departure from masculinist approaches to novel technologies.

My interview with Jennifer Wemigwans, "Toward a Media Theory of the Digital Bundle," offers a new perspective on how internet media logics are in tension with Indigenous knowledge protocols (chapter 12). Wemigwans uses McLuhan's theory of electronic media to argue that the internet is not a repository for knowledge but rather a tactile interface that can integrate all of the senses. Rethinking the impetus to decolonize the digital, Wemigwans suggests that we turn our attention to the technical specificities of digital technologies and consider how they intersect with Indigenous knowledge.

Feminist Retrievals for Further Media Study

In the very last pages of McLuhan's *Understanding Media*, he ends with a section on "Further Readings for Media Study." We know that the path he laid out has been well traversed. We also know there is yet another path for media study found within *Understanding Media*, a feminist one. In *Understanding Media*, McLuhan argues, "Man becomes, as it were, the sex organs of the machine world, as the bee of the plant world, enabling it to fecundate and to evolve ever new forms. The machine world reciprocates man's love by expediting his wishes and desires, namely, in providing him with wealth."[37] Flash forward to today and consider this often-repeated statement, which first appeared on the conservative website Breitbart in 2016, by one-time alt-right leader Yiannopoulos: "The rise of feminism has fatally coincided with the rise of video games, internet porn, and, sometime in the near future, sex robots. With all these options available, and the growing perils of real-world relationships, men are simply walking away."[38] This statement is astounding for how it reveals a misogynistic formulation of women as extensions of men, as technological tools there to take care of and reciprocate, in McLuhan's own words, "man's love." McLuhan posits a conception of women as pure information, like the light bulb. Thus, Siri is not a woman but an idea of woman. Feminists concerned with technology might take heed of McLuhan's patriarchal view and also avoid universalizing and fixing the category of woman in critiques of technology and gender. Technologies that are gendered as women are not extensions of women under patriarchy; they are, in fact, extensions of men. This allows us to consider how technologies are tied up with normative conceptions of gender. From such a perspective, we might argue that the toxic culture of Silicon Valley exceeds the issue of representation and inclusion.[39] This is a view that is in fact growing more dominant as the limits of representing and having a representative are harder to ignore. What this moment demands is the exact type of media study that McLuhan suggests. If we are interested in new objects like sex robots, we might treat them like McLuhan's light bulbs and think, along with feminist labor theorists, about the new technology constituting a shift in patterns of labor and types of work, giving rise to new pathologies.[40] There will be new forms of manual labor related to cleaning, housing, and assembling and new cultural anxieties that will demand new types of care labor.[41] This is only just one example for further feminist media study. A feminist approach to "the medium is the message" offers a virtually unlimited amount of politicized media study left to do.

This type of feminist media materialist and medium-centered theory has unexplored implications for thinking about gender and other inequitable social relations of power within not only the tech world but all sorts of institutional spaces. The media and topics examined here are by no means exhaustive—there is plenty more work to do. Rather, they are offered here as a starting point so that feminist media studies can assume its position as taking on, this time with credit, the expansion of "the medium is the message"—out of the hands of the tech-bros and the patriarchal culture they thrive on. To think about the technological as a form of power means also to rethink what might be designed and what sorts of new and better social worlds could be newly determined by feminist techno-logics.

Notes

1. McLuhan, *Understanding Media* (1994).
2. McLuhan, *Understanding Media* (1994), 39.
3. See, for example, Kroker, *Technology and the Canadian Mind*; Levinson, *Digital McLuhan*; Stamps, *Unthinking Modernity*; Theall, *The Virtual Marshall McLuhan*; Cavell, *McLuhan in Space*; Federman and de Kerckhove, *McLuhan for Managers*; Strate and Wachtel, *The Legacy of McLuhan*; Genosko, *Marshall McLuhan*; Hanke, "McLuhan, Virilio and Electric Speed"; Logan, *Understanding New Media*; Peters, "McLuhan's Grammatical Theology"; Peters, *The Marvelous Clouds*; Peters, "Reading over McLuhan's Shoulder"; Buxton and Bardini, "Tracing Innis and McLuhan"; Guins, "Themed Issue"; McLeod Rogers, Whalen, and Taylor, *Finding McLuhan*; Cavell, *Remediating McLuhan*; Krämer, *Medium, Messenger, Transmission*;

McLeod Rogers, "City as Techno-human Sensorium"; McCutcheon, *The Medium Is the Monster*; Berland, "McLuhan and Posthumanism"; Bollmer, *Materialist Media History*; Daub, *What Tech Calls Thinking*; Davis, *How Artifacts Afford*; McLeod Rogers, *McLuhan's Techno-sensorium City*.

4. Sterne, "The Theology of Sound"; Scott, "Critical Approaches to Advertising."
5. Shade and Crow, "Canadian Feminist Perspectives on Digital Technology," 161.
6. Enns, "Review of *Remediating McLuhan*."
7. Sterne, "The Theology of Sound," 207.
8. Peters, "Reading over McLuhan's Shoulder," 296.
9. Marchessault, "Mechanical Brides and Mama's Boys."
10. Marchessault, "Mechanical Brides and Mama's Boys," 57.
11. Balsamo, *Technologies of the Gendered Body*, 172.
12. Balsamo, *Technologies of the Gendered Body*, 29.
13. Towns, "Transporting Blackness"; chapter 1, this volume.
14. McLuhan, *The Gutenberg Galaxy*.
15. Young, "The McLuhan-Innis Field."
16. Young, "The McLuhan-Innis Field."
17. McLeod Rogers, *City as Techno-human Sensorium*; McLeod Rogers, *McLuhan's Techno-sensorium City*.
18. Hochschild, *The Second Shift*.
19. Slack and Wise, *Culture and Technology*.
20. Bivens and Haimson, "Baking Gender into Social Media Design"; Hicks, *Programmed Inequality*; Eubanks, *Automating Inequality*; Noble, *Algorithms of Oppression*; Benjamin, *Captivating Technology*; Brock, *Distributed Blackness*.
21. Crenshaw, "Mapping the Margins"; Noble and Tynes, *The Intersectional Internet*.
22. Innis, *The Bias of Communication*.
23. Jhally, "Communications and the Materialist Conception of History"; Angus, "The Materiality of Expression."
24. Coleman, "Race and/as Technology"; Chun, "Race and/as Technology"; Towns, "Black 'Matter' Lives"; Towns, "Transporting Blackness."
25. Wajcman, *Feminism Confronts Technology*; Oldenzeil, *Making Technology Masculine*; Wajcman, *Technofeminism*.
26. Wajcman, *Feminism Confronts Technology*.
27. Spigel, *Make Room for TV*.
28. Braithwaite, "Smart Home Tech."
29. Quinn, *Crash Override*; Chang, *Brotopia*; Wiener, *Uncanny Valley*.
30. Kate Conger, " Exclusive: Here's The Full 10-Page Anti-Diversity Screed Circulating Internally at Google," *Gizmodo*, August 5, 2017, https://gizmodo.com/exclusive-heres-the-full-10-page-anti-diversity-screed-1797564320.
31. Baudrillard, *The Spirit of Terrorism*; Virilio, *Ground Zero*; Žižek, *Welcome to the Desert of the Real*; Parks, *Rethinking Media Coverage*.

32. Browne, *Dark Matters*; Hall, *The Transparent Traveler*; Keyes, "The Misgendering Machines"; Noble, *Algorithms of Oppression*; Atanasoski and Vora, *Surrogate Humanity*; Benjamin, *Race after Technology*; Costanza-Chock, *Design Justice*.

33. McLuhan, *Understanding Media* (1994), 91.

34. McLuhan, *Understanding Media* (1994), 52.

35. McLuhan, *Understanding Media* (1994), 237.

36. McLuhan, *Understanding Media* (1994), 121.

37. McLuhan, *Understanding Media* (1994), 46.

38. Nolan, "Milo."

39. Ullman, *Life in Code*.

40. Cowan, *More Work for Mother*; Huws, "The Reproduction of Difference"; Gregg, *Counterproductive*; Gregg and Kneese, "Clock."

41. Hobart and Kneese, "Radical Care."

Part I
Retrieving McLuhan's Media

1 Transporting Blackness

Black Materialist Media Theory

ARMOND R. TOWNS

In the late eighteenth century, Great Britain decided to give up on the American Revolution, resigning its colonial hold over what would become the United States. For nearly a decade, the British forces fought against American rebels before defeat in 1783. However, before the British could fully leave, they still owed a favor to a large population of people: the enslaved people who escaped to British lines to fight against the rebels. In exchange for their fight against the rebels, the British promised to ship the enslaved people to freedom, away from the former colonies. Considered traitors by the rebels and Black loyalists by the British, those Black people who made it to British lines would be shipped to Nova Scotia, and their names were imprinted on Brigadier General Samuel Birch's log, famously called the *Book of Negroes*.

The *Book of Negroes* was not just a book about slavery, but also a book about media. Specifically, it was a book that detailed the ways that media transform who and what people are. For example, in the *Book of Negroes*, Black people's relations to transportation technologies (ships, or media) assumed that they did not free themselves, but were freed by the British act of transporting them to Nova Scotia. Indeed, taking an uncritical approach to race, the *Book of Negroes* could be read as marking Black people's transformation from slave to free via the media technologies monopolized by white people. Such an assertion somewhat mirrors remarks made by Canadian media theorist Marshall McLuhan, who argued that transportation technologies not only carried people and things but transformed them as well.[1] For McLuhan, transportation technologies were media because they mediated the traversal of space for people and things, transforming both in the process.

As McLuhan relied on colonial psychology, many argue that his media theory was inseparable from a larger Western racist, sexist project.[2] But in McLuhan's theory there is also the potential to push the discussion of race and gender beyond media representations and into materialist media domains. Thus, McLuhan's theorization of transportation as transformative can be applied to race and gender, though with caution. For example, the Middle Passage not only transported Africans to the Americas but transformed them into enslaved people (Negroes) as well, so much so that, even as the *Book of Negroes* marked the shipment/transformation of slaves into freed people, it could never fully undo that original, transatlantic-slave relationship. Thus, the shipment of Black people to Nova Scotia reinforced an older Western racial logic: white people control Black mobility.[3] Those tasked with shipping Black people to Nova Scotia could not fully imagine Black people outside the confines of slavery, suggesting a limitation to McLuhan's argument that transportation/media always transform people and things. Birch classified the Black loyalists as contradictions: as Negro and free, but only via the mobile and spatial capability of white people.

For Hortense Spillers, the legacy of white people violently kidnapping/moving Africans via ship and classifying them as "Black bodies" laid the foundation for a complex concern—the continual contradiction of Black gender in the West: "[The Africans'] New World, diasporic plight marked a *theft* of the *body*—a *willful* and violent (and unimaginable from this distance) severing of the captive body from its motive will, its active desire. Under these conditions, we lose at least *gender* difference *in the outcome*, and the female body and the male body become a territory of cultural and political maneuver, not at all gender-related, gender-specific."[4] It is in the violence of chattel slavery that the African body does not exist in or for itself, but now for another (the white), now as a Negro, whose Black body has "externally imposed meanings and uses" on it.[5] And one of those imposed meanings was gender.

As noted by the prevalence of the classification "likely girl" and "likely boy" inscribed throughout the *Book of Negroes*, specifically to classify those Black people being shipped to Nova Scotia, Black gender was classified by white authors, no matter if Black people were enslaved or freed.[6] For Spillers, racial slavery ungendered African people, making them commodities before gendered subjects. The ship signified a transformation from diverse, African gendered conceptions of the world to Western, white, binary gendered frames, largely structured around the reproduction (via rape and slave breeding) of more slaves for white, capitalistic profit. Black movement and Black gender were connected: both were deemed under the classificatory control of white people. It is via transportation (the ship, the Middle Passage) that *particular* conceptions of blackness and gender are made and unmade. Because African people were "removed from the indigenous land and culture, and not yet 'American' either," Spillers argues they were "captives, without names that their captors would recognize"; via their transport, "we could say that they were the culturally 'unmade,' thrown in the midst of a figurative darkness that exposed their destines to an unknown course."[7] The medium of the ship plays a central, violent role in the re/un/making of racial blackness.

McLuhan's definition of transportation technologies, as media that transport, translate, and transform people and things, is central to the ways that Black people continually re/un/make ourselves via transport. In short, the names listed in the *Book of Negroes* were classified as contradictorily *freed objects*; yet this classification did not capture the complexity of their movements toward their *own* concepts of freedom, those that General Birch could never understand or give to Black people. Indeed, if we use McLuhan's definition of transportation as media, then we can see that to be transported and transformed did not always require the same concepts of movement as white people or even the use of their technologies to become free. Combining McLuhan and Black feminist studies, we might ask, how have Black people used media to imagine new futures that their white counterparts could not? Many Black people were transported into new modes of liberation, without fully moving and/or by moving in alternative ways that were designed to prevent white people from discovering them. Thus, attics and wooden boxes could be rethought as McLuhan's transportation technologies, in that they played a central role in transporting and transforming some runaway enslaved people in ways that were not meant to be understood by those chasing them. Black feminist studies calls for us to consider how different modes and conceptions of spatial traversal and media transform the confines of blackness and gender altogether. To do so, we must consider that enslaved people understood the importance of ships for their transformation, but also reimagined other ways of moving toward freedom.

I put the work of McLuhan in conversation with Black feminist studies to consider the ways that Black people engage media in alternative fashions, often in the hopes of creating new modes of freedom that challenge the mobile supremacy of Western transportation technologies. In the process, we can think about McLuhan's definition of media (as any extension of the self) in ways that challenge his Western, gendered, and raced view, to point toward Black modes of self-making that are often misunderstood by those attempting to curtail any Black conception of freedom. I proceed by detailing McLuhan's media theory as it relates to transportation, showing its limits and use for thinking about blackness, gender, and technology differently. I then turn to the work of Black feminism to show how Black people have not only theorized space differently but have also used alternative media to traverse it. Specifically, by thinking through escape plans from former slaves like Henry "Box" Brown and Linda Brent, I focus on the ways that Black people during racial slavery rethought both geography and, by extension, media on their way toward liberation. I conclude by considering the centrality of media, such as transportation technologies, toward the production of new spaces and futures.

Transportation Technologies, Media, and Man

McLuhan's discussion of transportation technologies was highly influenced by Harold Innis's theorization of time-biased media and space-biased media. For Innis, time-biased media were media designed to last. Specifically, they were "durable in character, such as parchment, clay, and stone," and they were "suited to the development of architecture and sculpture."[8] By contrast, space-biased media were media designed to traverse distances. They were "light in character, such as papyrus and paper" and "suited to wide areas of administration and trade."[9] The media that Innis described were also representative of the political alteration of experience. For example, a space-biased culture would approach space as routes, roads, and passageways, often toward the materialization of profit, militarization, and administrative control of people at a far distance. Innis argued that roads were markers of imperialism, as they "facilitated administration and invasion" for the Roman Empire.[10] Similarly, the Persian Empire "developed an elaborate administration based on a system of roads and the use of horses to maintain communication by post with the capital."[11] Space-biased cultures sought to monopolize multiple modes of transportation toward their reproduction.

Likewise, for McLuhan, transportation technologies were concerned less with representations or content and more with the alteration of all human faculties. Transportation technologies were metaphors for media; they did not solely transmit information, but also altered the pattern, scale, and pace of life for those transported: "Each form of transport not only carries, but *translates and transforms* the sender, receiver, and the message," ensuring that "the use of any kind of medium or extension of man alters the patterns of interdependence among people, as it alters the ratios among our senses."[12] Rather than the search for a meaning, it is the capacity of new media to transform sender/receiver/message that I want to focus on for this chapter. Indeed, it is from this materialist approach to media that we can think about a Black feminist intervention into media theory, one that connects the Middle Passage (but also Black movement, in general) to the un/re/making of people. Transportation technologies mediate the transformation of some people into commodities and others into humans; but transportation technologies can also mediate Black radical fights against commodification and, by extension, Western humanism.[13]

If we take McLuhan at his word, that each new medium is an extension of man, a Western metaphor for humanness, then we must question if the human that he consistently focused on lay on the bottom of the slave ship or on the ship's deck. Indeed, a central question of media theory should be, who is this *man* and how is *he* transformed via *his* media? Even though McLuhan argued that both people and things were transformed via transportation/media, he was disproportionately more concerned with the humans on the deck of the ship than the *things* in the hull. Maybe McLuhan's examination of ships can give more insight into the human that he took for granted in his theory of transportation technologies as media: "[By 1826] the speedup of industry in England had extended business into the rural areas, dislodging many from the land and increasing the rate of immigration. Sea transport of immigrants became lucrative and encouraged a great speedup of ocean transport. Then the Cunard Line was subsidized by the British government in order to ensure swift contact with the colonies. The railways soon linked into this Cunard service, to convey mail and immigrants inland."[14] Here we see a continual link between McLuhan's thoughts on transportation technologies and Innis's: for a spatially biased culture, transportation over both land and sea is an administrative, imperialistic, and capitalistic concern. However, I want to add what McLuhan does not add: it is transportation, from England to the colonies, that further entrenched the power relations between immigrant and citizen, colonizer and colonized. Put differently, transportation was one important medium productive of raced conceptions of colonizer and colonized to begin with. Relatedly, the ability to colonize some people structured concepts of who was a shipmate and who was cargo, worthy of being chained to the bottom of the ship itself. An unexamined aspect of McLuhan's work on transportation is the transatlantic slave trade, that which Paul Gilroy argued was responsible for the unmaking of Africans via transportation (ships) to remake them as Negroes (raced and gendered bodies) or commodities.[15]

Unmentioned in McLuhan's above quote is that, although it was technically illegal shortly after the turn of the nineteenth century to transport Africans from Africa (which of course did not mean people did not try), the practice of racialized slavery in most Western countries was still in full effect. With or without the massive continuation of slave transportation, the Middle Passage lived in the memories, lives, and bodies of enslaved people and their descendants.[16] If transportation not only carries people and things but also transforms those people and things carried, there may be few examples of the production of racial blackness in the Americas better than the articulation of the social/political/physical violence of racial slavery with ships.[17] Indeed, we see both a Western production of humans (man) and nonhumans, of subjects and objects, of buyers and sellers and bought and sold that is inseparable from the movement of some at the expense of others.[18]

But Black feminist studies also illustrates that racial violence does not foreclose alternative forms of un/re/making. Black people have used ships, trains, boxes, and even attics as media to remake themselves/ourselves. There may be a white control of mobility in some cases, but it never closes new Black futures; blackness always escapes.[19] If transportation technologies are media that transport more than just information, but also transform people and things, then people and things can transport themselves in ways that remain outside the purview of dominant perceptions of what a person or thing is. People and things can create new media—oftentimes not viewed as media at all—toward their own aspirations of liberation. And these new modes of making, unmaking, and remaking are not only geographic concerns (the Middle Passage or fleeing to Nova Scotia), but media concerns as well.

Black Feminist Geographies/Technologies

Throughout her career, Katherine McKittrick has called for an interrogation of new futures, ones that exceed the destruction often associated with Black people via transatlantic slavery.[20] She argues that we must point toward alternative modes of Black living, which are often deemed unrecognizable within academic disciplines like geography; McKittrick has referred to these as "Black geographies," meaning Black women in particular have created spaces, often not deemed spaces in the traditional, dominant (white) geographical study sense. In McKittrick's rethinking of spaces, she suggests that the Western meanings associated with space are far from universal and often brush over alternative Black meanings of geography, new Black self-conceptions, and alternative modes of being. In other words, racial violence is important for white institutions (such as the field of geography), but it never fully forecloses Black women's ability to live and create alternative spaces.

McKittrick's Black geography work points to media concerns. For example, there have long been arguments that the electric telegraph created new conceptions of communication: whereas once communication and transportation were viewed as synonymous, the telegraph led to the idea that physical movement was no longer necessary to communicate at a distance. After the electric telegraph, concepts of communication moved from an engagement in a participatory, highly meaningful, shared connection to a lack of engagement in a nonparticipatory, cold, and mechanical task.[21] McLuhan argued, "It was not until the advent of the telegraph that messages could travel faster than a messenger. Before this, roads and the written word were closely interrelated."[22] More recently, media scholars have pushed back on the presumed complete separation of transportation from communication.[23] For them, the electric telegraph assumed an infrastructure of wires and telephone poles, set up by corporations via the traversal of contested, transforming spaces. In short, the traversal of space remained important, but the true change lay in our conception that no physical movement occurred. Because of the materiality of the infrastructure, so often ignored, Jonathan Sterne contends, not only are distinctions between transportation and communication faulty, but the fields of communication and geography are inseparable.[24] Sterne argues that media theorists "deride transportation as a mere instrumentality," elevating "communication as a constitutive social process," while "geographers have cast the problem the other way around: communication is a mere instrumentality;

transportation and movement are constitutive social processes."[25] Importantly, Sterne argues the truth is somewhere in the middle. Not only can transportation technologies be considered media, but such transportation technologies studied in media theory may also fill in the gap between the broader disciplines of communication and geography. Like McKittrick, Sterne argues that space is full of meaning; however, unlike McKittrick, Sterne's merger of communication with geography is not necessarily raced and gendered.

Building on Black feminist studies, we can consider the ways that alternative media transport and transform Black people outside of dominant norms. In short, I make a small addition to Sterne's argument, one that forces media theory into a conversation with McKittrick and Spillers: communication and (Black) geographies are inseparable. Where much of McLuhan's work (as well as media theory more broadly) examines space, I reposition this work as always about space, race, blackness, and gender, even when race, blackness, and gender are not explicitly mentioned.[26] McLuhan provides the backing for this argument, as he contends that people and things are transformed via the traversal of space; thus, McLuhan's transportation technologies as media can be reconfigured as transformative of some Africans into Negroes. Western transportation technologies were important for the transportation and transformation of a diverse population of people into commodities, bought and sold on the market.

But commodification is not all. To reconfigure communication technology for Black geographies points to the ways that alternative media forms (and their meanings) may go unnoticed by white people who profited off the reduction of the Black body to commodification. Indeed, Black feminist geographies open up new ways of theorizing media in relation to Black modes of survival in the face of racial violence. Put simply, if we rethink Black geographies at the height of racial slavery, then, I argue, we can likewise rethink what media meant for the Black freedom struggle at the same time. For example, Henry "Box" Brown was a former enslaved person who became famous for mailing himself in a box in 1849 from Virginia to Pennsylvania. For Brown, slavery was so bad that he would rather die in a box that was three feet long, two feet eight inches deep, and two feet wide than return to enslavement. Black studies scholars, such as Suzette Spencer, have turned our attention to the ways that Brown's movement "unmoored" him outside of dominant Western, US geographies of pure commodification for a "master"; instead, Brown's articulation of space, as well as his traversal of space via small box, resituated him as a transatlantic Maroon subject, one "whose elliptic movements within and beyond the U.S. nation-state and its laws correlate in many respects with the elliptic currents of resistance employed by African diaspora Maroon groups."[27] For Spencer, Brown's escape could be connected to a larger decolonial project that critiqued differing forms of commodification of all Black and brown bodies.

Brown can be examined via focusing attention on the multiple mediated representations of him, in the form of two slave narratives, several songs, a lithograph, paintings, and multiple illustrations. But media exceeded these depictions as well. Indeed, if we consider transportation technologies as media, as per McLuhan, then even Brown's box was an underthought medium. Brown, who traveled via wagon, railroad, steamboat, and ferry, can be reduced to these specific forms of transport, to these presumably linear, efficient forms of movement. Yet the small box, which may be deemed an irrational, inefficient form of mobility by those on the lookout for runaways, also mediated Brown toward a new conception of emancipation. To be "wrapped with five sturdy lengths of hickory wood, the box," and "marked 'THIS SIDE UP WITH CARE'" meant that Brown did not face the comforts of the wagon, railroad, or ferry, but he did face his own requirement to become something new: he *mimicked* a commodity, quietly shipped via box, to escape his actual commodification.[28] Where transportation can be viewed as a central transformer of Brown into a commodity, the box transformed him into a free person, beyond the racialized commodification placed on him by others.

McKittrick similarly points to another form of media in *Demonic Grounds*, one rarely if ever considered media. In the nineteenth century, Linda Brent sought to escape from her enslavement in North Carolina. Enslaved by Dr. Flint, Brent's life was always already shrouded in the "ideological and legal validation of rape, punishment, and racial-sexual subordination."[29] To be enslaved assumed gender, as Brent was viewed as a "reproductive technology," according to McKittrick, one meant to produce more technologies (slave children) toward enriching the bottom line of the white enslavers.[30] Indeed, the history of slave breeding and white male rape of Black women during chattel slavery is linked to a continual need to make better the lives of white people, providing gender to Black people when it could continually serve white wealth. Alternatively, Brent sought new ways of bettering her own life, which was a direct challenge to the entire institution that made her a Negro woman.

Instead of running away immediately, Brent hid in her grandmother's nine-by-seven-by-three-foot attic for seven years. Borrowing from Brent,

McKittrick reconfigures the attic as the "shape of mystery," or a "mapping of the terror and transparency of slave spaces that incorporates Brent's unique spaces of self-confinement (particularly in the attic), strategy, and critique."[31] The attic was a Black geography, one not deemed as essential to the traversal of space by those in pursuit of Brent. Yet it was still a central mediator between Brent's continued enslavement and her eventual escape to New York. While those seeking to recapture her may have used multiple transportation technologies, failingly, to search for someone who never left, Brent's technology changed her, even if it never fully moved her. For Brent, the attic was no transmitter of neutral information, but it was transformational of who she was; it was a physical embodiment of emancipation. Brent was moved, transformed forever, in ways unimaginable by those pursuing her. For Brent, "disabling, oppressive, dark, and cramped surroundings are more liberatory than moving about under the gaze of Dr. Flint who threatens her 'at every turn,'" and despite the physical pain the garret causes her, Brent "claims that in the garret she is *not* enslaved and that her loophole of retreat is a retreat to emancipation."[32] Brent states "that her emancipation begins in the garret—which she also repeatedly refers to as her dismal cell, her prison, and this dark hole."[33] The attic was transformative; it moved Brent into new self-conceptions for freedom, despite never moving her from the plantation. The attic, then, fit within McLuhan's definition of media, even as it is one that McLuhan may not have ever really cared to pay attention to. Indeed, to create new modes of being while Black has historically called for new mediations that white people (hopefully) ignored.[34]

The attic for Brent and the box for Brown were media, in McLuhan's sense: they were transportation technologies that mediated alternative experiences and movements toward Black freedoms and new self-conceptualizations. This is not to say they were the same forms of media as a railcar or a steamboat for McLuhan; but, like McLuhan's media, the box and the attic were representative of the ways that Black people invented movement as a mediator that unmade their commodification. We may begin to think about the ways that other media, often not considered media, transport and transform people in ways outside of dominant norms. Scholars like Spillers and McKittrick hint at a study of media that I explicate, illustrating that media may be used in ways that challenge dominant raced/gendered concepts of the world. Black feminist studies can be used to illustrate the importance of thinking media, communication, and geographies together.

On the Future/s

When McLuhan declared that transportation technologies, roads, and routes transported more than just messages, he did not consider the violent transportation of my ancestors.[35] McLuhan imagined a world where people and things were transported, but things were not people. Yet there is a large population of people whose capacity to be moved, rather than move themselves, has been "concealed beneath the overwhelming debris of the itemized account."[36] In such a world, transportation technologies, as media, transform people and things, but never in a neutral way, outside power. Combining media theory with Black feminist studies requires rethinking new forms of mobility, forms that Black people have used to remake humanness outside Western frames.

Such remakings of humanness are both geographic and media concerns. For example, in "Mathematics Black Life," McKittrick argues that the *Book of Negroes* can never fully capture the radical alternatives of Black life. In addition to its questioning of gender, the *Book of Negroes* likewise notes that many of the slaves say they were free. Of course, McKittrick argues the use of the word *say* suggests that the Black slaves were lying about whether or not they were actually free. Thus, to lie could be done with the intention of convincing the British that no one was searching for that enslaved person, making their transition to Nova Scotia easier. It is here that McKittrick argues that we must "trust the lies."[37] The archives are full of "truthful lies" that push us toward a place that "honors the ways in which blackness is archived as a violent beginning and, to be sure, does not consider this beginning as inevitably tied to trajectory that leads to something rightful or natural or ethical."[38] Brigadier General Birch could never fully monopolize the classification or transportation of Black people to Nova Scotia, even as he could not fully understand how blackness, gender, and freedom were supposed to go together. In fact, the "lies" and the movements that Black people made suggest that those marked in the *Book of Negroes* were moving in ways that were not meant to be fully understood by white people. White narratives of the enslaved as deceitful were irrelevant. What mattered was the creativity necessary to build a new Black life away from the horrors of commodification. And some of that creativity could involve the creation of alternative movements and media other than the slave catcher's. Today, those alternatives necessarily look different. Whether those movements entail Black Lives Matter Global Network protesters blocking freeway traffic or the efforts of youth climate activists like Isra Hirsi and Greta Thunberg, alternative conceptions of movement and media connect to rethinking and re-creating humanness.[39]

Notes

1. McLuhan, *Understanding Media* (2003), 127.
2. Hochman, *Savage Preservation*; Sharma, "Exit and the Extensions of Man"; Towns, "The (Black) Elephant in the Room."
3. Sharma and Towns, "Ceasing Fire and Seizing Time."
4. Spillers, *Black, White and in Color*, 206 (emphasis added).
5. Spillers, *Black, White and in Color*, 206.
6. Black Loyalist Directory Book 2, n.d., para. 57, http://blackloyalist.com/cdc/documents/official/black_loyalist_directory2.htm.
7. Spillers, *Black, White and in Color*, 214–15.
8. Innis, *Empire and Communications*, 26.
9. Innis, *Empire and Communications*, 26–27.
10. Innis, *The Bias of Communication*, 15.
11. Innis, *The Bias of Communication*, 40.
12. McLuhan, *Understanding Media* (2003), 127, emphasis added.
13. Towns, "The 'Lumpenproletariat's Redemption.'"
14. McLuhan, *Understanding Media* (2003), 143.
15. Gilroy, *The Black Atlantic*.
16. Gilroy, *The Black Atlantic*; Smallwood, *Saltwater Slavery*.
17. Packer, *Mobility without Mayhem*; Gilroy, *The Black Atlantic*.
18. Sheller and Urry, "The New Mobilities Paradigm."
19. Sharma and Towns, "Ceasing Fire and Seizing Time."
20. McKittrick, *Demonic Grounds*; McKittrick, "Freedom Is a Secret"; McKittrick, "Plantation Futures"; McKittrick, "Mathematics Black Life."
21. Carey, *Communication as Culture*, 157.
22. McLuhan, *Understanding Media* (2003), 127.
23. Packer, "Rethinking Dependency"; Peters, "Technology and Ideology"; Sterne, "Transportation and Communication."
24. Parks and Starosielski, *Signal Traffic*; Sterne, "Transportation and Communication."
25. Sterne, "Transportation and Communication," 124.
26. Cavell, "McLuhan and Spatial Communication."
27. Spencer, "Henry Box Brown," 117.
28. Spencer, "Henry Box Brown," 115.
29. McKittrick, *Demonic Grounds*, 39.
30. McKittrick, *Demonic Grounds*, 46.
31. McKittrick, *Demonic Grounds*, 39.
32. McKittrick, *Demonic Grounds*, 41.

33. McKittrick, *Demonic Grounds*, 41.
34. Towns, "Rebels of the Underground."
35. McLuhan, *Understanding Media* (2003).
36. Spillers, *Black, White and in Color*, 210.
37. McKittrick, "Mathematics Black Life," 20.
38. McKittrick, "Mathematics Black Life," 24.
39. Hamilton, "Protesters with Black Lives Matter Shut Down 405 Freeway"; Brady, "Teen Climate Activist Greta Thunberg"; Ettachfini, "Isra Hirsi Is 16."

2 Sidewalks of Concrete and Code

SHANNON MATTERN

When the motorcar was new, it exercised the typical mechanical pressure of explosion and separation of functions. It broke up family life, or so it seemed, in the 1920s. It separated work and domicile, as never before. It exploded each city into a dozen suburbs, and then extended many of the forms of urban life along the highways until the open road seemed to become nonstop cities. It created the asphalt jungles and caused 40,000 square miles of green and pleasant land to be cemented over.... Streets, and even sidewalks, became too intense a scene for the casual interplay of growing up. As the city filled with mobile strangers, even next-door neighbors became strangers. —MARSHALL MCLUHAN, *Understanding Media*

"This is the story of the motorcar," Marshall McLuhan explained in 1964, "and it has not much longer to run." He noted in *Understanding Media* a "growing uneasiness about the degree to which cars have become the real population of our cities, with a resulting loss of human scale, both in power and in distance. The town planners are plotting ways and means to buy back our cities for the pedestrian from the big transportation interests."[1]

The arrival of a new medium was making it possible for those planners to conceive of a new, less auto-centric form of urbanity. Television—that "hot, explosive medium of social communication"—would render meaningless such phrases as "going to work" or "going shopping," McLuhan predicted, because we would soon be able to do these things from our own homes, via video-telephone or two-way TV.[2] Television was collapsing distance in such a way that the car's extension of our corporeal mobility was no longer necessary—or desirable. "The tide of taste and tolerance has turned, since TV," McLuhan explained, "to make the hot-car medium increasingly tiresome. Witness the portent of the crosswalk, where the small child has power to stop a cement truck."[3]

If we update McLuhan's 1964 vision for, say, Toronto of 2030, when networked, ambient technologies will have supplanted the television, that small child most likely needn't even worry about finding a crosswalk. Autonomous vehicles, with their lidar and sonar and multidirectional cameras, will constantly be watching for her approach, ready to stop on a dime.[4] The crosswalk could potentially migrate, too, depending upon traffic patterns, the weather, the day of the week, or the time of day. Those shifting functions could be signaled by colored lights embedded in the pavers and linked to a digital hub that monitors and directs all the city's moving parts.[5] And our small child's caretakers needn't worry about shielding her from the curb, either—because there might not be one. "Shared streets," inspired by the Dutch *woonerf* principle, could call on pedestrians, drivers, cyclists, wheelchair users, skaters, and other moving bodies to share space and negotiate around one another's presence.[6] Technological innovations, like those embedded lights and situationally aware machines, could supply a necessary infrastructure for informal human navigation.

Negotiations of power and privilege, of competing uses and converging subjects, have long distinguished the sidewalk as a species of space (see figure 2.1). Yet we're entering a new era of sidewalk planning, use, and politics. In 2015, Alphabet (née Google) launched its Sidewalk Labs division to reinvent the city—sidewalks included—"from the Internet up."[7] As its name implies, the company claimed the humble sidewalk as its muse, métier, and medium. What pedestrian commitments are implied in such a name? If McLuhan reimagined the sidewalk for a television age, what might it look like in an era of ubiquitous connectivity and artificially intelligent, autonomous agents? How, in these evolving media milieux, does the sidewalk

2.1 Berenice Abbott, photograph of Radio Row, New York, 1936. Wikimedia.

continue to function as a networked medium, in multiple senses of the term: as a border between spatial conditions, as an interstitial site of exchange, even as a generator and harvester of data?

The sidewalk has historically denoted the boundary between private and public realms, between the professional purviews of architecture and urbanism, between biological and mechanical (i.e., pedestrian and vehicular) modes of transit. Its defining liminality is embodied in its distinctive materiality: surfaces and fixtures that separate it from the street, on one side, and the private lawn or commercial facade, on the other. What's more, the sidewalk is, and has been, home to marginal figures and mediated sites: sandwich-board hawkers and sex workers, used magazine vendors and street preachers, homeless encampments and stoop sales, window displays and stock tickers, graffiti and surveillance cameras, newsstands and digital kiosks (see figure 2.2). And today's sidewalk, embedded with sensors, blanketed

2.2 Alexander Alland, peddlers, 1937, Irma and Paul Milstein Division of United States History, Local History and Genealogy, New York Public Library Digital Collections, New York Public Library.

with cellular coverage, and trafficked by networked objects and subjects, has become a platform for data capture—a mediator between individualized actions and aggregated urban flows.

In nearly all of these qualities, the sidewalk embodies concerns that have been central to feminist urban planning for the past five decades. As Delores Hayden noted in 1980, in her germinal "What Would a Nonsexist City Be Like?," we've clung to false distinctions between public and private and between city and suburb, and we've associated those categories with dichotomous genders: male or female.[8] Western planners, designers, and policy makers have privileged home ownership over rentership (and often ignored homelessness altogether), and they've normalized single-family homes rather than cooperative neighborhoods. In so doing, they've essentialized the urban experience of the white male skilled worker. Yet here, by prioritizing mediation, liminality, and marginality—by attending to embodied socio-technical urban experiences, by validating disenfranchised populations and informal laborers—we have already aligned ourselves with feminist principles.

In what follows, we'll examine the history of the sidewalk as a mediator of built space, a social interface, a substrate or conduit for communication, a cultural medium, and a bridge between public and private realms. We'll attend to its role in negotiating gender, racial, and class dynamics, as well as its ability to highlight the importance of maintaining civic infrastructure. We'll then look to the future of the sidewalk in a post-COVID world of autonomous vehicles and smart cities, focusing in particular on how the sidewalk has been branded and instrumentalized by Sidewalk Labs and other technology companies—and how those projects diverge from feminist planning principles. We'll see that, throughout history, this liminal public zone has mediated not only spatial terrains but also the competing values, social dynamics, and communication logics of each age. By engaging with "the multiple uses of a space within a framework that is attentive to difference," Yasminah Beebeejuan suggests, perhaps we can "sustain a fuller sense of gendered rights to everyday life."[9]

Mud, Concrete, and Conviviality

The rudimentary spatial form has been around for quite some time, as Anastasia Loukaitou-Sideris and Renia Ehrenfeucht write in their 2009 book, *Sidewalks*.[10] The first sidewalks reportedly appeared around 2000 BC in central Anatolia, or modern Turkey. Ancient Corinth supposedly had sidewalks, and the Romans their *semita*, or footpaths. Yet in medieval cities and towns, pedestrians "mingled with horses, carts, and wagons."[11] These were among the original "shared streets," an innovation for which we typically credit twentieth-century Dutch traffic engineer Hans Monderman. And all the while, streets and sidewalks served as platforms for public communication: oratory reverberated through streetscapes, and building facades and statuary featured textual inscriptions.[12]

By the mid-eighteenth century, as a flourishing print culture spilled out of cafés and salons onto the sidewalks, some Parisian streets acquired foot pavements and *trottoirs*, and elevated walkways lined many boulevards. A few decades later, when sidewalks were becoming more common in London, a "border territory" emerged "between the footway and the carriageway": the gutter, that quintessential liminal space, became the place for all those who don't belong.[13] And by the early nineteenth century, many large cities, as part of larger public works projects, were paving and legislating sidewalks and occasionally including tax assessments for their provision. Wood and gravel eventually turned into concrete. Sidewalks "had become important elements of the urban infrastructure, and thousands of miles of [them] were paved in American cities."[14] Many urban sidewalks were also papered over with new print forms—newspapers, handbills, posters, and banners—and the infrastructures, like newsstands and hawkers, necessary for their dissemination.[15]

Because street improvements were known to increase property value, in the nineteenth century they were typically paid for by abutting property owners.[16] This is why one would commonly see breaks in the sidewalk along a given block, reflecting crests and troughs of entrepreneurialism (see figure 2.3). Those sidewalks also often served as extensions of commercial space, where grocers could display their produce, peddlers could lay out their wares, and plyers of licentious trades could advertise their services. But even now, when sidewalks are commonly regarded as public works, abutting property owners are still responsible for keeping them clear and in good repair. Some of those owners privatize the sidewalks, restricting particular uses and limiting access to particular people (typically those who can pay). As cities reopened after the COVID-19 lockdown, shops and cafés often annexed their sidewalks in order to adhere to social distancing guidelines. In many cities, sidewalks continue to serve as conduits for vibrant informal economies and cultural networks. In her *Sidewalk City* Annette Kim documents such uses—from street vending to motorcycle parking to improvised play—in Ho Chi Minh City, while Mitchell Duneir describes the social ecology created by sidewalk vendors selling used books and magazines on lower Sixth Avenue in Manhattan.[17] Duneir finds that "the entrepreneurial activities of the sidewalk"—which depend on a network of improvised survival skills—signal "what America has become for many poor people."[18]

Over the past several decades, as we've witnessed more widespread privatization of public space—through profit-driven urban renewal projects and speculative real estate development, for instance—our sidewalks have ever more precariously straddled the public and private. Likewise, "sidewalks are simultaneously public and parochial," Loukaitou-Sideris and Ehrenfeucht argue, "open to all and yet a space of which a group feels ownership."[19] Those social dynamics have shifted over time and varied by location. Sidewalks have mediated between subjects' identities and either

2.3 Eugène Atget, wooden sidewalks, Interborough Rapid Transit (IRT) construction, Twenty-Fifth Street and Fourth Avenue, New York City, 1906, Metropolitan Museum of Art, New York.

reinforced or allowed for challenges to traditional social hierarchies. As Loukaitou-Sideris and Ehrenfeucht describe the nineteenth-century sidewalk: "Acts of deference or domination were negotiated as people passed each other."[20] People of color and low socioeconomic class were expected to step aside, into the gutter, so as to avoid impeding the smooth passage of the elite. Yet the streets were also where the oppressed practiced small acts of resistance or engaged in political demonstrations to demand equality. The sidewalks were sites of contestation and media for resistance.

Meanwhile, nineteenth-century "women who wished to maintain middleclass propriety were relegated to private realms."[21] If they wished to walk the sidewalk, they typically needed an escort. But by the middle of the century, some cities had passed ordinances against sexual harassment (see figure 2.4). Safety and security have, for decades, been prime concerns for feminist urban planners—and today, geographer Ayona Datta works to highlight and mitigate gender-based violence on the streets of the informal settlements in India's "smart cities."[22] Yet sidewalks everywhere are still home to hate crimes and harassment, regardless of how "smart" a city is. What's more, the presence or absence of curb cuts and other accessibility measures, as well as a sidewalk's state of repair, can open up or close off a city to someone in a wheelchair, or a caretaker pushing a stroller, or a homeless person pushing their belongings in a cart.[23] Sidewalk politics are issues of access and equity—and, for those in underresourced areas, they're emblems of environmental justice, too. We witnessed such injustices amid the 2020 pandemic, when quarantined urbanites sought to escape their cramped apartments for a spring stroll, only to find that, in many areas, the sidewalks were too narrow and crowded. Some cities, including New York; Washington, DC; Oakland, California; and Seattle, Washington, temporarily closed miles of vehicular streets to accommodate pedestrians and cyclists. As urban planner Destiny Thomas argues, however, such quick fixes privileged "white comfort," green-(or white-)washed the long and continuing legacy of public streets as sites of Black death, and threatened to "deepen inequity and mistrust in communities that have been disenfranchised and underserved for generations."[24]

Jane Jacobs, writing roughly concurrently with McLuhan and often (yet, some critics charge, not often enough) in response to segregation, discrimination, and racism, regarded streets and sidewalks as "the main public places of a city," its "most vital organs."[25] Their conviviality, she argued, helped to maintain safety and stability—concerns that are particularly salient for women and minorities. Yet the car, rather than becoming "increasingly tiresome," she argued, instead commanded ever more terrain, stretching cities into suburbs and eroding urban public and play spaces. Perhaps then the rise of McLuhan's "hot, explosive" television—and, after it, countless smaller domestic and personal screens—diverted those "eyes on the street" that, according to Jacobs, once helped to "keep the peace" and maintain sidewalk order (an order that has long been gendered and racialized, exacerbating the marginalization of people of color, gender-nonconfirming people, and other noncompliant bodies).[26]

From ancient Anatolia to today, the rise of new media for transportation and communication has transformed how the sidewalk itself has served as a medium: a mediator of built space, a conduit for communication, a platform for economic activity, and a social interface. Appreciating the sidewalk's long media history helps us appreciate how publics are constituted there, how territory is claimed or commons are established, how public identities

2.4 J. Bennett, Broadway from the Bowling Green, 1828, The Miriam and Ira D. Wallach Division of Art, Prints and Photographs: Print Collection, New York Public Library Digital Collections, New York Public Library.

are constructed and interpersonal power dynamics are performed, how social hierarchies are negotiated, and how larger urban policies play out at the microscale, in the realm of the everyday. This history will also help us better understand how Sidewalk Labs has adopted and adapted the pedestrian qualities of its namesake—and how tomorrow's sidewalks will likely take on the datalogical and algorithmic qualities of computational media.

Street Protocols and Profiling

According to Sidewalk Labs CEO Dan Doctoroff, "Sidewalk Labs is a nod to both the rich mix of personal intersections that give great city streets their vitality and also the incredible ability throughout the history of cities to solve local challenges through innovation."[27] In pretty much any present-day Western metropolis, we'll find pedestrians strolling along sidewalks with their gazes fixed on smartphone screens. Sometimes they barely avoid collisions with folks in wheelchairs, dogs on retractable leashes, and seniors pushing assistive walkers and shopping carts, who in turn must navigate around other wheeled sidewalk species: Amazon hand trucks, Citibikes, and rentable electric scooters. This isn't exactly Jane Jacobs's "sidewalk ballet." But Doctoroff sees it as a "rich mix" of living and inanimate things that could be made even richer through the infusion of new sidewalk "innovation."

Sidewalk Labs wants to catalog and map the sidewalk ecology in order to offer cities a means of managing and monetizing this strip of public-private space. As Sidewalk's Willa Ng wrote in a 2016 blog post, a digital sidewalk inventory allows city departments and agencies to share data, facilitating faster planning and more efficient deployment of public services. We can install a new rental bike station without worrying that its placement will interfere with trash pickup or utility work; and we can optimally schedule maintenance and paving projects. We can also allow city residents and visitors to register potholes and sidewalk cracks via a civic app, then track their repair. With an accurate parking inventory, those apps can direct drivers to available parking—and perhaps prompt city officials to change parking rules to respond to evolving street uses.[28]

Yet recent attention has shifted from the sidewalk itself to the curb. Sidewalk Labs recognized that curbs—once merely marginal zones between sidewalks and streets, habitats for liminal urban characters—are "now delivery hot spots, bike-share or scooter parking and ride-hail pickup zones."[29] They're also often a key fixed reference for autonomous vehicles.[30] Even the crusts, the margins, can be capitalized and optimized in an increasingly privatized city. In 2018, Sidewalk Labs launched Coord, a platform for collecting, analyzing, and sharing curb data—bus stops, parking signs, fire hydrants, curb cuts, loading zones—both drawn from city registries (if they have them) and gathered via augmented reality and machine vision (see figure 2.5). Such an inventory, the company says, would allow city agencies, business improvement districts, and engineering firms to coordinate their work and enable cities to "manage curb access like air traffic control," liaising with mobility and logistics companies and orchestrating commercial and passenger pickup and drop-off activity.[31] Again, the COVID-19 pandemic, which dramatically expanded the demand for home deliveries, enhanced the appeal of such logistical oversight.

Cities need to "find new ways for increasing numbers of transportation options to coexist," CEO Stephen Smyth argues, "by better integrating mobility options into existing transit systems and identifying new avenues for revenue."[32] Bob Youakim, CEO of Passport, a Coord competitor, agrees that

2.5 Screenshot of Coord website (https://www.coord.co/).

"coding the curb" makes it possible for the same sidewalk-side terrain to take on a variety of uses at different times of the day and days of the week. For instance, truck loading zones, which are used as such for only part of the day, could possibly be transformed into parking or ride-hail pickup zones at night.[33] In order to "evolve the curb," to maximize and monetize it, cities have to map it, inventory it, disrupt it. Journalist John Lorinc describes how this "most quotidian kind of urban infrastructure," as it is embedded with sensors, monitored by cameras, and positioned within a network of data, becomes a financial instrument, with "its occasional condition of vacancy now assigned a [monetary] value."[34] It's precisely this mode of neoliberal planning that feminist proposals—for collectivism and justice—sought to counter.[35]

In 2017 Sidewalk Labs announced its plans to create a new test bed for urban technologies in Quayside, a waterfront site in Toronto, a city that, according to planning scholar Carolyn Whitzman, has long embraced participatory, feminist planning.[36] Among Sidewalk's core "street design principles" is that of the "dynamic curb"—which is essentially a noncurb (see figure 2.6). In place of the traditional elevated concrete boundary between street and sidewalk, Sidewalk would install "LED-embedded pavement that can—with the flick of a switch—signal a change in the number of lanes, the width of the 'sidewalk,' or even the direction of traffic."[37] Outside of business hours, the "sidewalk" could potentially command the entire street.

The Toronto plan elicited vehement opposition because of the unbalanced terms of the public-private partnership, the opacity of the development process, the lack of clarity over data governance, and suspicion that deeper ambitions of "surveillance capitalism" underlay Sidewalk's palatable

Street Design Principles v.1

These Sidewalk Labs Street Design Principles reflect our belief that cities can leverage new and emerging mobility technologies, such as connected and autonomous vehicles, to make their streets safer, more comfortable, and more efficient — for all modes.

2.6 Screenshot of Sidewalk Labs' Street Design Principles (https://sidewalklabs.com/streetdesign/).

public presentations.[38] Yet there was very little pickets-and-placards-on-the-sidewalk-style protest. The Quayside area's relatively inaccessible location and lack of symbolic sidewalks might have thwarted most attempts at on-the-ground demonstration. Local organizers told me that most dissent was contained within planned panel discussions, public forums, online petitions, *Medium* posts, and newspaper columns.[39] Nevertheless, their opposition efforts, which were led by several vibrant female leaders, ultimately prevailed, and Sidewalk Labs dropped their Quayside plans in May 2020. Many of the sidewalk innovations they proposed for Toronto will undoubtedly be applied in other contexts.

Meanwhile, in New York, where Amazon proposed to build a new campus, activists, union leaders, and lawmakers gathered on the streets to disrupt the company's promises of urban disruption. In early 2019, after facing weeks of sidewalk-level opposition, Amazon pulled out of the deal to build one of its two HQ2 campuses in Long Island City, Queens.[40] Yet it's Amazon who might ultimately realize Sidewalk's dream—of expanding the sidewalk to consume (and optimize and monetize) the entire street. In September 2019, Amazon launched Amazon Sidewalk, a low-bandwidth network connecting internet-of-things devices in and around the home; its "new protocol" for the 900 MHz spectrum, long used by emergency-service radios and pagers, would increase the connection range of smart devices like lights, speakers, doorbells, water sensors, mailbox sensors, and even dog tags "by more than one half mile."[41] Amazon also sees potential to build

Sidewalks of Concrete and Code | 47

neighborhood networks, which might sound like something Jacobs and Whitzman would appreciate. A test group of Amazon employees, friends, and family connected seven hundred Amazon Ring lighting products, and "in just days, these individual network points combined to support a secure low-bandwidth... that covered much of the Los Angeles Basin." That's a wide Sidewalk.

Yet Amazon's Ring products have raised an array of security concerns. The company has partnered with police departments to promote their doorbell security camera. And by flagging every visitor, squirrel, or waving branch as a potential intruder, the system tends to "inflame our great anxieties about crime" and potentially exacerbate racial profiling, among the many historical racial injustices that protesters took to the streets and sidewalks to decry in the #BlackLivesMatter protests of summer 2020.[42] Ubiquitous surveillance merely extends the sidewalk's role as a platform of imminent risk—just as it was when human bodies first encountered powerful new wheeled machines, and as it long has been, and still is, for women and other marginalized pedestrians who are commonly subjected to oppression and abuse. The same data that makes the sidewalk responsive and hospitable and conducive to myriad modes of movement also renders its pedestrians—particularly people of color—trackable and targetable.

"Coding the curb" for optimal monetization further reinforces the notion that the public sidewalk is a platform for private enterprise—a zone where profitability competes with values like accessibility and equity. Rather than "buying back our cities" from big corporate interests, as McLuhan predicted, many municipalities have instead been contracting with big technology companies—Alphabet, Amazon, Microsoft, Palantir—to build core urban systems and oversee development and discipline. In this world, electric scooters and surveillance cameras created more measurable value than street trees and sidewalk ballets. The sidewalk medium has thus come to embody the same neoliberal tensions that plague contemporary data-driven technologies and social media. Online, clicks and likes supplanted democratic engagement; filter bubbles and private groups repressed egalitarian commons. Both our Facebook feeds and our coded sidewalks, like McLuhan's motorcar, exercise "explosion and separation," dividing their "users" into those who can pay for private services and those who can't, those who can slip past the security camera and those who trigger the alarm, those who are favored by the algorithm and those who are penalized, those who can stroll unimpededly and those who are commonly subjected to harassment or arrest.

The Black Lives Matter movement and the COVID-19 pandemic turned a harsh spotlight on these concerns and prompted many urban planners and city leaders to reassess their priorities—to question their exorbitant police budgets and contracts with facial-recognition-based surveillance contractors, to reassess their prioritization of cars and corporations over people. At the same time, other technocrats dug in their heels, convinced that increased technologization and privatization of the urban realm are the solution to inequities in public health, public safety, and other injustices. These debates will play out in city halls, design studios, and tech labs over the next several years. Perhaps the new crosswalk portent in tomorrow's city is not the small child with the power to stop a cement truck, but the sidewalk protester, placard in hand, with the power to stop a tech behemoth, or a militarized police force, from remaking the city in its own optimized image.

Notes

1. McLuhan, *Understanding Media* (1994), 218.
2. McLuhan, *Understanding Media* (1994), 221.
3. McLuhan, *Understanding Media* (1994), 224.
4. See Mattern, "Mapping's Intelligent Agents."
5. Sidewalk Labs, "Street Design Principles v.1."
6. Ben-Joseph, "Changing the Residential Street Scene"; Crawford, "Bringing Up Baby."
7. Doctoroff, "Reimagining Cities from the Internet Up." See also Mattern, "A City Is Not a Computer."
8. Hayden, "What Would a Nonsexist City Be Like?."
9. Beebeejuan, "Gender, Urban Space, and the Right to Everyday Life," 331.
10. Loukaitou-Sideris and Ehrenfeucht, *Sidewalks*.
11. Beebeejuan, "Gender, Urban Space, and the Right to Everyday Life," 331.
12. Mattern, *Code and Clay, Data and Dirt*.
13. Loukaitou-Sideris and Ehrenfeucht, *Sidewalks*, 16.
14. Loukaitou-Sideris and Ehrenfeucht, *Sidewalks*, 17–18. As Clay McShane explains, some communities resisted the paving of their streets, which would turn "their only open social and recreational spaces into arteries for suburban travel" ("Transforming the Use of Urban Space," 290). See also Williams, Historic Pavement.
15. Mattern, "Steel and Ink: The Printed City," in *Code and Clay*, 43–84. See also Henkin, *City Reading*.
16. Loukaitou-Sideris and Ehrenfeucht, *Sidewalks*, 18.
17. Duneir, *Sidewalk*; Kim, *Sidewalk City*.
18. Duneir, *Sidewalk*, 314.

19. Loukaitou-Sideris and Ehrenfeucht, *Sidewalks*, 6.
20. Loukaitou-Sideris and Ehrenfeucht, *Sidewalks*, 86.
21. Loukaitou-Sideris and Ehrenfeucht, *Sidewalks*, 89.
22. Datta, "Gendering the Smart City."
23. Hamraie, *Building Access*; Kin, "NYC Agrees to Make All Sidewalk Curbs."
24. Thomas, "'Safe Streets' Are Not Safe for Black Lives."
25. Jacobs, *The Death and Life of Great American Cities*, 29. See Laurence, *Becoming Jane Jacobs*; and Schrader, "Reading Jane Jacobs in the Era of #BlackLivesMatter."
26. Jacobs, *The Death and Life of Great American Cities*, 54. Mock, "The Toxic Intersection of Racism and Public Space."
27. Quoted in Walker, "The Case against Sidewalks."
28. Ng, "The Importance of Coding the Curb."
29. Smyth, "Open Curbs." See also Barth, "Curb Control."
30. See Fernández-Abascal and Grau, "Learning to Live Together."
31. Coord, https://www.coord.co/. See also Westrope, "Coord Turns Street Photos into Curb Data."
32. Smyth, "Open Curbs." See also Barth, "Curb Control."
33. Kite-Powell, "Are Curbs the Next Frontier in Urban Mobility?" See also Small and Bliss, "The Race to Code the Curb." Coord has a number of competitors or complementary platforms, including Populus, Remix, SharedStreets, and Passport.
34. Lorinc, "A Mess on the Sidewalk."
35. Parker, "Gender, Cities, and Planning," 621.
36. Whitzman, "Taking Back Planning." According to Whitzman, the "Toronto School" of urban planning has been characterized by its commitment to "feminist analysis," participatory research and neighborhood planning, and the "integration of design improvement and community development."
37. Ng, "Four Principles for the Future of City Streets."
38. See #BlockSidewalk, https://www.blocksidewalk.ca/; and Zuboff, *The Age of Surveillance Capitalism*.
39. Shannon Mattern, Twitter, October 27, 2019, https://twitter.com/shannonmattern/status/1188467115478663168.
40. Del Valle, "New Yorkers Condemn Bezos"; Goodman, "Amazon Pulls Out."
41. Amazon Staff, "Introducing Amazon Sidewalk."
42. Guariglia, "Amazon's Ring Is a Perfect Storm of Privacy Threats."

3 **Hardwired**

NICHOLAS TAYLOR

Electricity is everywhere in *Understanding Media*: the world it portrays is one in which the immediacy and connectedness afforded by the speed and spread of electric signals lead to profound transformations across all aspects of life. In the "electric age" for which McLuhan is held up as a prophet, getting "wired" has at least two meanings. The first pertains to an abundance of energy: frayed nerves, affect that is perhaps precariously high. A wired body is overstimulated, perhaps in anticipation of something about to happen, perhaps from too many chemical stimulants. The second denotes connectivity. Rooms or devices or bodies get wired for sound, or entire regions of the world are wired up, stitched into global communications networks. In both senses of "being wired," a system (a body, a community, a location) is switched on, transformed into a node in broader circuits of affect, data, electrical power. As McLuhan points out throughout *Understanding Media*, these two meanings have become collapsed; the distinctions they present between technical and organic, local and interplanetary, are increasingly obsolete. Electricity connects our bodies to our media environments, coursing through and animating both. Wires are at once the most fundamental and the least remarkable components of these techno-organic electrical apparatuses, and yet they are nowhere to be found in McLuhan's work. As objects, wires are simply synonymous with their effects. What matters for McLuhan are the effects that electricity generates by powering light bulbs, telephones, radios, televisions, and so on; how electricity is distributed is less important. Indeed, at times McLuhan describes electricity as less a physical phenomenon and more a property—remarking, for instance, that "there is no longer any tendency to speak of electricity as 'contained' in anything."[1] The material infrastructures that store, transmit, and process electricity fade into the background, and wires—those most mundane of infrastructural components—drop from view.

During the Industrial Revolution, wires were the material catalysts for a transformation in communication that irrevocably separated it from transportation; the cables laid down under the oceans, along railroad tracks, and into homes laid the foundations for the technologically mediated immediacy that characterizes the contemporary world.[2] Now, like other infrastructural elements, we tend not to notice them until they break.[3] Wires are old news; when they are brought up, it is to consider their historical role in building empires or, more recently, to point out their stubborn persistence in the tech industry's faltering push toward wirelessness.[4] And yet, they are unavoidable. In their most visible and mundane forms, electric cords, Ethernet cables, audio-video wires, and so on string together our domestic media arrangements. They tether our bodies to our devices, and our devices to the global distribution networks and storage facilities that keep them running. They convert our homes into nodes in much broader circuits of power, data, and sense. They deliver pulses of electricity (and/or light) that are then translated by our devices back into content: a casserole recipe, fashion blog, pornographic video, the insults of a thirteen-year-old video gaming opponent, a friend's Instagram stories; all of these and more, immeasurably more, in speeds and scales far exceeding human perception and made possible, in part, by the translation of content into patterns that are only intelligible to machines. As technologies that consist of "pure information without any content"—a description that McLuhan gave to the electric light bulb that just as (if not more) aptly describes wires—they are the most McLuhan-ish of media, despite their near absence in *Understanding Media*.[5]

This chapter makes the case that wires matter; as conduits that tether our various electric extensions (and by extension, our bodies) to globe-spanning infrastructures of power and connectivity, they materialize social relations in certain ways. Particularly in domestic contexts, their properties shape the conditions in which we engage with our networked media: conductivity (will it work?), length (will it reach the outlet?), flexibility (can it stay coiled?), color (does it match the walls/floor/furniture?) all have a say over the "pace and pattern" of our domestic affairs. Exactly how these considerations come to matter, and for whom, is inextricably tethered to politics of (at least) gender and socioeconomic status; how we manage wires, and how they manage us, is therefore a matter of feminist concern. Follow the wires, and we can grasp how mundane considerations over the layout and arrangement of mundane devices, how and where we wire our habitats for power and connectivity, are absolutely integral for understanding the affects, relations of power, and subject positions that circulate in and are reproduced through our homes and other quotidian contexts of work and play.

An illustration from my early fieldwork: I am at the 2008 Major League Gaming (MLG) Summer Open in Toronto. The US-based competitive electronic sports (esports) organization, making one of its first (and last) forays into Canada, has partnered with Toronto's annual FanExpo convention to host a series of tournaments over the weekend for competitive team-based video games played on the Xbox 360. The main draw is *Halo 3*, and over one hundred teams of four have converged from around North America—including MLG's own stable of professional (fully sponsored) teams. Despite the vast size of the FanExpo venue, the portion of the floor given over to the MLG tournament feels cramped. Dozens of plastic fold-out tables are lined up in rows, on top of which sit hundreds of flat screens and Xbox 360 consoles, and thousands of wires: connecting the consoles to TVs, the TVs and consoles to power bars, power bars to outlets, consoles to access switches, access switches to the event's server, and, to the chagrin of many players, connecting consoles to individual controllers. Although the Xbox 360, introduced in 2005, marked the introduction of wireless controllers to Microsoft's consoles, this event—like most console-based LAN tournaments—does not permit players to connect their controllers wirelessly. The reasoning is logistical and infrastructural. If a single player presses the button on his controller to wirelessly connect it to a console, the signal is received by each of the hundreds of Xbox consoles in range. If four hundred players do this, four hundred controller connection prompts will appear on each Xbox: connectivity chaos. Devices designed for home use, Xbox consoles are not wired for receiving and managing multiple wireless connection requests in a networked environment.

The effects of these infrastructural arrangements of wires, tables, chairs, consoles, screens, and power adapters in a constrained space is to put hundreds of players—who are overwhelmingly young and male, and predominantly white—into close physical proximity. Tethering them to a cramped array of screens and consoles, their controller wires prevent them from having much, if any, room to spread out without coming into physical contact with other players (figure 3.1). Wired infrastructure produces wired affect; all that nervous energy required of (and manufactured by) the tense, violent bouts of action in *Halo 3* has nowhere to go. Knees shake, bodies lean in, fingers twitch, voices are raised. When teams win, members hug and high-five, their bottled-up energies temporarily released and the strictures around hetero male contact relaxed for a moment in celebration. When teams lose, members glance down at their feet, sagging further into shells of personal space that are already constrained by logistical arrangements. The wires connecting bodies to consoles channel affect and data in equal measure; gendered forms of power (the rules disciplining acceptable forms of proximity and contact between young, hetero, cis-men) traverse these circuits as surely as electrical power.

Playing through the Pain

Writing in the summer of 2020, well into COVID-19's rewiring of society, this fieldwork story seems almost nostalgic. The image of so many bodies together in close proximity, staccato chatter and trash talk from hundreds of throats

3.1 (X)boxed-in bodies at the 2008 Major League Gaming Summer Open in Toronto. Credit: Nick Taylor.

sending millions of aerosolized droplets into the turbulent and cramped space between players each second, seems both quaint and alarming. But even as playing video games in public might be a thing of our prepandemic past, playing games at home has never been hotter. The same physically isolating and time-intensive qualities that made the WHO warn of the psychological dangers of games in 2019 are now, for the WHO, crucial population management techniques for COVID-19.[6] Games are the pandemic's killer app, now that staying glued to the couch is a good, indeed socially responsible, thing to do. This is evidenced by the marked increase in video game sales in spring 2020 from the previous year.[7]

As helpful as video games might be to health authorities, they are resource-hungry. Internet and electrical infrastructures have had to work overtime during the pandemic, and video game livestreaming sites like Twitch, online game services such as Steam and Xbox Game Pass, and multiplayer games such as *Fortnite* and *League of Legends* are key contributors to these increasingly strained global networks. In response, a number of game companies and network providers started to bottleneck their services in spring 2020: to slow down the rate at which video gaming content circulates in and out of our homes, so as to make room for other kinds of data and their attendant practices and economies.[8] But playing through the pandemic involves further forms of maintenance beyond this infrastructural balancing act. We have to make space for games in our homes as surely as we do across continent-spanning infrastructures. They displace other domestic activities: cooking; housework; supervising children, pets, other family members; working at one's job; other screen-based leisure. It is now well established that the pandemic, for all its unprecedented conditions, has exacerbated long-standing inequalities: among households who are able to do their jobs from home, there has been renewed attention to the "grotesque" gender inequalities in domestic labor, to say nothing of the compounded vulnerabilities of service industry employees, food industry laborers, and "essential" workers unable to stay home.[9] The ability to carve times and places to play from these other practices—from the domestic work of social reproduction—is a privilege historically afforded to men. So, not surprisingly, the figure best positioned to play his way through these unprecedented times is a familiar one: he has plentiful access to gaming systems, sees games as his rightful terrain, has ample time and place to play them, and is used to the games industry catering to his whims.[10] He is wired into gender power, and his wires constitute the circulatory system for his techno-organic gender machine.

Man (Cave) in the Mirror

In my own domestic media arrangement, my PlayStation 4 and two computer monitors sit on a modern wooden desk adjacent to the TV, in a corner of the guest room on the third floor of our small house. The computer tower (a matte black slab) is tucked under the desk. On it sits a white rectangular plastic box with a faux-wood lid, with open slots on either end: a home for wayward, unruly, extraneous wires. When I am sitting at the desk, I am adjacent to the TV; if my partner is watching TV, I tend to sit with my chair pushed in tight against the desk, earphones on, so as not to distract her. I try to be a model game player in what is ostensibly a TV room, which is to say, to make my body, my screens, platforms, and input devices, and the coils of wires that bind and power all these things, as unobtrusive as possible.

We have moved this setup back and forth between our bedroom and our guest room a few times, always in an attempt to find an ideal balance between (the appearance of) cleanliness and organization, on one hand, and uncomplicated access to a main source of (predominantly, my) leisure and work, on the other. My partner despises wires. They spark irritation; they speak of disorder, clutter, and a lack of care. For me, they are an inevitable part of the domestic landscape. Each rearranging is a chance to reestablish order over the mass of wires that protrude out the back of the devices, down the wall, and along the floor; to balance my desire for ready access to my leisure technologies with my partner's desire for a tidy and uncluttered home. The wire management box with its faux-wood top is but one of the devices we've used in these efforts; others include tape, wire-bundling cords made of velcro and plastic, and translucent runners that adhere to walls and desks. While I have never fetishized wires to the extent seen among the masculinized cults of high-end audiophiles and home theater technicians, I have also never questioned their visibility—at least not until I learned of a whole industry of cord management for homes and offices. Sleeves, ties, clips, straps, covers, hooks, panels, boxes; made of nylon, plastic, silicone, rubber; in clear, matte black, faux wood; attached via magnets, glue, suction, velcro.... It seems, at least anecdotally, that wires and their management are a gender problem, one which the market is happy to both emphasize and address. These modes of living with wires, with rearranging the spatial and temporal patterns of our domestic media use around their length, width, conductivity, flexibility, and color (their capacity for disguise/camouflage), reproduce and circulate other forms of power: certainly gender, but also class, and possibly, race, age, and so on.

In Bart Simon's examination of the DIY computing cultures in the early 2000s, he sees in the aesthetic of "case modders"—who brazenly display the power and efficiency of their custom gaming rigs and the cleverness of their technical arrangements—a stance against a tendency toward "invisible" computing.[11] On one side is a masculine culture of hypertechnicity, a culture that finds pleasure and community in material performances of technical prowess. Case modders often house computers in PC towers that use custom lighting systems and transparent panels to show off the guts of their builds, the artful organization of wires, boards, and cooling systems. On the other side is an aesthetic of computing that Simon saw epitomized by Apple products (and perhaps more recently by flat-screen TVs that, when turned off, are indistinguishable from framed paintings): technologies that are barely there, that blend seamlessly into the chic, modernist décor of the hip, upper-middle-class North American home. Wires out in one, wires hidden in the other.

Wires also wend their way through Keir Keightley's research on audiophile magazines in the 1940s and 1950s. Across the editorials and advertisements Keightley draws on, midcentury male stereo equipment makers and consumers go to great lengths to disassociate their hobby from the emasculating influence of the television—that device that postwar suburban housewives were told would "glue" the family together.[12] Audiophiles were encouraged to set up their barely domesticated, military-grade stereo equipment in ways that let them sonically, spatially, and emotionally escape from the rest of the home and all its feminizing devices, obligations, and locations. As Keightley reports, masses of "bare wires" were celebrated by audiophiles who wrote to magazines like *High Fidelity* to boast of their masculine stereo arrangements. Wires worked in these arrangements to "underwrite the hi-fi man's pleasure in his sense of separation from feminine taste," forming material connections between "forceful masculinity, the reclaiming of domestic space, and audio-technology."[13]

Follow the Wires

Until recently, my own research has never been about wires. Over the last decade, I have attended dozens of gaming events in public settings—from massive LAN parties with tens of thousands of attendees to collegiate esports tournaments with a dozen players. Throughout this work, my main concern has been to document how changes in digital gaming's cultural significance, especially the cultivation of mass audiences for digital play, accompany and shape gendered relations and subjectivities. Wires have been a messy but unremarkable part of the technocultural landscapes I visit, under my feet (literally) and beneath my attention as I walk the grounds of LAN parties or internet cafés or esports tournaments, looking for more interesting, noteworthy, eye-level interactions between humans and screens.

In 2018, I departed somewhat from these walking explorations of public gaming events and began a study of gaming setups in domestic contexts, initiated in part by a fascination with the discourse around "man caves."[14] Informed by feminist research on portrayals of media domestication—whether hi-fi audio magazines in the 1940s and 1950s, television sets in post–World War II women's magazines, or home consoles in early 2000s lifestyle magazines[15]—I worked with a PhD student (Katreena Alder) to gather users' images uploaded to the gaming site NeoGAF, which runs an annual thread called "Post your gaming setup." We downloaded images from the first twenty-five complete posts for the 2007 and 2015 iterations of this publicly available thread, selecting these particular years as they preceeded the release of new console generations: the Playstation 3, Xbox 360, and Nintendo Wii, and the Playstation 4, Xbox One, and Wii U, respectively.

Users' posts to these busy threads varied in terms of amount and quality of photographs: some posted single photographs of their gaming setups; some posted multiple pictures, including both panoramic and close-up shots. Some were grainy, or blurry, or taken in low light. Others were well lit, in high definition. None showed images of actual humans, though we could reasonably presume that most of these users identify as male; this is based on what we know of the NeoGAF site and the casual use of male pronouns among those who posted to the thread, and by some of the excellent previous research on gaming in domestic contexts, which consistently points to arrangements in which consoles and gaming computers are monopolized by male family members.[16] We devised the following set of descriptors to mark the presence (or absence) of wires: "no wire management" for photographs of setups in which wires are visible, often in abundance, without any apparent semblance of trying to tame or organize them; "wire management: visible" for setups in which wires are clearly visible, but are contained and organized by the kinds of techniques described above (clips, ties, etc.); and "wire management: invisible" for setups in which wires are clearly present (insofar as the photographs depict technologies that require wires) but in which users have employed techniques for disguising wires entirely, such as wall panels, cord boxes, and so on. Upon further analysis, these terms proved to bundle together a host of other characteristics, such that we were able to discern three distinct kinds of gaming setup, which are discussed in more detail below: gaming hearths, gaming bunkers, and gaming cabinets. As the fulcrum of our analysis, wire arrangement forms the ground on which these three figures become intelligible.

HEARTHS

The first of these arrangements, associated in our data set with "wire management: invisible," directly connect to Spigel and Flynn's work on the 1950s television and early 2000s game console, respectively. Both authors draw from the figure of the hearth: sources of warmth and light in the home, sites for storytelling and bonding, and the nexus of feminized domestic labor. I describe as gaming hearths those setups in which wires have been tucked away out of sight (whether hidden behind special panels, housed in boxes, or corded cleverly behind desks and shelving units) in order to highlight their connections to these traditional arrangements of domestic media. Those NeoGAF forum images we coded as "wire management: invisible" often include multiple photographs of a given setup, usually clean and well lit: they depict large spaces, usually horizontally organized, with couches and/or multiple chairs oriented toward a large television (figure 3.2). Game

3.2 A gaming hearth, from the 2015 "Post your gaming setup" NeoGAF thread. Credit: NeoGAF user.

consoles are nestled discreetly on shelves, among DVD collections, books, musical instruments, and photographs. These setups are often beside windows, ensuring natural light, and the adjacent walls are frequently adorned by framed art; this suggests a prime location in the home, perhaps the den or basement of a house or the central area of an apartment or condominium.

The shared and negotiated nature of media use among multiple inhabitants (unseen in these photographs, but presumed) suggests that their function as domestic gaming setup is as much temporal as it is spatial: judging by the other media depicted in the photographs, these spaces are also reading nooks, home theaters, construction toy sites. We might imagine a parent playing Xbox after the children are in bed, or a couple curled up on the couch with their dog to watch a movie. The gaming technologies themselves are secondary to the TV, which remains the focal point of family media use. Gaming is one among a broad array of media practices centered around the shared screen; platforms and controllers recede into the background when not in use, unsightly wires moved out of sight.

BUNKERS

Where "wire management: invisible" became shorthand for gaming setups characterized by negotiated and communal use, images associated with "no wire management" exclusively depict setups that seem intended for and assembled by solo users. Furniture most often consists of a single office chair, maybe two, and a functional if unlovely desk or table on top of which perch multiple gaming platforms: almost always a desktop computer, usually with two screens, and often accompanied by a laptop and/or multiple gaming consoles. Wires are everywhere. They hang in clumps behind tables, snake over and under each other across desks, sprout in all directions from consoles, screens, and PC towers. As in figure 3.3, there is an abundance of peripheral devices (controllers, headphones, mice) and infrastructural nodes (charging stations, power bars) out in the open.

Often, the presence of a staircase, alongside other features like low ceilings and lack of windows, indicates that the setup is in either a basement or an attic. Decor is minimal, and wall hangings are almost always unframed. Hardware is front and center in these setups, supported by economical and often makeshift furniture: milk crates serving as a side table in one, the top of a pizza box used for a mouse pad in another (figure 3.4). And yet the gaming technologies themselves hardly speak of lack. Current-generation consoles, expensive input devices, and high-powered PCs all suggest a deliberate foregrounding of power and efficiency over aesthetics, of

3.3 A gaming bunker, from the 2015 thread. Credit: NeoGAF user.

3.4 Another gaming bunker, from the 2015 thread. Credit: NeoGAF user.

masculinized function over feminized form. As in Keightley's look at hi-fi setups of the 1940s and '50s, bare wires underscore this prioritization. I designate these setups as "bunkers" to emphasize the deliberate connections to wartime communications arrays: a fortified position, threadbare and functional, stocked with technologies of surveillance, command, and control; a safe place from which to coordinate computational counteroffensives in a world gone hostile. Such counteroffensives might take place in the digital battlegrounds of networked games and social media alike. Indeed, if the antifeminist Gamergate hate campaign had an interior design aesthetic, it might have looked something like the arrangements shown here, bare wires, hentai pictures, and all.

CABINETS

Hearths and bunkers—associated with "wire management: invisible" and "no wire management," respectively—are relatively straightforward. The third category of setup, associated with "wire management: visible," is less so. The setups in this category were almost always displayed across multiple photographs in a single NeoGAF forum post, their users capturing and sharing multiple, granular details of these immaculately curated media arrangements: a wide shot of a room with a modernist workstation and shelving units alongside close-ups of expensive LEGO sets, bobblehead dolls, game controllers both recent and decades old, all carefully posed (figure 3.5). Wires are visible, but they are as deliberately arranged as anything else: hanging discreetly down the back of a desk, gathered to run in tight formation along a wall to connect routers, consoles, power bars, screens. They are as much a part of the well-ordered landscape as the DVDs, toys, collectibles, curios, and framed images of gaming and sci-fi culture that populate the IKEA-style shelving ubiquitous throughout these images. Displays of multiple generations of consoles are frequent, as are expensive peripherals and speakers. These setups often include TVs, but they are not central; rather, they might occupy one shelf of a wall-length unit or sit on a stand to the side. The stuff—the curated and deliberately positioned objects from worlds of gaming, fantasy, sci-fi, and anime, either in their own compartment or mingling selectively with other elements—is the point. These setups are not just meant to be used; they are staged, intended for the admiration of visitors (perhaps) or, more likely, of other NeoGAF users. This is the setup elevated to a style, intended as much for visual consumption as for physical use, and reflective of a subculture that merges computational technicities with subcultural fandoms: what Bart Simon called "geek chic,"

3.5 A gaming cabinet from the 2015 thread. Credit: NeoGAF user.

before that term was appropriated by an unsuccessful maker of custom board game tables.

I call these cabinets in reference to a history of (particularly masculine) domestic curation that goes back to the Renaissance—entire rooms used by wealthy men to work and relax amid their amassed wealth. An orientalist bent further connects these Renaissance rooms to the brand of contemporary gaming setups shown here. In both instances, curios gathered from exotic cultures communicate the inhabitant's privileged location within globalized flows of media and capital. If the gaming hearth is characterized by negotiated and communal domesticity, and the gaming bunker by a kind of agonism channeled into distributed networks of gaming and social media, the cabinet is a site where play and display are productively conflated in support of showing off the users' cultural capital. Technologies of play (and their well-managed, visible wires) are all part of the exhibit, and the exhibit itself shows a kind of playful incorporation of curios, furniture, and hardware: a plush goomba squats among throw pillows on a couch; a poseable Master Chief figure manspreads in front of a row of *Halo* game boxes (figure 3.6).

3.6 Close-up of a gaming cabinet from the 2015 thread. Credit: NeoGAF user.

Our Setups, Our Selves

Hidden or visible, messy or managed, wires are how the elements of all these gaming apparatuses talk to each other; they are material conduits for these local infrastructures of networked leisure and sociality. Wires are also how these arrangements join up with globalized infrastructures of power and connectivity. Thus far, I've explored what we might learn by following the wires into these dens, home offices, and bedrooms. Perhaps we might follow them on their way out of these domestic arrangements as well, to see how they connect to broader flows—of electrical power and connectivity, but also of power relations and networked communities. What sorts of subjectivities, and what kinds of politics, are being cultivated and deployed in these hearths, bunkers, and cabinets? How might these gender politics circulate, become amplified, disrupted, transformed, weaponized, in other kinds of spaces? Properly addressing these questions would likely require a much more nuanced and ambitious study than the kind of online window-peeking I did here. It might, for instance, look to the domestic recording studios of Twitch streamers and YouTubers popular among certain communities, operationalizing T. L. Taylor's insight that streaming platforms make particular domestic gaming contexts visible in very particular ways.[17]

At the minimum, however, we can follow Paul B. Preciado's lead in his consideration of how Hugh Hefner's media empire helped craft an "indoor man" through both the pages of *Playboy* and the design of Hefner's own dwellings.[18] I am less interested in drawing connections to the gaming setups I explore here, on one hand, and the swinging bachelor pad with its sexually predatory inhabitant on the other, than I am in Preciado's sensitivity to the formative role of space in shaping subjectivity. In a continuation and feminist application of McLuhan's insistence that domestic spaces "shape and rearrange the patterns of human association and community," Preciado writes that Hugh Hefner "had somehow understood that in order to sculpt a new masculine subjectivity, one had to design a habitat: to create a space and invent a series of practices and uses of the domestic that could function as technohabits of the male body."[19] Following this, we can begin to imagine what sorts of "technohabits of the male body" we might associate with a domestic arrangement in which high-end gaming gear mixes with shoddy furniture, where a towel might serve as a curtain, blocking the natural light from hitting a newly purchased computer monitor, and where wires in their tangled multitudes vie for surface space with fast-food wrappers and energy drink cans. Conceptually at least, if not empirically, this is taking us into the territory explored by Sarah Sharma in her work on "Mommy's Basement": those locations, both in our cultural imaginary and in everyday domestic and organizational settings, in which young men rail against the evils of feminism, social justice warriors, and progressive politics from spaces that are kept comfortable and safe for them through feminized labor.[20] Taking this a step further, we might begin to get a better sense of how networked socialities and spatio-technical arrangements shape each other in the production of (among other things) hyperreactionary masculinities and their associated gender politics. This is perhaps where current accounts of the "manosphere" are in need of a bit more support.[21] For all of the rich insights afforded by research on the manosphere, its operant metaphor—a self-contained and geometrically perfect shape—does not help us access the lived realities of its proponents. The texts that constitute the manosphere—whether memes, subreddits, YouTube videos, or games—are certainly ripe for critical analysis, but following *Understanding Media*, such analyses stop short of questioning the technological conditions that make these texts possible in the first place. The machineries of contemporary masculinity that generate and circulate these texts are powered by the kinds of spatial and temporal arrangements portrayed on the "Post your gaming setup" threads: techno-habitats that, through their arrangements of wires, screens, peripherals, furniture, and so on, permit inhabitants' escape into worlds untouched by feminism. Rewiring these machineries is messy and complex work but involves, at the very least, a more earnest consideration of the material technologies that tether us to our masculinized media.

Notes

1. McLuhan, *Understanding Media* (1994), 384.
2. James W. Carey, "Technology and Ideology: The Case of the Telegraph," in *Communication as Culture*, 155–77.
3. Graham, *Disrupted Cities*.
4. McLuhan, *Understanding Media* (1994), 246–58; Bollmer, *Inhuman Networks*; Mackenzie, *Wirelessness*.
5. McLuhan, *Understanding Media* (1994), 52.
6. Canales, "The WHO Is Recommending Video Games."
7. Smith, "The Giants of the Video Game Industry."
8. Cimpanu, "Akamai to Slow Down Video Game Downloads"; Farokhmanesh, "Sony Is Now Slowing Down PlayStation Downloads."
9. Gross, "Pandemic Makes Evident 'Grotesque' Gender Inequality."

10. Harvey, *Gender, Age, and Digital Games*; Salter and Blodgett, *Toxic Geek Masculinity in Media*; Taylor and Voorhees, *Masculinities in Play*.

11. Simon, "Geek Chic."

12. Spigel, *Make Room for TV*, 68.

13. Keightley, "'Turn It Down' She Shrieked."

14. See, for instance, Rodino-Colocino, DeCarvalho, and Heresco, "Neo-orthodox Masculinities on *Man Caves*."

15. Keightley, "'Turn It Down' She Shrieked"; Spigel, *Make Room for TV*; Chambers, "'Wii Play as a Family'"; Flynn, "Geography of the Digital Hearth."

16. Bryce and Rutter, "The Gendering of Computer Gaming"; Harvey, *Gender, Age, and Digital Games*; Tobin, *Portable Play in Everyday Life*.

17. Taylor, *Watch Me Play*.

18. Preciado, *Pornotopia*.

19. McLuhan, *Understanding Media* (1994), 127; McLuhan, *Understanding Media* (1994), 180. Preciado, *Pornotopia*, 19.

20. Sharma, "Going to Work in Mommy's Basement."

21. "Manosphere" is the name given to a loose network of forums, social media accounts, YouTube channels, podcasts, and so on that are unified by a vociferous opposition to feminism and by a valorization of reactionary and very often white supremacist masculinities; see Ging, "Alphas, Betas, and Incels."

4 Textile, the Uneasy Medium

GANAELE LANGLOIS

What counts as media? McLuhan's famous answer is that anything that extends human capacities counts as media, from wheels extending legs to glasses extending sight, from radio extending the ear to electricity extending the brain. Textile, which is the medium I focus on in this chapter, extends the skin both in its physical capacity to provide warmth and as a "means of defining the self socially."[1] The question of extension, however, has over time been narrowed down in two ways. First, McLuhan's original formulation suggests a unidirectional extension from the human outward, and not, for instance, from nonhuman entities, dynamics, and processes inward. Second, the term *man* encapsulates the overall focus on examining the link between media and power as absolute control over environments. This comes as no surprise: the study of media in general has mostly been the study of dominant, Eurocentric media. I do not mean this as an accusation, but to highlight that one of the central questions in media studies is how media in turn fold into, shape, and extend the capacities for dominant power to organize all aspects of life and to mobilize resources through time and space. For Innis, media were inseparable from the rise of Eurocentric, Western, colonial empires: writing in particular enabled new forms of control over resources, time, and space that made the exercise of centralized European power across vast spaces possible, up to the colonial land grab of resources for global trade.[2] Closer to us, we can think about the mobilization of mass media as tools to assert a capitalist mode of productivity over social life. McLuhan expanded this angle in his analysis of *The Gutenberg Galaxy*.[3] Within such a framework, what counts as media is what fits into this specific concern with Western, Eurocentric, and colonial power.

Contemporary textile production and consumption by and large fits within this logic: the production of cloth for global trade has long involved land grabs, technical appropriation, and erasure of non-Western forms of knowledge, mass production, enslavement, and worker exploitation. All these culminate in an industry that, being built on overconsumption through short fashion cycles, is one of the key environmental polluters and causes of global warming, and is well known for its brutal labor practices. In this chapter, however, I want to focus on how textile as a medium has operated outside of this Eurocentric, Western, colonial framework. I do this to address three limitations of the media as Eurocentric power framework. First, historically, the articulation of media and empires existed long before the invention of alphabetic writing, and I want to point out here the importance of textile as a medium that is historically inseparable from the formation of non-Western empires, from China and India to pre-Columbian civilizations. The power of textile as global medium in that regard was multifaceted: from the times of the Roman Empire onward, intricately woven silk and cotton from Asia, adorned with exotic colors such as indigo (blue) and madder (red), profoundly impacted consciousnesses, tastes, and cultural identities, shaping vast global networks of exchange (e.g., the Silk Road) of commodities, cultural tastes, values, and practices.[4] Second, what about the relationship between media and nondominant sociocultural groups, such as Indigenous, non-Western groups and women? Here, the interrogation is not only about how dominant media are adopted by these subaltern groups, but also about the media practices developed by subaltern groups as their own practice in the first place. Interestingly enough, textile as medium fits in this perspective as well, albeit demoted by Eurocentric, Western, neocolonial frameworks as local domestic handicrafts mostly made by women that express cultural identities and make for colorful souvenirs. And finally, the question of extension beyond control invites us to consider more multidirectional flows of exchange: what happens when we consider media as that which enables new extensions, not only from the body outward, but from the environment in, or from one environment to another, or from one world into another? And textile fits here as well: it is an extension of the skin, but the skin is not only what delineates me from the world, what encloses me. It is also porous, breathing, that is to say; it enables the outside—the air, a touch—to penetrate into me. The skin, and by extension textile, is about resonances that blur the boundaries between what we usually think about the individual, the internal, the world of intimate sensations and the external world, understood here as including the material environment, social world, and cosmos.[5]

Indigenous textiles such as those from the Shipibo-Conibo group in the Peruvian Amazon throw our preconceived analytical categories of what constitutes media, and what media can do, into profound and liberating disarray. In focusing on Shipibo-Conibo textiles as media, I explore how a medium that is oftentimes ignored or at best understood as a minor craft in the West actually enables a new form of lived politics, especially for this Anthropocenic moment when meaningful worlds teeming with life and possibilities keep disappearing before our eyes. At the same time, I explore how media capacities to have transformative effects at a distance are curtailed by global communication and discourse infrastructures and practices—in other words, a system of distribution of media objects and their exchange and translation as economic and symbolic value—that systematically work to negate and neutralize possibilities for change. The kind of critical media politics that result from this requires recognizing that as much as media can extend into the uncertain space of new worlding practices, there is significant work to be done in dismantling the neocolonial systems within which media practices and objects circulate.[6] In other words: it is not enough to focus solely on media as the site of new extensions and relations, but to pay attention in turn to the systems of distribution and exchange that in turn amplify or negate effects at a distance.

From Skin to Cosmovision: The Shipibo-Conibo Practice of *Kené*

My case study is located in the city of Pucallpa in the Peruvian Amazon, on the Ucayali River, along which lives one of the largest Indigenous groups in the Amazon—the Shipibo-Conibo (est. 35,000). The combined pressure of mining, logging, climate change, pollution, and need to access educational and health resources has meant that a significant number of

Shipibo-Conibos have moved from distant villages to the city of Pucallpa. The Shipibo-Conibos are well known for their cosmovision, including their healing and shamanistic practices, which are anchored in a deep knowledge of the Amazon ecosystem and the medicinal properties of local plants. Since the 1970s, a combination of policy changes allowing Amazonian Indigenous groups in Peru to claim land ownership and greater interests in Shipibo culture from scholars and tourists have led to a renewal and reinvention of Shipibo identity and ways of life as clearly distinct from mainstream Peruvian society.[7] Tourism in the region is not as developed as in Cusco and Machu Picchu, for instance, but Shipibo culture enjoys an international notoriety. Most visitors come with an interest in Shipibo ritual practices, which were popularized in William Burroughs and Allan Ginsberg's *The Yage Letters*. Descriptions of drinking ayahuasca (a brew of hallucinogenic plants) during ceremonies to gain transcendental, mystical experiences and understanding of self, other, and the world have proliferated ever since. Today, many foreigners come to participate in healing rituals led by *médicos* (shamans), which involve consumption not only of ayahuasca but also of local medicinal plants and foodstuffs. Foreign tourism in the region therefore tends to be a specialized one that involves interest in spiritual issues, dissatisfaction with Western ways of life, including never-ending material consumption, and desire to seek radically new experiences and ways of being in harmony with the environment. As well, Shipibo medicine has a deep appeal—an alternative to Western medicine, it is acknowledged by the scientific community (and further demonstrated by reckless patenting of local Amazonian plants by the pharmaceutical industry) that the Shipibos have sophisticated medical knowledge.

Shipibo ceramics and textiles offer a continuation of such experiences, as they are adorned with designs—or *kené* in Shipibo—that are commonly described as the visual translation of spiritual and intangible encounters. Only women engage in *kené* as a spiritual and artistic practice, and usually from a young age. Developing the capacity to dream and imagine designs traditionally requires a ritual consisting "of placing a few drops of piri-piri plant (*Cyperus* sp.) juice in [the] eyes and navel" of young girls.[8] This eventually allows Shipibo female artists to access designs in their thoughts, visions, and dreams that they then translate onto skin, ceramics, and cloth. The finished designs are characterized by lines of various thickness forming a web of labyrinthine paths (figure 4.1). *Kené* designs are quite unique and difficult to classify—there is no equivalent for them in the Western world. What they mean is an ongoing discussion, and many anthropologists have attempted to decipher them, with at times confusing results that highlight the incommensurability of *kené* when it comes to trying to make it fit within a Western perspective on art and communication. *Kené* has been described as transcriptions of spiritual visions and therefore as the materialization of the intangible.[9] It has also been said to represent the skin of the cosmic serpent that created the world, and therefore the paths that lead to other strata of reality. More recently, *kené* have been said to be transcriptions of healing songs, but this a recent interpretation that is not widely shared among Shipibo artists.[10] It is agreed that kené designs are about transformation because they are the pathways to different worlds, different realities. They materialize being granted access to other worlds and realms, communicating with the nonhumans, traveling through different times and spaces. Some design components have names—for instance, piranha, fish, bird, and human—but these are conventions that can change from one group to the next. There have been propositions, from both anthropologists and their Shipibo interlocutors, that *kené* could be compared with writing. Yet here lies the main difference: a *kené* design expresses a changing multiplicity of references, some that are related to myths, others to emotions or desires, others to personal histories, others to the communities, and others to the very specific context within which they appear.[11] In that sense, they are the complete reverse of writing, which (apart perhaps from poetry) is about precision of meaning and fixing things in linear, rational sequences, or what McLuhan called "typographic" civilization.

Further, *kené* designs are not figments of one's imagination only—they are communication with other realms and other entities that have no equivalent, again, in the West. Let's focus for a moment here on Amazon cosmologies. To refer to Viveiro de Castro, *kené* is to writing what Amazonian cosmology is to Western ontology: its inversion. Here lies its relevance: it is the materialization of an Other, not as representation but as expression of other modes and possibilities of relating to other worlds—it is, for the foreigner, an indecipherable map of other modes of being. Viveiro de Castro, addressing the problem of Western anthropology encountering Amazonian people and their cosmology, states, "the problem doesn't reside in seeing the native as an object, nor does the solution reside in casting him as a subject. That the native is a subject is beyond doubt; but what the native forces the anthropologist to cast into doubt is precisely what a subject could be."[12] The point of studying Amazonian Indigenous culture is about throwing into question the limitation of the very concept of the subject, on which any capacity for knowledge and meaningfulness is based, in two ways. First, such a statement both highlights the limitations of the Western epistemological framework—the assumptions about what the other is supposed to be—and allows for casting into doubt the Western subject itself, thus severing the ties between dominant modes of subjectivation and the self. Second, if encountering the native forces us to reconsider what a subject is, then encountering Indigenous modes of expression means casting into doubt what communication, and by extension meaningful relationships with the world, is about. In short, *kené*, because it is so visible, tangible, and material, is not craft: it is also a medium through which Western subjects can engage in a practice of casting themselves, and their understanding of the world, into doubt in order to encounter new possibilities. For all their incomprehensibility to the Western subject, *kené* designs are nevertheless impactful—the closest analogy I can think of here is that they create a punctum that suspends and pierces through visitors' preconceptions and apprehensions of what spiritual communication is about.[13] It is this very equivocation of *kené* that allows openness to take place. The question, in turn, is about how this interface of openness and encounter between incommensurable worlds and modes of being, and the space of equivocation and doubt that it opens up, is both colonized and deterritorialized, in short, how new extensions

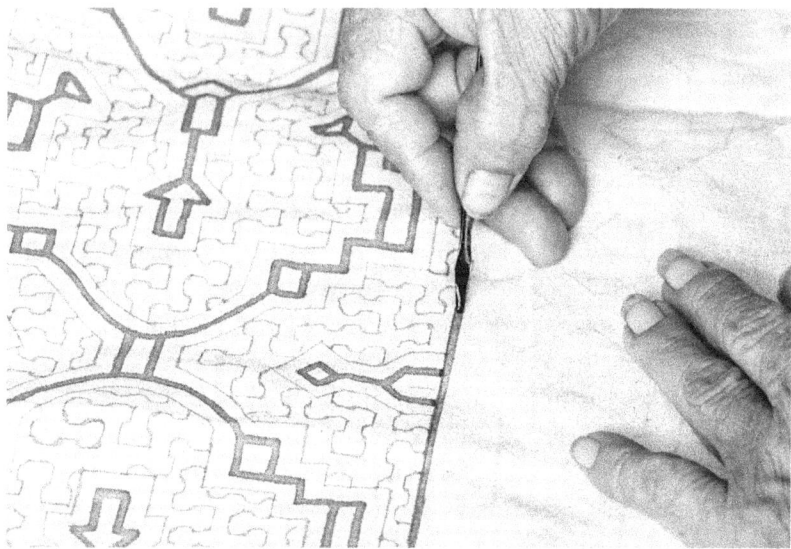

4.1 *Kené* practice at Maroti Xobo, Pucallpa, 2018. Natural dye on cloth. Credit: Ganaele Langlois.

are by and large captured and neutralized within global systems of distribution and exchange.

Indigenous Women's Media Goes Mainstream: Systems of Appropriation and Alienation

The development of Shipibo-Conibo textiles as a commodity for external markets is fairly new, as traditionally *kené* designs were for domestic use only, adorning skin, clothes, ceramics, and houses. The selling of textiles is now important to Shipibo women, and it is estimated that 80 percent of them derive some income from their craft, which helps cover basic food, educational, and health needs for their families.[14] The production of textiles for use outside the community fulfills important needs: it provides a source of income, with the hope that this will translate into social mobility and better living conditions; it offers an incentive to younger generations to train and continue with Shipibo *kené* artistic production rather than assimilate to mainstream society; and it plays a central role in showcasing Shipibo culture and cosmovision on the international scene. There are therefore significant opportunities for Shipibo women to gain socially and economically from their textile artistic practices. However, in reality, Shipibo textiles illustrate a central problem with the development of Indigenous women's media: message, practices, and women makers become sites of appropriation and exploitation as textiles enter the global craft market and its attendant media infrastructure.

There are several factors that enable appropriation and exploitation. First, it is incredibly challenging to get handmade textiles to be recognized as meaningful, and therefore as demanding more value, including economic value, than the vast majority of machine-made textiles that can easily create cheap imitations of handcrafted goods. This is particularly apparent at the Shipibo women's craft group Maroti Xobo in Pucallpa, where members gather to embroider or paint on textiles, and sell their textile art pieces to visitors. These include small, medium, and large wall hangings, either painted, sometimes with natural pigments, or embroidered in bright synthetic colors; smaller painted or embroidered pieces such as patches; clothing; and bags. Maroti Xobo textile makers experience the same tension as traditional textile makers elsewhere: as their pieces are handmade, they have a higher price point. The priciest are the ones made with local hand-spun cotton woven on a backstrap loom, on which the artists paint *kené* designs using local natural dyes and pigments. The higher price point is a turnoff for the local market, and so most purchasers of medium and large textile pieces tend to be visitors and foreigners.

Inevitably, problems of cultural and economic appropriation of Indigenous textiles have arisen as they enter a global market, in several ways. Visitors will record the designs and copy them back in their home country, so that they can be found on garments for the psychedelic scene in North America, for instance, or on apparel destined for the spiritual, hippie, and yoga markets. Others purchase a large number of Shipibo textiles and then sell them in stores or online. A few foreigners have asked to be trained in Shipibo embroidery, to then start their own businesses selling their embroideries, mostly online. Etsy is the main online platform where one can see the circulation of Shipibo textiles on the global market and where we see the tensions between a neoliberal feminist ideology of individual competitive entrepreneurship and communal, cosmological, and value-based approach to women's media practices. While some sellers state that they are working in collaboration with Shipibo artists through commissions and giving back a percentage of the sale, the vast majority of online sellers are located in Europe and North America and do not claim any form of collaboration, giving back to the community, or awareness of fair-trade practices at all. But many of the descriptions of Shipibo or Shipibo-inspired items on Etsy will claim a kind of magic power in the items being sold, a link to some kind of cosmic energy, a way to tap into some kind of spiritual understanding. Some of the Western makers claim that their embroidery practice is a spiritual one as well—the textile objects they sell are thus imbued with a capacity to communicate with some mystical spiritual realms. Through such statement, the interface of openness through *kené* mentioned earlier turns into a polysemic vagueness around some kind of access, through the mere purchase of exotic designs, to undefined well-being and spiritual power. In other words, ontological incommensurability between two worlds (the West and the Indigenous Amazonian world) is transformed into commodity fetishism, with the original makers—the Shipibo women and their communities—being completely erased in the process and the actual Shipibo cosmovision being transformed into personal well-being. The interfaces of openness therefore are captured and colonized through both distribution and discourse networks that redistribute meaningful potentials—for extending to other modes of existence and of relating to the world and to others—as personal consumption of commodities.[15] It is interesting to note as well that this process pits makers against makers and is not primarily about big fashion companies stealing designs to mass produce them. Rather, we can note the radically different forms of engagement and relationalities between mostly women makers and artisans cast as micro-entrepreneurs inhabiting niche fashion and craft markets online, and Indigenous women artists and artisans. The former engages in commodity production for personal consumption through cultural appropriation; the other is, at this point in time, much more indeterminate and by and large open to experimentation with alternative networks, as will be discussed shortly.

Last, there has been a colonization of the general desire of Shipibo artists to explore new avenues for dissemination of *kené* designs. Neoliberal multiculturalism has opened up this possibility of economic sustainability through craft production, only to reinscribe it within dominant infrastructures of commodification and alienation. The idea here is that Indigenous groups should become entrepreneurs capable of marketing their identities and ways of life in order to protect them. This has led, on the ground, to various collaborations with foreign designers. These collaborations carry some important contradictions: the development of products that the makers themselves will never see or use (e.g., high-end Western-style furniture), and the presumption that through projects that are short in duration, Shipibo makers will become savvy global textile designers and marketers. The problem is that while these collaborations showcase Shipibo art, they do so for a very remote and rarefied Western audience, therefore alienating the Shipibo makers from the very objects they produce. Furthermore, these collaborations generate a lot of hope in terms of enabling Shipibo makers to make economic gains, but by and large they are usually one-offs and at best sporadic, offering no long-term economic stability. What they highlight in turn for Shipibos is the need for long-term collaborations, but these would involve a fairly profound rethinking of textile objects away from commodities that have to fit into the dynamics of alienation and appropriation of the mainstream fashion and design market.

We therefore find in Shipibo textiles destined for external markets a common dynamic of cultural and economic appropriation of not only the design, but also rituals and cosmovision, mixed with a system of distribution and exchange that alienates Shipibo makers from their media objects. This is further enabled by the impossibility, for the vast majority of Shipibo makers, of gaining direct control over this system of distribution and exchange that organizes the circulation of Shipibo textiles worldwide. Most Shipibo women do not have computers, let alone high-speed internet access. As well, most of them, like most Shipibos, are in situations of poverty and thus cannot afford the services of marketers and lawyers. As it is, Shipibo people, like many Indigenous groups, do not receive much in terms of institutional support (local and national) for protecting their intellectual property, even though they are encouraged to market their arts and crafts. If we were to map out the network of cultural appropriation of Shipibo textiles, we would therefore see two dynamics at play. The first one would be the transformation of a set of transformative extensions—Shipibo textiles—into commodities for personal consumption, thus separating the spiritual from the sociopolitical context, the item from its network of makers, the cosmovision from the actual relations and acts of engagement and composition that make it alive and meaningful. The second one is control, by mostly Western actors, over systems of distribution and exchange of Shipibo textiles, which encompasses (1) the infrastructure of material distribution (shipping, mailing, customs, online payment systems, etc.); (2) the online networks that allow an imposition of a discourse that circumscribes the meaningfulness of Shipibo textiles to individual acts of consumption, leading to some kind of vague individual empowerment; and finally (3) the legal infrastructures that Indigenous groups cannot access and that enable such appropriation to take place. From this situation, it thus seems that Shipibo textile arts for the external market are stuck in a dynamic of appropriation and colonization.

Indigenous Women's Media and the Freedom of Not Knowing

In producing textiles for an external market, Indigenous groups aim to establish a set of relationships with the world outside of their communities, which transform textile objects originally meant for domestic use into uneasy media interfaces where Indigenous values, rights, and claims, themselves changing and evolving, meet an outside that by and large is traversed by and struggles with postcolonial and neocolonial capitalist logics of exploitation and appropriation. In such a context, it is tempting to see Indigenous communities as victims of global capital, by being either dispossessed by it or forced to adapt to its demands, and only surviving in the margins, in niche markets. However, such an understanding would not do justice to the capacities of Indigenous textiles, as media objects open up an uneasy space of encounter between two radically different actors—the local, Indigenous maker and the Western visitor—and through confronting modes of existence and being (Indigenous versus capitalist ones) that are incommensurate. In these confrontations, there is an opening where the possibilities of relations not based on exploitation and objectification can arise and be experienced, however briefly. Dwelling in these moments of confrontation is a way to engage with Viveiro de Castro's perspectival anthropology—to experience moments of doubt that allow for preconceptions as to what other people are and what the world is like to fall apart, to acknowledge "the virtual presence of Another ... who, prior to being a subject or object, is the expression of a possible world."[16]

I argue that such a task of letting one's knowledge structure fall apart is definitely not meant only for the Westerner encountering Shipibo objects, but for any media theory scholars actually wanting to engage with decolonizing media studies. By this, I mean not only understanding how media theory has been focusing on Western media and power by and large, but also inviting non-Western media to the stage and in that way letting some of the core assumptions about media fall apart. What would happen, then, if rather than folding Indigenous media into dominant media infrastructures or judging them for their incapacity to become dominant media in turn, we Western subjects were to recognize and cultivate the space of uneasiness and not knowing that they open up in the first place?

Doing so highlights how thinking of Shipibo textiles as uneasy medium rather than craft could have transformative existential effects. My analysis builds on ethnomusicologist Bernd Brabec de Mori's assertion that "an 'orthodox' western understanding of most processes of change makes the Indigenous people appear very passive, likewise reacting to the intruding forces of the globalising world. However, a deeper understanding of the Indigenous structuring of time reveals that their role is much more active."[17] There has been a rise in an essentialist discourse around Indigenous identity, so much so that, for instance, Shipibo cosmovision is commonly assumed to be an ancient tradition that has remained unchanged throughout time. Such romantic visions of Indigenous people abound in the Western imagination, especially for people in search of spiritual answers. As well, mobilizing an essentialist version of indigeneity has been a successful strategy to claim rights to space, land, or natural resource wealth. It is however a mistake to settle on an essentialist understanding of Indigenous cosmovisions as fixed and unchanging. In the case of the Shipibo, Brabec de Mori explains that the emergence of a discourse centered on a "singular" and fixed Shipibo Indigenous identity, as opposed to the plural cultures and "histories of various sub-groups," serves several actors, including "natives, missionaries, NGOs, researchers, and tourists in a surprisingly consistent mutual agreement."[18] As Brabec de Mori further explains, this preoccupation with tradition and authenticity is intrinsically a Western imposition—original authenticity as a concept does not even exist in most Amazonian societies, which have a completely different understanding and experience of time and of the relationships between past, present, and future. In particular for the Shipibo, the past is "flexible" and "un-fixed" and, just like the future, has an "immanent presence" that is often "not felt directly" but "located in . . . remote strata of realities" that only specialists such as *médicos* can "visit," "access," "manipulate," and use to transform everyday life through rituals.[19] Brabec de Mori further argues that this understanding of time allows Shipibos to be quite creative and "innovative" in their use of rituals and culture, concluding that "the structuring of time and distance in Shipibo understanding allows for complete freedom in maintaining, transmitting, creating and changing of 'tradition.' . . . History is in the making."[20] An anecdote illustrates this tension: I was told of a Westerner commissioning a Shipibo textile artist for an embroidered piece, but specifying that only local materials should be used—local, hand-spun, and hand-woven cotton and thread, hand-dyed with local dyestuff. While there are painted textile pieces using local dyestuff and handwoven cotton, Shipibo embroideries typically use bright synthetic colors, which correspond more to their current aesthetic sensibility. The resulting piece was, in the eye of the Westerner, an authentic Shipibo textile that went back to some kind of original roots when Shipibo arts were unsullied by external forces. For the Shipibo maker, on the other hand, the constraints imposed were entirely artificial. Here again, we find two positions with regard to Shipibo arts and crafts that are the reverse of each other: from the Western perspective, an alignment between the spiritual, understood as sacred, and therefore unchanging and rooted in some kind of pure origin. On the other hand, a fluid and unfixed approach to transformative cosmologies, based on playfulness and practices of composition and recomposition, that is, of creative linkages with actors, elements, and processes that are heterogenous.

In actuality, Shipibo textile practices evolve, responding to external input and in that way redefining themselves as media interfaces of experimentation and dissemination, rather than obeying the Western ideal of centralization and fixity. For example, the quality of lines for *kené* designs has evolved—there are at least two different styles in existence, with the older one being more angular, and the newer style being more curvaceous. Shipibo textile artists in turn sometimes combine these different styles in order to produce different aesthetic effects. Shipibo makers have begun to use new support for *kené* designs, particularly garments. They now sell T-shirts and pants with *kené* designs that are often perceived by visitors as the proper kind of apparel for taking part in ritual ceremonies. These garments have very little in common with traditional Shipibo garments but find a place in the reinvented rituals. Interestingly as well, some Shipibo textile makers have also started to mix in pictorial representation with *kené*. Such integration of pictorial representations is a shift toward finding new ways to communicate with visitors and foreigners. It would be a mistake to see such changes as either disingenuous or imposed adaptation to market demands only. Rather, it would be more accurate to see these changes as an effort to find bridges between radically different modes of existence. This echoes many efforts on the ground to develop ways to enable visitors to experience Shipibo cosmovision, not only through ayahuasca and other rituals, but also through lived experience—sharing the daily life of a village, being educated in the Amazon ecosystem, and so on. The efforts, in other words, are toward creating something that will enable visitors to gain something meaningful from Shipibo rituals and cosmovisions, beyond surface experiments with psychedelic drugs. For this reason, it would be more appropriate to consider these changes and experiments, including ones around Shipibo textiles, as practical engagements with the kind of perspectival anthropology that Viveiros de Castro argues for. Overall, then, in Shipibo textiles we find a medium that does not fix but rather is always changing, that relates to time and space as fluid, that has its own formality, but can experiment without constraints, overall, a medium that functions in ways that are radically opposed to a Western conception of media.

System Politics for Crossing the Abyss

I have to confess that as a media scholar, it is difficult to encounter this space of not knowing and to admit that one is missing some key conceptual tools that have yet to be invented through further dialogue with Shipibo makers. There is cause for careful appreciation of the failures of Western modes of extension that have traditionally enabled us to comprehend, grasp, and assimilate other forms of knowledge. The key mistake, indeed, would be to dismiss Shipibo textiles because they do not act or have effects at a distance like Western-dominant media. In that sense, it is tactical to acknowledge media scholarship as part of the system of distribution and exchange examined above. Our job as media scholars might be to critique, but also to recognize our positionality in a complex system that is notable for its capacity to index anything and everything to its own capitalist and postcolonialist neoliberal logics, including critique, in the search for new market opportunities. And the first step in disengaging from this system of distribution and exchange is to investigate the construction of other systems. What could happen then if, rather than focusing on defining what Shipibo *kené* is as media practices, forms, and objects, we turned our attention to the constitutions of new systems of distribution and exchange? If rather than extending ourselves and imposing our epistemologies outward, we were to welcome extensions coming at us? This kind of dynamic is present on the ground: quite a few anthropology researchers ended up settling in with Shipibo groups and decided that the most important tasks were, for instance, providing language instruction and building sanitation systems, something that might seem far away from theory as can be, but in actuality is a profound and essential commitment to establishing structures of sustainability that enable, in turn, experiments with new exchange processes.

In that regard, the situation concerning the propagation of Shipibo textiles demonstrates, at least in Pucallpa, an incredibly wide variety of ideas and experiments that are often prevented from happening because of lack of support and infrastructure, because they indeed fall outside of the system, from fashion education to long-term financial investment. One example is a proposed project for a Natural Dyes in the Amazon workshop open to non-Shipibo artists. The project aims to fulfill several goals: first, to offer a way for non-Shipibos to experience more than the finished *kené* designs, that is to say, to experience the environment and context that shape Shipibos' cosmovision. Second, the project offers a way for Shipibo artists to be exposed to other artistic and design practices. Third, it aims to strengthen the use of local materials for artistic practice, especially for younger generations, thus strengthening identity building through contact with the Amazonian environment. Finally, this helps promote knowledge of Amazonian plants and materials, as many local dyes and pigments have medicinal properties as well. In all, the transitions toward mobilizing Shipibo textile practices, as interfaces for forging new relationships, reveal attempts to establish new and different networks and systems to mobilize different dynamics and actors. Such projects, which might seem small in scale, are actually cosmotechnical in their approach: through small gestures of having to deal with and relate to the Amazonian environment in order to gather creative materials and try out techniques, one is forced to engage with the question of cosmovision, including not only Shipibo cosmovision but a cosmovision for the Anthropocene.[21]

In Lima, there are many murals that include *kené* designs, some made by the Shipibo diaspora, but many made by other non-Shipibo artists.

The inclusion of *kené* in these murals and street art involves a call to other modes of being outside the Western, colonial legacy, a call to refusal of destructive capitalism and commitment to the Amazon as the most diverse place in the world, teeming with so much life. Through *kené*, the calling of the Amazon in the desert where Lima is located represents a bridge toward new ways of being together and new solidarities that do not and will not fit into the dominant system of distribution and exchange. *Kené* breaks apart the system and calls for new modes of communication, of relationalities, of existence to and with each other.

I follow Boaventura de Sousa Santos to offer that the incommensurabilities between the Indigenous and the Western world delineate the abyssal line that separates the world of those subject to colonization and the world of colonial power.[22] But the question is, in turn, about the capacity for Indigenous media such as Shipibo textiles to create uneasy bridges (new extensions indeed) to open up a space of uncertainty and doubt for us Western scholars who are, by and large, and just because of our positionalities, extensions (albeit at times critical and reluctant) of a Western system of knowledge. Such uncertainty and doubt constitute the necessary ground on which new transformative alliances and potentials can be formulated and does require that as a scholar, one lets oneself be extended in new ways and directions. I want to be clear that I am not arguing that in and of themselves, Shipibo textiles are capable of the kind of deep transformation of existence that the current age of the Anthropocene requires of us: ultimately, this is a political choice and commitment requiring rethinking the systems within which media are able to fully extend, with no guarantee of measurable deliverables. Embracing not knowing as a political media engagement is not an easy proposition, but it also offers the space for much-needed ontological and epistemological creativity. One could perhaps start imagining the possibilities of collective dreaming, like the *kené* practice, of worlds to come, worlds to be made, of detaching oneself from unilateral extensions of control and becoming in turn extended, transformed into something else entirely.

Notes

The author would like to thank Alianza Arkana for their generous help and support. The research for this project was made possible through a grant from the Social Science and Humanities Research Council of Canada.

1. McLuhan, *Understanding Media* (1994).

2. Innis, *Empire and Communications.*
3. McLuhan, *Understanding Media* (1994).
4. Frankopan, *The Silk Roads.*
5. Tanaka, *The Power of the Weave.*
6. Franklin, "Staying with the Manifesto."
7. Brabec de Mori, "The Magic of Song."
8. Wali et al., "The Shipibo-Conibo," 81, 82.
9. Belaunde, "Diseños materiales e inmateriales."
10. Brabec de Mori, "The Magic of Song," 181.
11. Wali et al., "The Shipibo-Conibo," 85; Feldman, "Evolving Communities," 51.
12. Viveiro de Castro, "The Relative Native," 473.
13. Barthes, *Camera Lucida.*
14. "Welcome to Shipibo Joi," Shipibo Joi, August 29, 2011. https://shipibojoi.wordpress.com/2011/08/29/hello-world/.
15. Kittler, *Discourse Networks.*
16. Viveiro de Castro, "The Relative Native," 473.
17. Brabec de Mori, "The Magic of Song," 186.
18. Brabec de Mori, "The Magic of Song," 180.
19. Brabec de Mori, "The Magic of Song," 185.
20. Brabec de Mori, "The Magic of Song," 186.
21. "Cosmotechnical" from Hui, *The Question Concerning Technology in China.*
22. Santos, *The End of the Cognitive Empire.*

Part II
Thinking with McLuhan: An Invitation

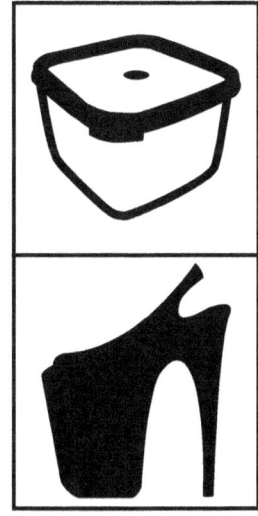

5 Dear Incubator

SARA MARTEL

Dearest Machine:

I hope this letter finds you well. It has been a few years since my son was discharged from the neonatal intensive care unit where he lived inside of you for many months. I have to say, it all feels like yesterday. He was born three months too early, long before he or I were expecting or prepared for him to transition violently from the inside of my body to the outside. Thank goodness *you* were ready, dear incubator, always reliable, clean, warm. How can I thank you enough?

    My labor unfolded in a complicated mix of shock and panic that was still considered "natural childbirth" by virtue of it not involving surgery. Perhaps the physical pain was "barbaric," but I would take it many times over the anguish of pushing out a baby without really knowing if I was birthing or deathing.[1] I barely caught a glimpse of him after he exited my body. The obstetrician's hands moved him swiftly from between my legs to the neonatologist's hands, who had been watching the birth alongside her team through a large rectangular observation window looking into the delivery room.[2] It was surreal to be gazed upon like this in such a vulnerable state. Was I actually a patient in premature labor or was I just playing one on TV?

I waited for someone to tell me my baby was alive after he had been rushed to the adjacent room. Then suddenly the television screen suspended on the ceiling above my head turned on, projecting the image of the neonatologists' hands working on and around a tiny baby on a table. In all the quick and decisive action, he hadn't quite become my baby just yet. He was wrapped entirely in plastic except for his tiny cone-shaped head and had the ventilator attached on his face.[3] All I could see were blue latex gloves darting purposefully across reddish-pink skin. Every once in a while, I would see my partner's hands move into the frame to take a picture with his phone. My newborn appeared on so many screens before I even got up close to see, smell, hear, or feel him. I wondered if he was making sounds. I wondered what the physicians were saying. The screen above my head had no audio.

A few hours later, I was finally taken to the neonatal intensive care unit to see him—or, more accurately, to see him inside of you. Narrowly squeezing through the doorway of his small room in my postdelivery wheelchair, you were the first thing I laid eyes on. The lights were off and there was a blanket draped over you to shield the baby from any light or disturbance. The blanket wasn't just one of those starchy generic flannel types found in all hospital rooms; this blanket was a soft, quilted material with light pastel swirls. I suppose it was chosen to give this cramped pod—stacked with monitors, IV poles, packaged needles, sterile bandages, tape, breathing apparatuses, thermometers, a mobile breast pump, a refrigerator for medications and donor milk—the feel of a nursery. You were not the machine in the nursery so much as this soft quilted blanket was the nursery in the machine.[4]

I tried moving in closer, but the wheels of my chair clanged against the base of your cart. This was the first of many times I was reminded you came first. Of course, it only made sense. I needed to let you do your job. Your regulated embrace never fluctuated or faltered. You never had to leave the hospital to shower or sleep the way I did. You never lost power. You never got sad or scared. You never risked infection. At first, I felt quite inferior in comparison. My body was permeable, unsanitary, unpredictable, failed at unfolding the seemingly clockwork biomechanics of gestation: What is more useless than a broken clock? Maybe a broken clock with swollen ankles and rampant postpartum anxiety. But oh, how I craved the close contact you had with my son that I did not have in those first many days. You held him long before I could. I would watch him sleeping inside of you, still curled up tight as if unaware he was no longer constricted inside my fleshy belly.

The only thing illuminating the space around him in the darkened room were the screens of his vital sign monitors and other small flickering LED lights on the various machines. Little did I know how many hours I would spend staring at those monitors over the next few months, contemplating the tone of its different alarms and shifts in the numbers and graphs that told me what his heart and lungs were doing.[5] "Look at your baby, not at the screens!" the nurses would scold. The monitor lines, the IV line providing him antibiotics through his belly, and the ventilator over his mouth were the only things you let near him. Getting closer, I noticed two circles on the side of your wall with doors latched shut on each. Those were for human hands to enter and exit. Would I get to touch him? Maybe I could even hold him, I wondered.

The necessary wires and tubes entered your space through ports at each end of your plexiglass box, reminiscent of the tangled cords one finds at the back of a television set. But these cords did not join gadgets to each other. They tethered his body to the machines keeping him alive—the body that just hours earlier was inside of me but was now inside of you. You created your own environment.[6] To me, you as a biomedical medium—one of many that pumped and dripped and shocked and counted and visualized and beeped and wheezed the production of the intensive care space where near-death was transformed into almost-living[7]—you were a whole planet and my baby was the whole world.

Eventually, I got up the nerve to ask: Could I hold him? The nurse's patient response was "not yet"; too much stimulation was not good this early on. It would stress the baby. But as he stabilized, they showed me how to unlatch your doors and slide my hands in to touch his small back or place his impossibly small hand on one of my fingers to make me feel like he was reaching for me, even though he never did. "Hand hugging" is what they called it when you put your hands on him, the realignment of the boundaries between embrace and touch based on the contours of your openings.[8] I would have loved to keep my hands in there all day to feel his warmth and his body moving with breath. But your doors couldn't be kept open too long. Your air needed to stay clean and warm.

You are a tricky medium, aren't you? You were hot with visual information that lit up every sensorial spark in my body with the affect of longing and anticipation. Yet, you were frustratingly cool in touch, sound, or smell, leaving me to fill in anything that was missing. You demanded and denied my participation. I suppose that makes you a uniquely *warm* medium, just as you like it.[9] You are a participant form that demands a partner.[10] I was happy to oblige. You reconfigured the boundaries of living, dying, and the space and time of reproduction, demanding decision making, intervention, care, investment. You may act shy, like a static object that only creates and controls negative space, but you and I both know you will never be a background instrument.[11] That's not your way.

Sitting there staring through your walls, I recalled the historical photos I had seen of the "child hatchery" sideshows at the turn of the twentieth century across Europe and America.[12] How far you'd come since those days when your value wasn't quite common sense. The doctors-turned-showmen would arrange for sick and low-birth-weight newborns from local hospitals to be placed in shiny new incubators that the public could pay to see. Highly skilled nurses would provide care and mothers would breast-feed between shows. They weren't the stars of the show though.[13] Nor were the babies or other incubators exactly. It was the inseparability of the babies-incubators. I suppose I wasn't much different than the carnival gawkers, staring through your wall day and night, always in awe. But my baby never felt like spectacle to me. And you never felt like a screen projecting my newborn as ex utero content the way many imagine the ultrasound visualizing the fetus in utero.[14] You were more.

Other mothers of premature babies have said they felt replaced by you.[15] I suppose in some ways you are an artificial womb, a prosthetic to complete my womb-work like a domestic robot might help me finish my chores.[16] But you aren't a uterine appendage in any simple terms, moving the gestational process from the biomechanical to the mechanical. You revealed my experiences of reproduction—from initial desire, to infertility, to thwarted desire, to surprise conception, to unexpected preterm labor, to the desire to see my baby live, to the physical labor of keeping my baby alive—as technological. *We* the reproductive assemblage are a happening, a phenomenon.[17] This can't be separated out into who is natural (me I guess?) and who artificial (obviously you) or who most deserves to hold the baby. We are machinic coparents, you and me.[18]

Through you, I emerged as Mommy Martel. It was disorienting at first. I hadn't even adjusted to the idea of mothering, never mind being erased as anything other than Mother.[19] "Mommy Martel, the ultrasound will tell us if there is bleeding on his brain. Mommy Martel, do you want us to move him off the ventilator?" Once we were out of the woods, the questions started to change: "Mommy Martel, do you want to try bathing him? You're going to have to learn so you can do it at home. Don't worry, we'll unhook all his wires first. Mommy Martel, do you want to take him out of the incubator to hold him? Skin-to-skin contact is very important. Mommy Martel, are we going to try breast-feeding today? Breast milk is very important. Mommy Martel, do you want to be a good mother or do you want to be a bad mother?"[20]

In keeping my baby alive, you demanded my skin and my milk and my smell and my microbes and my eye contact and my time and my sleeplessness and my anxiety and my fear. You did not replace me, dear machine, you created more work for mother.[21] Technoscientists might indeed be driven to produce new monsters, but it's safe to say they've shown less interest in changing the little one's diapers through two holes in the side of an incubator, waking every four hours around the clock to pump breast milk, medicating to increase lactation, providing skin-to-skin contact, standing by helplessly during painful procedures on tiny bodies, or experiencing the complicated turmoil of not doing any of these things because they can't or don't want to.[22] The urge to continuous use means you are always on.[23] And if you are always on, mommy is always on—or carrying the judgment of being off.

I apologize if my tone sounds resentful. Who am I to complain? Each moment with my wished-for baby has been a privilege—that's not lost on me in the least.[24] This is in fact what compelled me to write to you. I wanted you to know I don't think of you as a technology of separation, like some kind of ectogenetic adversary disconnecting me from my baby. I think of you as a technology of attachment. You tether with wires, sure, but also with feeling. In transforming the threshold between birth, life, and death, you transformed the psychic and social grounds of wishing, hoping, failing, losing, and grieving. The partner you demand is one who cares—dare I say it, the one who loves. In reconfiguring reproduction, you reconfigured reproductive loss. How can one's conception of the medium account for wishes? Isn't desire what gets the structures of reproduction under our skin in the first place?[25]

When we were finally sent home from the hospital, the urge to continuous use did not suddenly stop. The hardest part about leaving you behind was that I had grown to desire the security of the sterile space you provided my son's immune system, severely compromised by his prematurity. You revealed the world to me as risky and full of infection, making it hard to adjust to organic life again. No one tells you to expect this when you're expecting, but maybe they should. Maybe it would have been less lonely. Sometimes I miss you—how strange does that sound! Sometimes I wondered, would it be that crazy to have you come live with us just for cold and flu season? But I knew I needed to move on. All the stickers with our baby's first name we used to decorate your cart were peeled off. You were sanitized for another baby to call home. I get it; you are not ours any more.

Anyway, I think I've said what I felt I needed to say. I don't get to talk much about life in the NICU these days, so I appreciate your attention. You, after all, are such an important part of our story. Thank you for keeping my baby alive. That's all I really wanted to say.

Warm regards,
Mommy Martel

Notes

This chapter is an autoethnographic piece, written in the format of a letter to the incubator that housed my son for weeks after his premature birth. Endnotes have been provided to orient the reader to the critique woven into my performative correspondence with the machine.

1. Shulamith Firestone famously declared that "pregnancy is barbaric" (*The Dialectic of Sex*, 180) in challenging the mystification of childbirth and physical pain it entails. She proposed that women ought to be liberated from the tyranny of traditional childbirth through automated ectogenetic gestation. Firestone's and contemporary feminist work could be expanded to question more thoroughly how reproductive "failures" such as miscarriage, stillbirth, and perinatal and infant death—in addition to the more frequently engaged experience of maternal pain or risk of death—are socioculturally constructed as outside of the natural reproductive order, whether assisted or not. The silence around reproductive loss in Western society and in feminist scholarship reflects a challenge of critically navigating questions of unborn life without reinforcing antiabortion rhetoric. This silence in turn compounds a lack of social or emotional support for mothers who experience high-risk reproduction and/or reproductive loss. As an example of work bringing reproductive loss into feminist dialogue, Sophie Lewis takes up reproductive loss among other "life-enabling forms of holding and letting go" in her piece "Cyborg Uterine Geography," calling for the "deromanticization" of "uterine relations." See also Earle, Komaromy, and Layne, *Understanding Reproductive Loss*.

2. My birth took place in a high-risk obstetrics ward in a Canadian hospital that housed a Level III neonatal intensive care unit (NICU). A NICU is a specialized care unit providing high-level intensive care to newborns requiring medical attention, including, frequently, those born prematurely. It is common practice for neonatologists to be on hand at high-risk births so care can be transferred from the obstetrical team to the neonatal team immediately upon delivery.

3. It is current practice in many hospitals to wrap the bodies of preterm infants with plastic bags immediately after delivery to reduce heat loss and the chance of

hypothermia before transferring the baby to an incubator. Hypothermia is associated with increased morbidity and mortality rates among preterm infants. Many preterm infants also require help breathing due to immature lungs, so breathing machines such as ventilators are often applied by an endotracheal tube placed down the baby's windpipe through the mouth or nose.

4. The term "machine in the nursery" here is an allusion to the title of Jeffery Baker's book *The Machine in the Nursery: Incubator Technology and the Origins of Newborn Intensive Care*. Baker explains how incubators were involved in shifting responsibility for premature newborns from mothers to physicians, as part of the evolution of the complex system of contemporary neonatal intensive care within which incubators evolved from warming devices to life-support technology. I switch Baker's phrasing to the idea of the nursery being in the machine to capture the temporal-spatial expanse of the NICU as a technological environment within which the material cultures of motherhood (e.g., knitted blankets, stuffed animals, rocking chairs, etc.) are the interlopers, not the machine. The presence of baby blankets such as the one in my son's room (often homemade and donated by volunteers) also call to mind Linda Layne's work on reproductive loss such as miscarriage, stillbirth, and early infant death, which illustrates how consumer goods are circulated to construct the personhood, or the "realness" of the unborn or born babies, and the identity of the mothers as "real mothers," often otherwise erased in reproductive loss. Layne, "'He Was a Real Baby with Baby Things.'"

5. Babies in the NICU are attached to cardiopulmonary monitors via wires with electrodes on the chest and abdomen to detect heart activity, respiratory rate, oxygen levels, and blood pressure.

6. The incubator creates its own environment by way of its enclosure, as well as the material assemblage of neonatal intensive care, an environment for human sensory experience, as per McLuhan's conceptualization of the medium in his adage "the medium is the message." McLuhan, *Understanding Media* (1994), 7.

7. I refer to the incubator as "biomedical medium" to situate its use in neonatal medicine within the broader economic, bioethical, and technoscientific transformation of Western medicine within the same time frame, often termed biomedicalization. See Clarke et al., *Biomedicalization, Technoscience, Health, and Illness*. The widespread adoption of incubators by contemporary hospitals emerged through the development of neonatal medicine as a specialty and intensive care units as specialized spaces across the latter half of the twentieth century. See Lantos and Meadow, *Neonatal Bioethics*.

8. Hand hugging has been introduced in many NICUs as part of an increased focus on the therapeutic benefits of skin-to-skin contact between the baby and caregivers, understood to help with physiological regulation and psychosocial development. Hand hugging is used in the many cases in which babies cannot leave their incubators for extended periods of time, making full skin-to-skin contact difficult.

9. McLuhan defines a hot medium (e.g., radio, film) as "one that extends one single sense in 'high definition'" versus a cool medium (e.g., cartoons, telephones) as "one of low definition, because so little is given and so much has to be filled in by the listener" (*Understanding Media* [1994], 22, 23). While McLuhan's theorization of the sensorial experience of media is arguably light and overly universalizing, I have used it here believing it provides an interesting framework for thinking about the incubator's interface that is simultaneously deeply engaging and distancing—a warm medium, both in its sensorial experience and in its temperature-controlled functions.

10. McLuhan, *Understanding Media* (1994), 268. This citation and the following citation in the same paragraph are taken from McLuhan's description of the telephone. I draw on his explanation for why the telephone is a medium that can "create an intense feeling of loneliness" to think through the incubator's sensorial and affective tensions: "Why should we feel compelled to answer a ringing public phone when we know the call cannot concern us? Why does a phone ringing on the stage create instant tension? Why is that tension so very much less for an unanswered phone in a movie scene? The answer to all of these questions is simply that the phone is a participant form that demands a partner, with all the intensity of electric polarity. It simply will not act as a background instrument like the radio." Like the telephone, I argue the incubator is a technology that can call us to answer and leaves us tense when unanswered. This call can be experienced through many senses, for example, sound (e.g., the muffled cries of the baby through the plexiglass or the beeping of the vitals monitors when heart rates, oxygen saturation, or breathing slows to dangerous levels), sight (e.g., the baby making eye contact, seeing the baby squirm in discomfort and needing tending, looking at the data visualization on the monitors, reading the temperature levels of the incubator or the baby's body), smell (e.g., smelling a soiled diaper through the openings, smelling vomit, smelling the baby's skin), or touch (e.g., hand hugging, the feel of leaking breast milk when near the baby). And yet, by the nature of the incubator's enclosure, the potential for response to these calls is limited. While I would argue against the notion of a universal affective response to babies in incubators, the biomedical space of neonatal medicine demands such maternal responses. As I will return to farther down, I question if this imperative toward maternal response can be understood drawing on Sarah Ahmed's work on capitalism's demand for happiness in *The Promise of Happiness*. In figurative terms, we might also think about the baby in the incubator as the Child of reproductive futures (Berlant, "America, 'Fat,' the Fetus"; Edelman, *No Future*), demanding economic and emotional investment. A lack of complete maternal participation in the NICU is constructed as postpartum pathology or negligence, thus connecting the incubator to other technologies of social reproduction, such as the state's removal of infants from their bio-parents or caregivers.

11. McLuhan, *Understanding Media* (1994), 268.

12. European obstetricians created "infant hatchery" sideshows at World's Fairs as a means of garnering public fascination and support for the investment into

neonatal innovations. American obstetrician Dr. Martin Couney created a standing exhibit at Coney Island that remained open until the 1940s. The exhibits consisted of rows of incubators holding premature babies on loan from local hospitals. See Silverman, "Incubator-Baby Side Shows"; Baker, "The Incubator and the Medical Discovery"; Baker, *The Machine in the Nursery*; Reedy, "Historical Perspectives"; Raffel, *The Strange Case of Dr. Couney* for accounts of the incubator as medical innovation and sideshow spectacle.

13. Historian Gina Greene suggests literature on the topic of incubator sideshows does not commonly reference the babies' mothers, as "they were likely indigent, or in poor health themselves, and thus consigned their premature infants over to the temporary care of physicians who then placed them in the exhibits" ("The 'Cradle of Glass,'" 88). Although parents were not always present during the shows, many were eager to let their premature and underweight babies participate, as it would ensure they would be cared for by highly trained nurses and increase their otherwise narrow chance of survival. Social oppressions similar to those facing the sideshow mothers make many parents invisible in literature on the efficacy of biomedical intervention into prematurity and high-risk reproduction.

14. See Petchesky, "Fetal Images"; Jordanova, *Sexual Vision*; Berlant, "America, 'Fat,' the Fetus"; Newman, *Fetal Positions*; Mitchell, *Baby's First Picture*.

15. Writing about the experience of having her prematurely born daughter's life sustained by an incubator, Jaimie Smith-Windsor, in "The Cyborg Mother," describes "the displacement of my own motherhood by the machine." She suggests that within "cyborg consciousness," which she explains as the complete mediation of experience by the technological, "the Mother becomes redundant: technology becomes the external womb."

16. I borrow the term "womb-work" from Sophie Lewis and the concept of gestation as work more broadly from Lewis and Emre's dialogue in the *Boston Review's Once and Future Feminist* (2018); Lewis, "Mothering"; Emre, "On Reproduction.". Although Sarah Sharma's contribution to the same dialogue (see Sharma, "Going to Work in Mommy's Basement") does not look at the automation of gestation directly, her probes into the technological expansion of and simultaneous devaluation of maternal labor (for example, through domestic robots, sex robots, and care apps) can inform a critical reading of the incubator's role in expanding maternal labor, normative regimes, and the oppressive nature of reproduction for many women. To be clear, however, the incubator needs to be conceptualized distinctly from artificial womb technologies designed for ectogenesis (i.e., embryonic development outside of the human womb), as incubators assist preterm babies with bodily functions but do not simulate the uterine environment exactly, which makes me hesitant to use the womb in my figuration of the incubator as medium. For a bioethical take on this distinction, see Romanis, "Artificial Womb Technology and the Frontiers of Human Reproduction," and for critical feminist exploration of ectogenesis see Aristarkhova, "Ectogenesis and Mother as Machine."

17. Returning to McLuhan's notion of the medium as environment, the incubator can be thought of as an entity within a material assemblage. I have brought together the notion of reproduction as a "happening," to use McLuhan's term employed in "Education in the Electronic Age," with the notion of reproduction as "phenomenon," taking up the language of Karen Barad's feminist materialism in *Meeting the Universe Halfway*. In Baradian terms, the parent, the baby, and the incubator would not preexist each other, then come together in an "interaction," but rather emerge through their "intra-action," that is, the phenomena of biomedical or technoscientific reproduction. I believe Barad's formulation of phenomenal entanglements lends McLuhan's media environments an ontological angle that brings into focus the connectivity between the medium, the body, the social, the spatial, and the temporal.

18. By highlighting the contingency of my baby's survival on the incubator, I acknowledge how my motherhood is not directly unfolded from my own uterus/womb or any natural process of gestational completion therein. Contextualizing this acknowledgment is Merve Emre's ("On Reproduction") assertion that all reproduction is assisted and that assuming otherwise "occludes the many individuals who carry or care for children. They include lesbians, trans people, and gender non-conforming people, as well as single women, women who cannot conceive or carry, women who have had miscarriages, adoptive parents, mothers of premature babies, and surrogates" (13). The incubator is an example of one of the seemingly "mundane" (8) technologies that xenofeminist Helen Hester (*Xenofeminism*) has pointed out could be used for the further oppression of laboring bodies or turned toward the feminist refiguring of social relations. I use the term "machinic coparents" to expand reproductive justice beyond questions of technological conception and gestation (e.g., who has the right to pregnancy, who has the right to end pregnancy) to include reproductive care practices that are not entirely uterine but perhaps uterine-adjacent, such as incubator parenting and/or other forms of medically complex caregiving. As Hester suggests in relation to reproductive justice beyond abortion rights specifically: "we must persistently embrace a more holistic concept of reproductive justice. Such a characterization is necessary to ensure that protocols are not unwittingly limited to the concerns of middle-class, able-bodied, white, cishet women. Reproductive justice is as much about support for having and raising children in conditions of safety and freedom as it is about resisting personally unwanted births" (*Xenofeminism*, 125–26)—and I would add achieving personally wanted births in the face of infertility. NICU spaces are prone to being limited to concerns of the dominant voices Hester calls out above, as the biomedical and maternal merge in the construction of the good NICU mommy who is economically and psychosocially resourced to be present in the NICU and who enacts attached mothering via extensive kangaroo care and lactation work. Patricia Hamilton's critique of neoliberal parenting philosophies in "The 'Good' Attached Mother" is useful here, as is research connecting preterm mothers' feelings of distress, failure,

and inadequacy with the NICU's technocratic structures (see Palmquist, Holdren, and Fair, "'It Was All Taken Away'").

19. I am making a distinction here between mothering as a practice and being a Mother as a normative social identity—the latter of which machinic coparenting could serve to dismantle. I refer to myself here as "Mommy Martel" because that is what medical staff called me in the NICU. Parents are generally referred to as Mommy Surname or Daddy Surname rather than by their first names. Babies are also often referred to as Baby Surname, as per the information sheet taped on or near each incubator. Although likely a practical measure to help clinicians match caregivers to babies in units that hold multiple patients, it also echoes the Mommy of Sharma's "Mommy's Basement" in that it was, in my observation, a terminology informed by gendered and biologically determined notions of maternal (and lack of paternal) labor.

20. Again, expectations of mothering in the NICU include much of the economically undervalued yet socially expected care practices within neoliberalism, such as exclusively breast-feeding (or at least providing human milk), attachment, and constant physical contact.

21. This is an allusion to Ruth Schwartz Cowan's *More Work for Mother: The Ironies of Household Technology from the Open Hearth to the Microwave*. Reproductive technologies might appear to liberate women from certain labors, but they also introduce new forms of labor as part of the medium's environment. These labors are not equally or equitably experienced, as they unfold within the same well-documented racial, gendered, and classed discriminations defining good or bad motherhood outside of the NICU.

22. Rosi Braidotti's handling of reproductive technologies in the chapter "Mothers, Monsters, and Machines" in *Nomadic Subjects* offers an example of feminist work concerned with ectogenesis as patriarchal desire for autogenesis that makes the mother's body obsolete: "On the imaginary level . . . the test-tube babies of today mark the long-term triumph of the alchemists' dream of dominating nature through their self-inseminating, masturbatory practices. What is happening with the new reproductive technologies today is the final chapter in a long history of fantasy of self-generation by and for the men themselves—men of science, but men of the male kind, capable of producing new monsters and fascinated by their power" (88).

23. McLuhan, *Understanding Media* (1994), 68.

24. Any preterm baby's survival must be contextualized within structural inequities related to health outcomes and health care.

25. Sarah Ahmed has said, "feelings might be how structures get under our skin" (*The Promise of Happiness*, 216). Although I do not offer a complete theorization of McLuhan's urge to continuous use through Ahmed's affect theory, I include this reference as an opening to future work that might consider how medium theory might draw from the idea that "emotions . . . create the very effect of the surfaces or boundaries of bodies and worlds" (Ahmed, "Affective Economies," 117) and vice versa.

6 Wifesaver

Tupperware and the Unfortunate Spoils of Containment

BROOKE ERIN DUFFY
AND JEREMY PACKER

Introduction

Few consumer commodities are more emblematic of feminine, domestic life in postwar America than Tupperware, the line of vibrantly hued plastic storage containers. But in 1954, Tupperware was cast as more than just a desirable commodity. It was, simply put, a "Wifesaver" (figure 6.1). To the housewife whose life needed saving from seemingly endless responsibilities, Tupperware promised to be a technology that "works for you" and "makes life easier." Tupperware's appeal thus drew from its capacities for extension—prolonging the shelf life of food, furthering the sprawl of the middle class away from urban centers, broadening women's roles into the (paid) labor market. We contend, however, that Tupperware is more fruitfully understood not by looking outside or afar, but by focusing *within*, namely into the process of containment. In what follows, we offer an analysis of Tupperware as container media that collected, stored, and processed the spoils of consumer capitalism during the Cold War era. Tupperware as a "Wifesaver" offered a helping hand of support—even as it seemed to

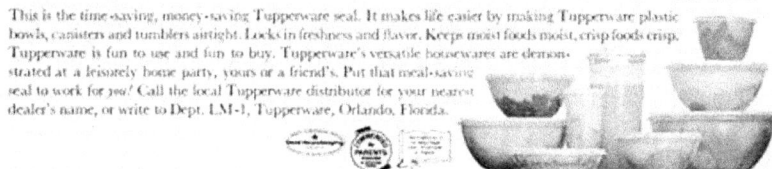

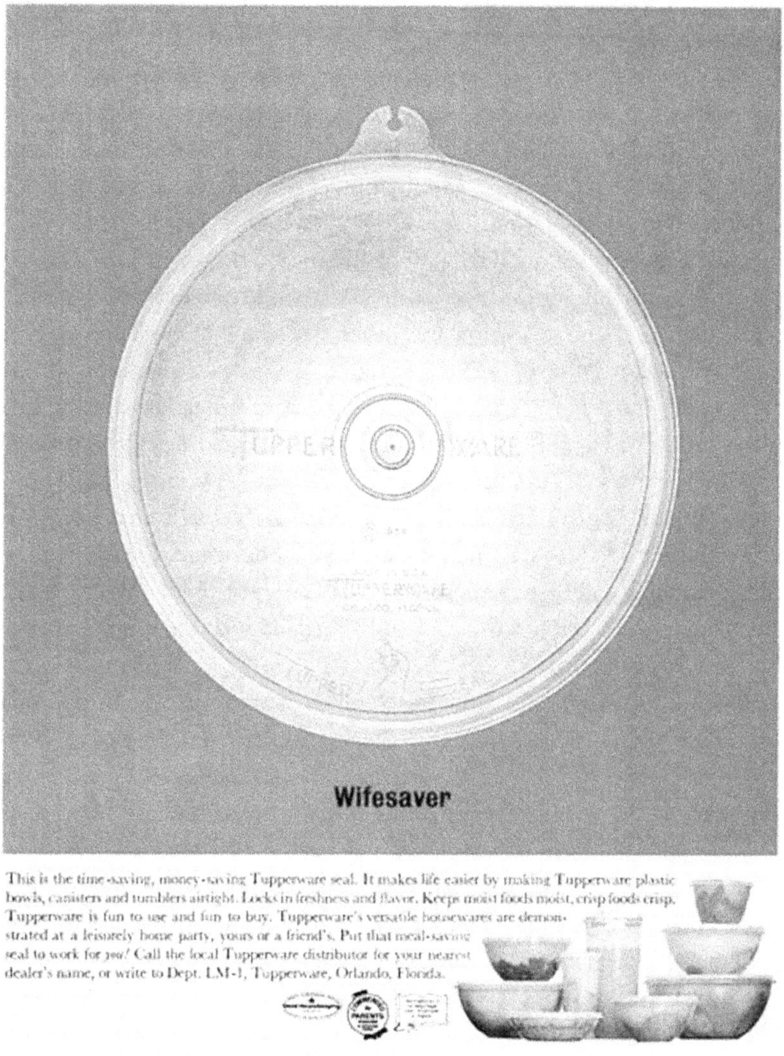

6.1 1954 Tupperware advertisement.

ensure that wifely duties would be structurally saved, organized, and preserved ad infinitum.

The concealment of Tupperware's inward systems of preservation with a rhetoric of outward progress—or extension, in McLuhan's terms—can be observed in a full-color ad published in the August 1969 issue of the men's sporting magazine *Field & Stream* (figure 6.2). The ad depicts flannel-clad outdoorsman "Harry" admiring his rifle; scattered across the table before him are Tupperware containers full of ammunition. Harry's wife, who approaches to present him with a snack, is stunned to find his arsenal of supplies in her kitchenware. Below the visual, the ad copy touts Tupperware's exclusive technical properties: "Airtight. Waterproof. Moisture-proof. Dustproof. Rustproof" before cataloging a list of potential uses. At first blush, an ad for Tupperware stands out from the magazine's standard promotional registry of machismo: beer, cigarettes, automobiles, and sporting equipment. But surely, as McLuhan's *Mechanical Bride* made patently clear, all such ads reveal something essential about gender roles. Indeed, the concluding call to action prods readers to enlist their wives as provisional suppliers: "Ask her to be a good sport and pick some up for you at her next Tupperware party."

Indeed, the ad's barely concealed hunter-gatherer metaphor is similar to the one that structured McLuhan's perspective on technology: he invoked this binary to downplay the active nature of gathering as well as to reaffirm the tenet of technologies as extensions. Such a masculinist bias, which is discernible in early determinists' perspectives on technology, fundamentally elides attention to those tools and devices used for containment.[1] Not only is this gendered dynamic of masculine-extension/feminine-containment problematic in terms of historical accuracy, but the binary itself, we contend, is not so clear-cut. Take the fishing net, for example: Is it a technology for hunting or gathering? Describing it as one or the other hinges on the degree to which the tool offers up the possibility to exert power over other objects or actors. Whereas hunting implies the exertion of force upon another agentic force, gathering suggests an action upon a passive object.

We can see how Harry's use of Tupperware still functions through properties of (masculine) extension, even as he seems to be engaging in the (feminine) work of sorting, arranging, and preserving. Rather obviously, the items Harry will store relate to his still-productive leisure pursuits of capture (bullets for hunting; flies for fishing; film and gun scopes for targeting visual data), or they will extend the life of his neuro-stimulants (pipe tobacco).

"Harry, what on earth are you doing with my Tupperware?"

What all smart sportsmen are doing. Using Tupperware, their wives' favorite food containers, for their favorite hunting and fishing gear. Giving it the protection it deserves. And gets only in Tupperware.

Tupperware is airtight. Waterproof. Moistureproof. Dustproof. Rustproof. And that's proof enough.

Besides, Tupperware won't rattle, dent or break. Tupperware has containers you can use for everything from scopes to spinners. From flies to film. From pliers to pipe tobacco.

Best of all, you don't need a license to buy Tupperware. And there's no limit either.

Your wife knows what wonders Tupperware works for her. Now, find out what Tupperware can do for you. Ask her to be a good sport and pick some up for you at her next Tupperware Party.

TUPPERWARE®

IN THE YELLOW PAGES UNDER "HOUSEWARES"

Guns Courtesy of Remington Arms Co., Inc.

6.2 1969 Tupperware advertisement.

More substantially, what Harry's deployment of Tupperware makes clear is that containers are necessary elements in other technological pursuits. Tupperware, like all socio-technical systems, depends upon containers; the more complex the system, the more elaborate the containers. Containers make possible supply chains, assembly lines, networks, cities, and space travel. Containers are the infrastructural elements that furnish the "hidden systems of maintenance and supply" as well as the structuring capacities for addressable systems of organization.[2]

This chapter uses Tupperware as a heuristic to show how media theorists' preoccupation with properties of extension has come at the expense of acknowledging the importance—and even primacy—of containment. Before a letter can be sent, it must first be contained by an envelope; an email, similarly, is contained within network packets. Further, containers are often overlooked as technologies, even by those media theorists carefully attuned to the technical dimensions of media systems. For instance, as we discuss below, Wolfgang Ernst suggests that the importance of a Greek vase is not its technical capacities, but its ability to represent cultural traits. Such assumptions imply that containers are aesthetic, rather than technical. This is not to say that the wider academic community has ignored containment as an organizing concept; some historians of technology, and especially feminist technology scholars, have challenged such assumptions. Lewis Mumford argued more than six decades ago: "historians of technics have overestimated the role of tools and machines, the dynamic, mobile, masculine components of technics. . . . By the same token, they have overlooked the more passive, static, feminine aspects, so conspicuous in neolithic culture: the role of the container and the internal transformer."[3] While Mumford's appraisal has been elaborated on by other technological theorists, Judy Wajcman provides a sharper-edged feminist critique: "A greater emphasis on women's activities immediately suggests that females, and in particular black women, were among the first technologists. After all, women were the main *gatherers*, *processors* and *storers* of plant food from earliest human times onward."[4] We can see in Wajcman's description an implicit overlap with what Friedrich Kittler has identified as the three key components of all media systems, namely selection, storage, and processing.[5] For us, Tupperware can be usefully understood as "container and the internal transformer" used to select, gather, store, and process food and other items in a regularized fashion. John Durham Peters goes so far as to suggest that containers were the fundamental means for transforming elemental media, such as fire, into something humans could use by managing, prolonging, and quelling its immense ability to reconfigure the material world.[6]

While there are various technologies of containment that can help us understand reconfigured power relations, our decision to focus on Tupperware speaks to its location at the intersection of a series of gender-coded binaries: hunting/gathering, active/passive, technical/social, public/private. Further, our examination of Tupperware reveals how containers function as information systems that are systematically used to organize and provide addressability in space through the manipulation and codification of size, shape, and color. Finally, containers have since their inception been used to manipulate the "time axis" by extending the life or usability of objects.[7] From a media theory perspective, Tupperware preserves food in a fashion similar to how writing preserves thought. It doesn't merely make it last longer, but opens it up to different kinds of use, analysis, and processing. Tupperware reshapes cooking and kitchens, while writing reshapes thought and enables the circulation of knowledge.

More broadly, the example of Tupperware reveals how containment functions as a mode of power that is anything but passive, as a McLuhanist perspective would suggest. As Zoë Sofia's critique makes clear, containers in general and, for our analysis, Tupperware is not simply an "extension of woman's" capacity to contain or nurture life through care and protection.[8] Nor does Tupperware merely function as a means to enable the feminine-coded labor of domesticity. However, it has certainly been treated as if both are true. In what follows, we recast Tupperware as a medium and reveal how its strategy of containment has been implicated in patriarchal notions of domesticity, labor, and the fraught doctrine of separate spheres. In so doing, we highlight the active properties of containment, wherein it furnishes a strategy for preserving, dividing, securing, and/or enclosing.

Space and Time: Containing Women's Domesticity and Labor

To understand Tupperware as a system of—and strategy for—containment, it seems necessary to briefly trace the cultural history of the home products line, from its emergence in postwar America to its recognition as one of the "greatest inventions of the 20th century" by the *Guinness Book of Records*.[9] Biographical writings on the company's founder, Earl Silas Tupper, construct him as a plucky inventor who saw the potential of a seemingly useless wartime waste product—hardened polyethylene slag—which he purchased at minimal cost from his then-employer DuPont.[10] The first product in the Tupperware line was the now-iconic Wonder Bowl; like many of the brand's products, the Wonder Bowl featured an airtight lock system that would protect perishables from the microclimate of the refrigerator, which quickly dried food out. As a design technology, then, Tupperware functioned to contain both time (by prolonging the state of its contents) and space (by allowing contents to maintain their properties while being transported). It also promised organizational efficiency through stackable products that would maximize the refrigerator's capacity for storage.

In this way, Tupperware capitalized on a wider cultural moment that emphasized design imperatives that helped make possible the "scientific management of the kitchen." Indeed, by the 1950s the relationship between kitchen storage and efficiency was cemented through the notion of "kitcheneering."[11] Such modular design-thinking constituted a mode of information management through aesthetic patterning within a host of interrelated container systems, such as cupboards, dishwashers, refrigerators, closets, iceboxes, root cellars, attics, and garages. Kitchen cabinet manufacturers, for example, explained that "the storage units and working surfaces . . . are the framework into which all other elements are fitted," such as shelving, drawers, inserts, racks, files, bins, boards, trays, rails, attachments, and receptacles, all of which promised "to give most efficient use of space."[12] Tupperware adhered to this broader commitment to configurability with systems of size, color, and shape that became defining features of the various lines. Tupperware, in other words, became the technology du jour for further modularizing the postwar kitchen.

Tupperware's staggering rise to success was, of course, as much cultural as it was technological, and a confluence of socioeconomic factors provided the necessary backdrop for the brand's ascent. This includes a postwar economic boom that roused consumers to "keep up with the Joneses"; a suburban sprawl that nurtured new forms of leisure and mobility; and a revival of codes of domestic femininity that had been temporarily hampered by women's wartime service efforts.[13] To the last point, Tupperware advertising often emphasized the social (i.e., feminine)—rather than the technical (i.e., masculine)—features of its product line. Even the patented "Tupperware burp" (a descriptor for the sound Tupperware lids would make to signal a locked seal) can be understood as an invocation of the "metaphor equating women's faculties solely with a predisposition for nurturing and domesticity."[14]

Take, for instance, the 1960 print ad in figure 6.3, which deployed a prominent advertising appeal of the time equating newly introduced domestic technologies with women's liberation.[15] With stacks of pastel-hued containers juxtaposed with iconic symbols of American patriotism—an eagle statuette, ballot box, and red, white, and blue banner, among others—the ad hails Tupperware as the "best thing that's happened to women since they got the right to vote." As the copy reads: "Less work—more leisure! . . . These light, bright modern plastic containers go all out to give women new kitchen freedom. With Tupperware you can fix food way in advance—even days ahead—and it'll stay fresh till you're ready to serve. . . . No wonder Tupperware's a woman's choice—a woman's right to own." Here, Tupperware's potential as a labor-saving device is unambiguous, and other ads similarly described the products' ability to shift homemakers into a "work-saving wonder world" and allow them to enjoy such leisure-time activities as reading the Sunday paper. Of course, much like the other labor-saving devices introduced to women—or, more aptly, white women—in the nineteenth and twentieth centuries, these technologies didn't necessarily involve time saving. Rather, as Ruth Schwartz Cowan has illustrated, such innovations often translated into an increased demand on women's time and energy.[16] Further, as Sarah Sharma explains, the very gendering of such technologies is a means by which structural inequities are built into the infrastructures of everyday life.[17]

One crucial way that Tupperware transplanted women's labor was through the company's iconic party system of product distribution, which recast "housewives" as self-enterprising "hostesses."[18] The Tupperware party was born in the late 1940s, after Tupperware's initial launch on the retail circuit was met with lackluster sales results. Consequently, Tupper agreed to replace his traditional strategy with a mode of direct-to-consumer sales spearheaded by single mother and sales ingenue Brownie Wise.[19] Wise's idea was to bring women together in each other's homes for a convivial product demonstration; such parties were orchestrated by trained hostesses. With Tupperware hostesses earning commissions based upon their sales records, the party model was hyped as a path to women's financial independence and, tacitly, a source of fulfillment outside the home. As Christina Bax contends, Tupperware allowed middle-class women to "balance society's expectations of them as wives, mothers, and homemakers with their desire for economic autonomy and self-realization."[20] Wise herself was widely celebrated for her entrepreneurial prowess: she was the first woman to appear on the cover of *Businessweek*.

Perhaps not surprisingly, Tupperware's feminine-coded model of self-enterprise was touted in the company's advertising and promotional

6.3 1960 Tupperware advertisement.

communication. As the headline of the ad in figure 6.4 assures, earning money and having fun can be one and the same for Tupperware hostesses. Social metaphors, moreover, abound in the ad copy: Tupperware is the "best friend a kitchen ever had" and provides the opportunity for women to showcase the "wonderful family" of products through "friendly" home parties. By invoking traditionally feminine discourses and ideals, the ad seems to downplay the instrumentality of these interactions. In this way, these texts contributed to a broader ideology of "women's work"—a concept that is historically fraught, given its patterned economic devaluation and its disregard for the politics of race, class, and sexuality.[21]

Crucially, Tupperware's reliance on traditional codes of white, middle-class femininity made for a more socially acceptable category of work outside the home, providing what Susan Vincent describes as "an initial step into the commodification of labour by exploiting the skills they had developed as housewives."[22] Moreover, work as a Tupperware hostess was billed as something that would enrich—rather than supplant—women's more primary roles as wives and mothers.[23] In this way, Tupperware contributed to much wider processes of consumer capitalism identified by Susan Strasser, wherein commodities seemed to fulfill the functions of the private sphere, including provisions of "cooking, childcare, and emotional life.'"[24]

Through the lens of containment, then, we can see how Tupperware's appeals to women's empowerment were superficial, at best, supplying a model of work outside the home that was still largely confined to the domestic realm. In other words, the Tupperware party's reliance on sociality and consumerism helped to ensure that women's extension into the masculine-coded public sphere was rerouted into the feminine, private sphere in order to compel participation in the commodity circuit.[25]

At the same time that the social dynamics of the party system downplayed crass associations with the economy, the materiality of Tupperware technology was also strategically underplayed. As Alison J. Clarke notes, references to the containers' material properties and chemical compounds were conspicuously absent from the promotional appeals targeting women.[26] In this way, Tupperware advertising allows us to see how particular technologies—especially those linked to domesticity—are feminized through a patterned disavowal of their associations with machinery and mechanization.[27] The history of media technologies, of course, follows a similar trajectory, with women's use of (masculine-coded) technologies vilified or rendered frivolous.[28]

She's earning good money—and having fun, too!
[*So could you!*]

She's a Tupperware dealer, introducing her friends and neighbors to the "best friend a kitchen ever had"—Tupperware.

Tupperware is the wonderful family of plastic food containers with the exclusive airtight seal that locks *out* air, locks *in* all of food's freshness, flavor and aroma. It keeps leftovers "just-cooked-fresh" for days.

And Tupperware is available only at friendly home parties from a local Tupperware dealer. (That could be *you!*)

It's easy being a Tupperware dealer. You show Tupperware at parties in the homes of your friends and neighbors. You show them how Tupperware can make their homemaking much easier, and save food, money and time. Then you simply pick up their order cards.

Being a Tupperware dealer is a happy business, and one you can conduct either in your spare time or full time. Best of all, it can fill your hours with fun and fellowship—as well as with profit.

Would *you* like to get more fun out of life—and add $40 to $60 a week to your family income? You can do *both* as a Tupperware dealer. Start by calling your local Tupperware dealer or distributor. Or write Dept. J, Tupperware Home Parties Inc., Orlando, Florida.

6.4 1960s Tupperware advertisement.

Media Theory Packs a Lunch

The following comparison of a vase and a transistor radio by Wolfgang Ernst provides an opportunity for us to clarify our thoughts and elaborate how containers should be considered technical objects and analyzed as such.

> But what drastically separates an archaeological object from a technical artifact is that the latter discloses its essence only when operating. While a Greek vase can be interpreted simply by being looked at, a radio or computer does not reveal its essence by monumentally being there but only when being processed by electromagnetic waves of calculating processes.[29]

We suggest that the "essence" of a Greek vase is not so immediately clear—though, much like the original medium, sunlight, vases do produce clarity.[30] One of the earliest uses of containers was, of course, to capture, store, and transport water. This process reformatted space and time by allowing humans to survive further away from natural water sources and over greater periods of time when water was not otherwise available. Water containers, moreover, clarify water through the process of settlement to make it clearer, to give it clarity. Clarification is the very process that makes water safe for human consumption. Due to the particularities of ingenious design, sediment from lakes and streams would filter to the bottom of vases, working to clean the water on top while minimizing evaporative loss. When turned upward for drinking or pouring, the vase gripped unwanted detritus via its concave shape. These technical capacities were built into the shape of the vase. Later developments in water container composition would lead to the use of copper and other materials to leach out unwanted substances.

A thorough media theory treatment of the vase might consider it a kind of "filter media" used to select one substance as opposed to another, store said substance, and then process it into something more valuable for human use. Ernst's oversight could be interpreted along disciplinary lines (the vase is an aesthetic object to be interpreted by art historians or cultural anthropologists) or gendered lines (domestic tools are not considered technologies). Tupperware was by no means the first domestic technology to be discursively positioned in this way. As Cowan reminds us, "Because of our peculiar set of cultural blinders, we do not ordinarily associate 'tools' with 'women's work'—but household tools there nonetheless are and always have been."[31] The patterned omission of the technical properties of the objects—along with the overemphasis on the social dimensions—testifies to an implicit hierarchy of tools that extend, rather than store, time and space. Regardless, investigating containers from this media technical perspective elucidates the centrality of containment as a strategy.

Our description of the vase thus clarifies that there is intelligence engineered into container technologies that manifests in their ability to select, store, and process material elements of the world. Further, one means by which we can approach a container's ability to effect change is to approach it, as McLuhan suggests, in terms of "the change of scale or pace or pattern that it introduces into human affairs."[32] Adhering to rudimentary definitions of these three terms is incisive, seeing as taken together they elaborate a range of considerations that are fundamental to media theory. Pace refers most directly to the speed at which something happens, changes, or develops. It implies a measured tempo or distance in between steps. Something can lead by setting a pace or create distance by falling off the pace. Pattern, a term used extensively in the domestic and aesthetic realms, suggests a repeated decorative design and an intelligible arrangement or sequence found in comparable objects, actions, or situations. Patterns are epistemological outcomes of recognizing similarity (pattern recognition) as much as they are a set of instructions to be followed to create or re-create material objects. Scales create standards and norms in terms of size and shape. A scale can clarify the number of something, or the degree to which, or the extent to which something happens.

Against this backdrop, we can understand containers as a fundamental means by which humans engage in altering the tempo at which things happen; reconfigure and arrange objects in the world; and create the norms and standards by which things cohere, adhere, and appear as objects. Let's begin with the notion of pace. When most media theorists approach the question of pace, it is almost universally to point out how media "speed things up."[33] Tupperware advertising has incorporated this doctrine of speed in earnest; early ad copy thus emphasized Tupperware's potential to save time spent in the kitchen, consequently speeding up women's processes of domestic labor. But, crucially, what containers such as Tupperware are fundamentally created to do is to slow things down. Their ability to preserve is a means of postponing natural processes that diminish the usefulness to humans of what is contained. Containers are often anti-inertia technologies. Through the process of selection, containers partition the world to segregate forces that act upon each other in an entropic fashion. While the layperson is simply happy their sandwich stays fresh, Tupperware's "burping" forces oxygen out of the container, so it is not available for mold and bacteria.

Further, this process seals in moisture, negating dehydration via evaporation. Selection manipulates the time axis through remixing which elements work together—either speeding up or slowing down differing chemical and biological processes. Harry wants to prolong the capacity of his bullets by ensuring the gunpowder stays dry and the metal casing does not rust.

In a broader sense, containment is often meant to protect what is inside from the threat of what is outside via the active creation of a barrier. Containment attempts to preserve the integrity and composition of that which it holds and thereby maintains the very existence of an object. And while for communication theory, this means maintaining the coherence of a signal, for humans at the end of life, it can be the feeble attempt to stave off complete dissolution of the body's recognizable form.[34] Peters suggests that graves may be the oldest of container technologies—a point not lost on the minds of cartoonists who have played up the idea of Tupperware as the ideal casket for the consumerist age (figures 6.5 and 6.6).[35]

While the promises of time-saving technologies found in the kitchen have proven illusory, the notion of saving something, or preserving over time, is something altogether different.[36] Saving time—extending the life of something beyond its natural limits—is not merely ideological; rather, it is a technical feat with a sound basis in fact.

As Sofia notes to this end, containers process and, upon emptying, something new appears.[37] One true gift of the container is therefore the outpouring of time—the giving of the preserved, which is still there, still useful, still lovely, still alive. The container creates ongoing aliveness. But what sort of container processes aliveness? We can see in Sofia's feminist analyses that container technologies—the earth, for instance—process that which they also contain, in part by existing as a void capable of taking, shaping, and keeping.[38] Applying a media-theoretical perspective to Sofia's analysis, we suggest that containers used to store things are also used to select and process things. The leftover is not merely what is left, but more profoundly that which is not over. Implanted in the freezer, Tupperware invites in the cold, creating temperature stasis through the outside, itself, and its cared-for foods. Its will to contain remains unthwarted by thermal expansion. Sealing out freezer burn, it patiently waits, ceaselessly doing the work of upkeep—literally the process of keeping something in good condition. As a medium, Tupperware's processing is never done.

Containers also reformat scale and pattern in spatial terms. In media history, this tends to mean extension of an ever-greater scale. But containers point to the ways in which scales can be shrunk, nestled inside each

"Edna would be so pleased... look - Tupperware!"

other, broken down into smaller and smaller pieces to work collectively in a concerted systematic fashion. The "extensions of man" that McLuhan most famously outlined expressly reformat spatial orientation in terms of a bringing-together, hence the metaphor of the Global Village and the notion of time/space compression.[39] Both reference a shrinking of the world via the speed at which media (radio signals as well as automobiles) move across space and extend the distances they can cover (the whole globe). Yet containers are often not meant to extend or speed up, but rather to limit the speed of movement, if not outright stop it altogether. Further, they work to create boundaries, some of which have entry points and exits, but many of which do not. Sofia envisions the planet not as a Global Village, but as a kind of global container.[40] For Sofia, following Lefebvre and Massey, space should not be seen as passive but productive and reproductive of relations of power. Thus, the patterned spatial arrangement of containers (houses, cities, and nation-states) is always already an exercise of power. McLuhan's planet isn't unified because the globe has been able to contain humans (and their co-constitutive technologies) over the longue durée of evolutionary development, but because media enable a global network of simultaneous stimulation. Sofia, however, imagines the planet itself an active

6.5 and 6.6 Arnie Levin, Tupperware cartoons.

container that shapes all that there is to human life and its various processes of inscription. Earth as container is not a mere metaphor for Sofia, and neither is it metaphorical when Chris Russill suggests the Earth is a medium.[41] Space and time are the ultimate containers, but they are anything but inactive playgrounds or prisons.

The scale of containment and the various containers that work in unison are necessary to all modes of local and global organization. This is to say that they are fundamental to the patterns of social, economic, and material life. At the very local level, we can see Tupperware as a medium by which the kitchen is meant to be reorganized according to the products' aesthetic, technical, and logical modalities. As noted earlier, society at large was going through an "organization revolution" at the time of Tupperware's emergence; discourses about this seeming revolution often entered the public world of labor.[42] A dishwasher is a container that washes dishes, but still demands feminized human labor to fill it and to transfer dishes into other containers after they've been washed. In simple terms, Tupperware fit into the "time saving" modern and modular kitchen that continued to take shape in the 1950s and beyond. Containment from such a perspective starts from an understanding that containers process the world in specific ways, are dedicated to different kinds of labor, and provide organizational epistemologies.

The incoherence of containers and washers—that is, the inability of a container to do all of the processing—led feminist architect and designer Frances Gabe to reenvision the home not as a place that contains a feminized laboring subject, but rather as a container that does all domestic processing on its own. Known as the "self-cleaning house," the Gabe house was furnished with "specialized cupboards using water, steam, and air and a series of pipes and sprinklers for cleaning, allowing dirty dishes to be cleaned and left in cabinets where they are ready for next use, clothes to be washed, dried, and left hanging in situ, and the floors to be cleaned automatically."[43] While Gabe's still-vital envisioning of the smart house more than thirty years ago offered an emancipatory potential for the smart home/container, recent iterations extend capacities for the smart home in profoundly disinhibiting ways. For example, smart home technologies have been deployed to harass women or even lock them into their own homes.[44] This transplants the idea of home into a technology-enabled machine for domestic containment.

Containment as Strategy Plus Technics in the Digital World

Housing as shelter is an extension of our bodily heat-control mechanisms—a collective skin or garment. Cities are an even further extension of bodily organs to accommodate the needs of large groups. —MCLUHAN, *Understanding Media*

In reconsidering the (in)activity of containers, we contend that a focus on containment as an active process can help us think through broader changes in contemporary systems of media and technology. Whereas McLuhan interpreted houses and cities as extensions of human bodily organs, our formulation of containers sees them as technical systems or "machine(s) for living"[45] that exert agency in ways that tend to reinforce power relationships. McLuhan's humanist orientation always leads him back to the human body as referent, and it overdetermines his essentialist assessments of the gendered nature of labor and the kind of extensions that are worthy of analysis. Hence for McLuhan, housing is not something that contains family expectations or patriarchal power relations, or more broadly reproduces classist and racist spatial divisions, but rather extends from the natural capacities of bodies to regulate temperature. For us, containers contain the capacity for containment: Containment is an active strategy for accomplishing goals. Containers are the technical systems by which containment is activated.

Even in its most banal form, such as Tupperware plastics for storage, containment preserves boundaries and preserves content as a means of addressing an imagined future. In its selection mode, it functions to determine what belongs and what does not. In its storage mode, it serves to maintain a fixed relation in time. And in its processing mode, it works on the content and responds to its environment in such a fashion that it induces changes to produce a desired outcome. It modulates to maintain the boundary between outside and inside that is expected to occur in the temporal horizon.

By approaching containment as a technique or technology in the broadest sense, we open up the possibility of seeing linkages from large-scale forms of geopolitical spatial containment (Cold War detente and the notion of a "Closed World"[46]) down to the microlevel of food containment enabled by Tupperware. Containment is the ur-form of postwar American culture. As Alan Nadel contends to this end, "Because of the United States' unprecedented capacity in the decades following World War II to deploy arms and images . . . containment was perhaps one of the most powerfully deployed national narratives in recorded history."[47] What we see is a set of nesting systems in which relationships of power organize technical systems and spatial arrangements that are consistent with geopolitical dynamics, competing forms of industrial production, patriarchal family structures, red-lined neighborhoods, and the like. NATO, the Soviet bloc, and the containment of communism take place in the kitchen and in the famous Nixon versus Khrushchev Kitchen Debate of 1959. The suburbs contained the single-family home, which contained the "time saving" modern kitchen, which contained the "fruits of capitalist production" such as the refrigerator, which of course contained the leftovers from a Campbell's Soup can, safely nestled inside a Tupperware bowl. The white suburban housewife, whose labor was also contained by these dynamics, is not present during the debates, which took place in a manufactured kitchen built in Moscow to represent what the typical American home was supposed to look like, though her generalized good fortune ("hardly working in this modern marvel of efficiency") is presented as a pinnacle of US superiority. Entirely invisible in this vision are the contained bodies of laboring black women who made the domestic labor done in the kitchen seem to disappear altogether for the wealthier white homes in which the kitchen typically was completely closed off from the rest of the residence.[48]

Lest we forget that containers are essential to human survival, Peter Galison reminds us that few containers are more explicitly important, nor more temporally challenged, than those that contain nuclear waste.[49] The half-life of frozen chicken soup is easily exceeded by Tupperware; the soup will lose its ability to produce its intended effect—the provision of safe caloric energy—long before the Tupperware's seal will break or its polymers dissociate. The biggest challenge may be marking time so as to know how long the soup has been in the freezer. As Galison points out, the half-life of nuclear waste will almost certainly outlast the efficacy of any container made to hold it. The waste will escape its bonds. Equally problematic is the fact that the waste will likely outlast any communications system used to warn future humans, aliens, or other sentient entities as to the danger contained within.[50] No current written human language has lasted more than ten thousand years, so there is no historical precedent that warnings will be legible to future generations. Containment in this instance is not merely a technical feat, but also a corresponding communicative one; it demands that humans not forget what they have contained.

What these final two examples suggest is that containers cannot be disarticulated from adjacent conditions and commitments that are themselves maintained through forms of containment. Containment, and the containers by which it operates, is quite clearly not a passive strategy, nor a natural state of things. Rather, it is an active strategy that is implicated in broader structures of power and should compel us to interrogate who contains, and to what ends. Accordingly, we close with a call for media theorists to take seriously these questions as they engage with the broader conceptual applicability of containment.

While we have already suggested some of the concerns that either have or could be framed as containment—for example, feminist approaches to technical systems; elemental media, from Peters's example of containing fire to Russill's example of the earth as medium, to the role of container media in extraction[51]—other research agendas could similarly benefit from an inward rather than an outward-facing lens. Indeed, the supplanting of physical storage systems with the seemingly infinite realm of 0s and 1s and "the cloud" has been complicated by enduring logics of containment, including the norms, formats, and standards of media systems, digital enclosures, and infrastructures.[52] Alternatively, the feminized modes of entrepreneurship that dominate social media platforms—amplified by a logic that involves "a strategic deployment of recommendations and social networks to sell goods or services" could benefit from a renewed focus on technologies of containment.[53] From the sprawling culture of Instagram influencers to networks of Facebook users hawking face creams and diet pills among their networks of friends, today's social media platforms seek to keep us all contained within their algorithmic, surveillant systems. The most successful platforms—amid a sprawling social media ecology—are those that contain our attention and, consequently, our datafied selves. These and other efforts to deploy the heuristic of containment, we conclude, can be incredibly productive for scholars of media and technology who seek to better understand the sociopolitical stakes of ever more pervasive, oft-invisible, systems that capture, enclose, and repurpose the worlds we inhabit.

Notes

1. Mumford, "An Appraisal of Lewis Mumford's 'Technics and Civilization'"; Sofia, "Container Technologies"; Sterne, "The mp3 as Cultural Artifact"; Peters, *The Marvelous Clouds*.

2. Peters, *The Marvelous Clouds*, 142.

3. Mumford, "An Appraisal of Lewis Mumford's 'Technics and Civilization,'" 529.

4. Wajcman, *Feminism Confronts Technology*, 17.

5. "The network of technologies and institutions that allow a given culture to *select*, *store*, and *process* relevant data," Kittler, *Discourse Networks*, 369.

6. See especially the sections "Container Technologies" (139–44) and "Settlement and other Containers" (144–48) from Peters, *The Marvelous Clouds*.

7. See Sybille Krämer's highly influential essay "The Cultural Techniques of Time Axis Manipulation."

8. Sofia, "Container Technologies."

9. Castronovo et al., "One of the Best Last Lists of the Century."

10. Watson-Smyth, "Secret History Of: Tupperware."

11. St. Charles Manufacturing Co., *Your Kitchen and You*.

12. St. Charles Manufacturing Co, *Your Kitchen and You*, 3.

13. Cowan, *More Work for Mother*; Cohen, *A Consumers' Republic*; Bax, "Entrepreneur Brownie Wise."

14. Clarke, *Tupperware*, 5, 57.

15. Spigel, "Designing the Smart House."

16. Cowan, *More Work for Mother*; Strasser, *Never Done*.

17. Sharma, "Exit and the Extensions of Man."

18. Clarke, *Tupperware*; Vincent, "Preserving Domesticity."

19. Bax, "Entrepreneur Brownie Wise."

20. Bax, "Entrepreneur Brownie Wise," 171.

21. Federici, *Revolution at Point Zero*; James, "Women's Unwaged Work."
22. Vincent, "Preserving Domesticity," 85.
23. Clarke, *Tupperware*.
24. Strasser, *Never Done*.
25. Strasser, *Never Done*.
26. Clarke, *Tupperware*, 57.
27. Cowan, *More Work for Mother*.
28. Marvin, *When Old Technologies Were New*, 23.
29. Ernst, "Media Archaeography."
30. Kittler, *Optical Media*; Cubitt, *The Practice of Light*.
31. Cowan, *More Work for Mother*, 9.
32. McLuhan, *Understanding Media* (1994), 1.
33. Sharma, *In the Meantime*.
34. On communications theory, see Shannon and Weaver, *The Mathematical Theory of Communication*.
35. Peters, "Proliferation and Obsolescence of the Historical Record."
36. Cowan, *More Work for Mother*.
37. Sofia, "Container Technologies."
38. Sofia, "Container Technologies," 191.
39. McLuhan, *Understanding Media* (1994).
40. Sofia, "Container Technologies."
41. Russill, "Is the Earth a Medium?"
42. Boulding, *The Organizational Revolution*.
43. Sofia, "Container Technologies," 183.
44. Small, "How Smart Home Systems and Tech Have Created a New Form of Abuse."
45. Le Corbusier, *Toward an Architecture*.
46. Edwards, *Closed World*.
47. Nadel, *Containment Culture*.
48. Cowan, *More Work for Mother*; Wajcman, *Feminism Confronts Technology*.
49. Galison, "The Future of Scenarios."
50. Galison, "The Future of Scenarios."
51. Cowan, *More Work for Mother*; Wajcman, *Feminism Confronts Technology*; Sofia, "Container Technologies"; Peters, *The Marvelous Clouds*; Russill, "Is the Earth a Medium?"; Galison, "The Future of Scenarios"; Parikka, *A Geology of Media*; Tollefson and Barney, "More Liquid Than Liquid"; Young, "Salt, Fragments from the History of a Medium."
52. Sterne, "The mp3 as Cultural Artifact"; Peters, "Proliferation and Obsolescence of the Historical Record"; Edwards, *Closed Worlds*; Andrejevic, "Surveillance in the Digital Enclosure"; Parks, *Cultures in Orbit*; Parks and Starosielski, *Signal Traffic*; Starosielski, *The Undersea Network*.
53. Duffy and Pruchniewska, "Gender and Self-Enterprise in the Social Media Age"; Van Dijck and Poell, "Understanding Social Media Logic," 9.

7 "Will Miss File Misfile?"

The Filing Cabinet, Automatic Memory, and Gender

CRAIG ROBERTSON

"Will Miss File misfile?" Drenched in the sexism of the 1920s, this question was asked by an American office equipment company in an attempt at humor on the back page of an in-house magazine.[1] It was the headline to a single-sentence article that along with a cartoon and a poem filled up space in a monthly magazine that published stories about the company's direct sales to large businesses: "Mr. Clarke tells us that one of the big insurance companies has an expert file clerk named Miss File." At the center of the question was a woman who filed papers in a filing cabinet in an office. In 1920, all of these things—filing cabinets, file clerks, and women—were new arrivals in offices. Invented in the United States in the 1890s, it only took a couple of decades for the vertical filing cabinet to become a common fixture in offices. In this period, women arrived in a workplace in which ideas of gender and efficiency divided the time and space of clerical work into particular tasks, such as filing; this was also when management emerged as a profession to give men more career opportunities in the new employment hierarchy.²

In the early twentieth-century business imagination, the answer to the question about Miss File, if taken seriously, was no. This was not due to any presumed skill on her part. Instead the answer represented the dominant understanding of office equipment such as filing cabinets. Represented as a machine, the filing cabinet functioned to ensure papers were not lost. It automatically guided a person to the correct place for papers. Therefore, if misfiling somehow occurred, it was Miss File's fault, with her age and sexuality disrupting the efficiency of the filing cabinet.

However, while some general anxiety about young unmarried women working alongside men in offices lingered into the 1920s, it rarely turned into a concern that Miss File would misfile. Any regular acknowledgment of the possibility of misfiling would have undermined the faith in system and efficiency that made the modern office modern. The intended humor behind questioning Miss File's ability spoke to, and sought to negate, any suggestion that misfiling was a problem in a workplace increasingly populated by machines.

As a machine, the filing cabinet was activated in particular ways, an object that did some things and not others. As a response to a set of problems, it generated a set of processes that affected thought and action. The way it stored paper shaped an encounter with information that constituted "information labor." Both the information contained in a filing cabinet and the labor required for operating the cabinet were products of the late nineteenth-century articulation of efficiency that made saving time one of the defining problems of the twentieth century. Through drawers, tabs, and folders, the filing cabinet broke knowledge into bits of information that could be more easily stored, retrieved, and circulated. Mechanization, specialization, and gender divided work into discrete tasks that removed skill and introduced the faith that tasks would be completed as planned. In each case, an investment in particularity supported the claim that a filing cabinet made a clerk more productive because it reduced the time it took to file. This encounter with information required neither thought nor interpretation and did not directly produce knowledge; as Miss File suggested, it was an experience coded as feminine. This was labor that came to be represented by disembodied women's hands, not their minds; a filing cabinet thought and a woman felt.

Therefore, this chapter offers an argument about the materiality of technology, but it does so through a specific critique of techno-determinist readings of media materialism. To think about the filing cabinet as an object that is active, that is not inert, is to offer a more nuanced understanding of the relationship between technology and society. In this chapter I use the filing cabinet and the file clerk to explore the centrality of power dynamics to the conception and functioning of media technologies, specifically the intersection of gender and capitalism, but also age, sexuality, and gender.[3]

As the editors of this volume make clear, this approach to media materialism is a project that can exist in relationship to Marshall McLuhan's flawed but productive understanding of media; from this perspective, the critique is indebted to the feminist technology studies scholarship the editors outline in their introduction. It is a critique that foregrounds power dynamics to prioritize an analysis of the specificities of media forms. That is, to explore the power relations critical to the filing cabinet is not to forgo a focus on its physicality or to downplay how the filing cabinet as an object mediates relations in time and space. This analysis of the filing cabinet emphasizes that storage is not a neutral practice; particular technologies, practices, and ideas shape storage.[4] In making objects readily available, storage technologies create a specific relationship to those objects; decisions about what to store and how to store adhere to social values. In the context of McLuhan's world of concepts, to argue that storage technologies are not neutral fits with Sarah Sharma's argument that the reorganization of labor is part of the message of every medium.[5]

Although this chapter is historical in focus, it is important to note the technologies associated with filing continue to structure twenty-first-century interactions with information. Files, tabs, manila folders, and filing cabinets remain integral not only to the comprehension of information and data, but also to understanding the relationship between technology and gender. To acknowledge the power relations integral to these technologies is to offer another dimension to critiques about the materiality of information and data. Rather than an infrastructural tubes-and-wires critique, this history makes information and data material by showing that the concepts through which people are asked to imagine their interactions with information and data (files, folders, tabs) originated in highly gendered understandings of labor and information. It critiques the materiality of information via media theory to reembody information by showing that the properties of the information technologies associated with filing are a product of power relations so that, whether she misfiled or not, only Miss File filed (figure 7.1).

7.1 From filing cabinet catalog, c. 1910. Courtesy of the Smithsonian Libraries, Washington, DC.

Automatic Filing

Miss File could not misfile because the filing cabinet provided what prescriptive literature called "automatic filing" or an "automatic memory." Creating an association between a filing cabinet and a machine, the claim to be automatic emphasized the regularity, consistency, speed, and reliability critical to this piece of office equipment; it also informed the attempt to bring Frederick Taylor's ideas of the scientific management of machines and labor from the factory into the office.[6] The word *automatic* only came into general use in the nineteenth century. As Lisa Gitelman argues, derived from *automaton, automatic* brought "lingering connotations of resolving the organic and the mechanical—of human forms and functions built into machinery and of mechanical responses by human beings."[7]

Proponents frequently anthropomorphized the filing cabinet to reinforce claims to precision and speed, implicitly echoing the relationship between *automatic* and *automaton*. According to one filing manual author, "in a large file of about 150 four-drawer units, the conspicuous red, blue, green, and white labels fairly cry out their divisions."[8] Another simply stated that an effective filing system "will explain itself automatically."[9] In crying out or explaining the location of a letter to a person, a filing cabinet became automatic because it performed the mental work associated with remembering location and content. A filing cabinet took on the task of remembering; it replaced personal memory with procedure and a system that could store and recall on a scale beyond the capability of the human mind.

How did a rectilinear stack of drawers remember? As the quotes above suggest, the answer was mundane. A filing cabinet remembered, it cried out, through paper technologies designed to subdivide other pieces of paper. Each drawer was shaped to hold loose paper stored in manila folders, with tabs identifying the content of the folders according to indexing systems. Guide cards, taller than folders, used tabs to establish larger divisions within which folders were placed.

The filing cabinet's utility came from this combination of index and papers. It did not require a separate index or registry; everything needed to find the proper place for papers was inside the drawer, available to direct the user. How-to literature quickly identified the key principle of vertical filing as "the filing of papers on edge, behind guides, bringing together all papers, to, from, or about one correspondent or subject."[10] The "to, from, or about" made vertical filing valuable in comparison to existing methods that stacked papers on top of each other in files or kept incoming and outgoing correspondence separate in bound volumes; inside the filing cabinet, subject trumped chronology in the name of efficiency.

Therefore, the vertical filing cabinet broke the bound book into fragments to allow easy access to pieces of paper no longer stored as bound pages (figure 7.2).[11] Although contemporaries celebrated its innovation, the filing cabinet developed a preexisting "cabinet logic." This labels the development of interior compartments to organize storage space in cabinets according to classification and indexing systems that came to prominence in the early modern era.[12] This division of space in the name of order is often linked to the development of type cases for printing; the fragmentation critical to the classificatory project McLuhan attributes to "typographical man."[13]

At the end of the nineteenth century, corporate capitalism co-opted cabinet logic to solve the problem of information storage and access. Cabinet logic, articulated via efficiency, highlights the increasingly pervasive faith in granular certainty. Within an economic context, *granular* signifies the belief that breaking things down into small parts to produce a high degree

Are letters on your desk in stop-watch time?

DON'T blame your file clerk when she's slow in bringing you something you ask for—until you are sure the fault doesn't lie with the file.

What kind of filing equipment has she got to work with? Anything as efficient as the Art Metal 6700 File shown above?

There's a file that's planned for modern business! You get every inch of filing space you pay for... patented ball-bearing roller suspensions make drawers accessible to full capacity. Make them slide smoothly, too... they literally *coast* in and out.

The 6700 File has a special *positive lock* compressor that keeps papers smooth and firmly in place—yet a slight pressure of thumb and finger releases it. That compressor wastes no space, either.

And this Art Metal File will last a lifetime. It's framed of electrically welded steel... with cross bars at each drawer to make the whole cabinet rigid.

There are nine different 6700 styles. And they are only one group of the 81 types of Art Metal vertical files that cover every possible filing need — just as the complete Art Metal line covers every office equipment requirement. Every Art Metal product is of lasting, warp-proof steel... finished in fine wood graining or rich olive green.

We shall be glad to furnish information on office equipment for your type of business. Or, if you need more equipment for your present office, just check below the kind you want and we will forward a catalogue.

Art Metal Construction Co.,
Jamestown, N. Y.

☐ Fire Safes   ☐ Horizontal Sectional Files
☐ Desks   ☐ Upright Unit Files
☐ Plan Files   ☐ Counter Height Files
☐ Shelving   ☐ Postindex Visible Files

Steel Office Equipment, Safes and Files

7.2 Filing cabinet advertisement, 1930. Courtesy of the Fenton Historical Society, Jamestown, New York.

of detail or specificity would produce efficiency. *Certainty* indicates the conviction that this increased specificity would reduce individual discretion and increase the confidence a task would be completed efficiently.[14]

The ability of a filing cabinet to allow unbound paper to stand on its long edge was critical to how it enacted granular certainty. Loose paper does not stand on its edge on its own. The filing cabinet was innovative because it provided the technological support for paper to stand on its edge; this was the source of the name vertical, in contrast to flat (or horizontal) filing.[15] Stored vertically, paper took up less space and could be more easily retrieved.

With paper stored, standing at attention, advertisements regularly included the phrase "at a glance" to convey the claim that tabs and guides made an effective filing system, visible to anyone who needed to use a cabinet. In an "age when every moment counts," office equipment companies collapsed visibility and accessibility to assert that an open filing cabinet drawer allowed someone to find papers "at a moment's notice" or "almost instantaneously."[16] According to a satisfied customer, the "almost" of *instantaneously* was twenty seconds to find one letter and ninety seconds to file five folders (figure 7.3).[17]

This speed in filing depended on the precision a filing cabinet produced. In one of its promotional booklets, the office equipment company Library Bureau explained how an alphanumerical system worked to ensure accuracy through the following scenario: "The file clerk about to put the correspondence of Jones marked 113 carelessly in the files, sees that her hands rest on the folder marked 117. And naturally she is checked at once, and is reminded that Jones's correspondence should go into a folder marked 113. The LB Automatic actually makes it difficult to perform an error in filing."[18] In this instance, positioned as a machine, the filing cabinet protected an organization from human failure. It "guaranteed" accuracy "because it checks itself" and therefore "prevents misfiling."[19]

Operating a Filing Cabinet

Filing was an example of a form of clerical work that emphasized the necessity of particular bodies interacting with a machine.[20] In the name of granular certainty and efficiency, the actions of these bodies were also separated into discrete parts to better manage their labor. In the words of one how-to-file author, "mind, eye, and hand can soon be trained so that they automatically act together and do team work that is invaluable."[21] As Library Bureau ad copy shows, advertisements and catalogs frequently implied that

7.3 From filing cabinet catalog, 1919. Author's collection.

an important function of filing equipment was to train mind, eye, and hand in this teamwork; filing textbooks made this explicit with lessons framed as instruction in efficiency and dexterity.[22] Filing cabinets integrated mind, eye, and hand to make them suitable for repetitious and routine work, to make the act of filing a matter of habit performed properly and without hesitation or thought.

James McCord, who founded the New York School of Filing in 1914, used his textbook to stress the need for a clerk to possess physical dexterity:

> Use your hands for selecting the proper guide and filing. Should the guide be far back in the file, draw the bulk of the other guides and folders forward by grasping at the sides. Remember that the tab is the weakest part of a guide, and while you will often have to finger it directly, remove as much weight as possible from the front of it before doing so. In putting material in the folders, lift the folders up if not entirely out of the file, otherwise papers may be placed in the wrong folders or between folders. This will train you to check what you are filing with the notations on the folders.[23]

Although the filing cabinet lacked the mechanical parts that grounded scientific management's celebration of dexterity in the factory, McCord's description illustrates the importance of hands and fingers to filing in the office. Filing demanded more than the mere handling of paper; it involved selecting, grasping, removing, lifting, placing, fingering, drawing.

However, the focus on hands also underscored what filing did not involve: understanding the content of files. In the binary world of mental and manual work that helped organize the office, the filing cabinet turned mental work into a form of manual work. As Harry Braverman argues, to the extent that clerical "work is still performed in the brain . . . the brain is used as the equivalent of the hand of the detail worker in production."[24] The "teamwork" of mind, eye, and hand needed to successfully operate the filing cabinet constituted thought as an action equivalent to manual manipulation defined in relation to a machine.

An image used to promote office equipment presents filing as an efficient form of manual labor distinct from thought or so-called mental work. Manufacturers sometimes used a close-up of the interior of a file drawer to illustrate how a cabinet worked to claim their folders, guides, and tabs as unique. Occasionally the image of the drawer also included hands. While the close-up of the drawer was necessary to show the guides and tabs, it meant that it was not possible to show the body attached to the hands (figure 7.4).

THE GENERAL GF FIREPROOFING CO.

The Super-Filer Way
—Four Simple, Easy Steps Instead of the Usual Eight.

The Drawer is Opened

Step No. 1 — A light finger pull opens the Swing Front, unlocks the buttonless safety latch, and the drawer coasts out on balanced, ball-bearing suspensions. The Swing Front plus the mechanical action of the Throw-Back slope the material backwards and make every guide and folder visible. Contents cannot fall forward accidentally.

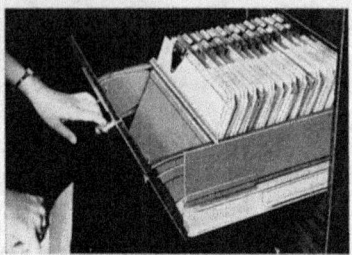

Contents are Parted

Step No. 2 — The contents are parted in one simple, effortless motion. As the finger touches the index tab of the required folder, the Throw-Back Compressor locks automatically against the Swing Front, releasing compression and freeing both hands of the operator. Note the orderly arrangement of the contents and the instant accessibility and visibility of the records.

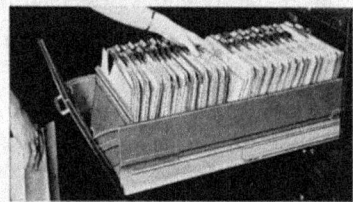

Letter is Dropped Into Place

Step No. 3 — The letter is dropped directly into its position—no necessity for removing the folder, as in ordinary filing cabinets. The wide angle, book-like spread permits the letter to drop to the bottom of the folder speedily and accurately. No pinching of contents; no wrestling with guides or mutilation of folders to gain working space. Errors of misfiling are minimized.

The Drawer is Closed

Step No. 4 — A light push closes the swing front, releases the Throw-Back Compressor, applies compression to the records and the drawer glides back into the case, safely latched. The filing has been done. These four simple and effortless operations not only reduce the time factor in filing and finding, but also reduce the mental and physical fatigue of the operator — minimize errors — speed record handling — preserve records and indexing in the least space — reduce costs.

7.4 From filing cabinet catalog, 1940. Courtesy of the Hagley Museum and Library, Wilmington, Delaware.

The result was disembodied hands that not only pointed out how filing equipment functioned, but also represented the relationship of labor and technology that underwrote automatic filing. A disembodied hand highlighted a filing cabinet as a machine to be operated on, not a machine to think with. Therefore, the visual use of disembodied hands established filing as manual labor. It emphasized this by not showing a connection to the body and mind; in filing, the process of choice and deliberation (thinking) is transferred to the predetermined pathways of tabs; as one advertisement put it, tabs were "the intellect of the filing machine."[25]

Disembodied hands in filing advertisements represented work that was neither independent nor constructive. As Janet Zandy argues, "truncated hands represent metonymically, an ignored whole, a lesser human element and species."[26] Since the seventeenth century, this truncation has been applied to workers when they are identified as "hired hands" or simply "hands." The fact that the disembodied hands in advertisements for filing cabinets were gendered as women's hands further established the lowly value of filing.

A catalog description for the "Efficiency Desk," which included file drawers, summarizes the gendered organization of work that supported the distinction between manual and mental work in the modern office (figure 7.5): "Each compartment should represent a fixed place, so that the hand of the executive will reach automatically for desired records without interrupting the continuity of brain action."[27] The male executive did not have to think about retrieving documents. He reached over as a matter of habit, while the file drawer, as a machine, worked to locate papers. A file drawer took on mental processes (such as remembering) deemed unproductive. It allowed the male executive to keep thinking about other matters deemed critical to the productivity of the office. When the scale of business produced so much paper that it had to be stored beyond his immediate reach, filing cabinets further freed the male executive by creating a mode of storage that generated work for women. Filing, as a discrete task, was women's work because it did not directly contribute to the productivity of the office—women worked in the office to assist men to think. As historian Delphine Gardey reminds us, "to be a boss is not to be disturbed; it is to be served and liberated by technology (and by others' work) rather than be constrained by it."[28]

Therefore, the filing cabinet was very much an "extension of man."[29] The "our" that McLuhan uses when he talks about technologies as extensions of physical and nervous systems needs to be situated and embodied. The filing

WOOD FILING EQUIPMENT

"Y and E" Efficiency Desks

Your Workbench Should Be a Desk and Filing Cabinet Combined

THE "Y and E" Efficiency Desk enables you to keep your vital current records *at your finger tips*—classified and instantly accessible. It adds the convenience of a well-built desk to the advantages of a high-quality filing cabinet—at the price of a desk alone.

Leaving your desk to refer to distant files—requesting information from subordinates—telephoning to different departments to secure facts—all these annoy, waste time.

The upper right hand drawer, shown above, is the logical card-record drawer. It permits the desk user to hold the telephone receiver to the ear with his left hand and draw out cards or other information from this drawer with the free hand—making for speed in transmitting information. The need of "holding the line" or telling an inquirer that you "will call back later" is obviated.

Features That Speed Up Your Work

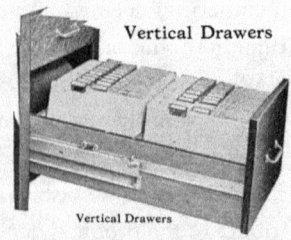

Vertical Drawers

Vertical drawers, both on the right and left side of the desk, offer an ideal place in which to keep sizable current papers, telephone books and advertising literature.

In the illustration, notice that the papers are filed *across* the drawer, so that the files face the desk user.

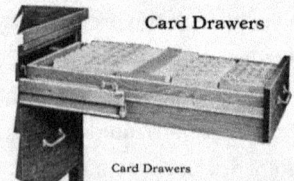

Drawers are $11^{15}/_{16}"$ wide, $11^{1}/_{2}"$ high, $27^{5}/_{8}"$ deep inside. Partitions are adjustable so that compartments can be set up for different size material.

Card Drawers

The Card File Drawers measure $11^{15}/_{16}"$ wide, $5^{5}/_{8}"$ high, $27^{5}/_{8}"$ deep inside. They have movable partitions so that compartments can be set up for the standard 5x3, 6x4 or 8x5 card sizes. In each compartment there is a depth of

7.5 From filing cabinet catalog, 1916. Courtesy of the Hagley Museum and Library, Wilmington, Delaware.

cabinet provides a nonelectronic extension of the memories and thoughts of a male executive, manager, or owner. The increased scale of multiple filing cabinets created an organizational memory but for an office designed to cultivate the agency of men, with women present to serve them. This technology depended on female hands to operate it, but the cabinet and these hands (gendered but disembodied) functioned as a "technological conduit for male thoughts."[30]

The operation of a filing cabinet needs to be understood as an example of "information labor." This is not a distinct occupational category but a label for the instrumental encounter with information that became more common in offices at the turn of the twentieth century. It is a gendering practice; to perform information labor is to do woman's work. It is a historically specific product of discourses of systems and efficiency that positioned work with information within a gendered conception of labor that depended on rational and calculative procedures. This locates information labor as a specific instance within a longer history of "the gendered context of working on, with, and around paper."[31]

In constructing the specialized tasks of twentieth-century clerical work as feminine occupations, advocates invoked the commonsense association between a woman's hands and dexterity; this successfully naturalized the changes taking place in the office. By 1943, Evelyn Steele, editorial director of Vocational Guidance Research, could confidently note, "It is generally agreed that women do well at painstaking, tedious work requiring patience and dexterity of the hands. The actual fact that women's fingers are more slender than men's makes a difference."[32] Adherents linked this belief to leisure activities and work. For the former, it was often noted that socially acceptable practices in the home provided ways for women to enhance their natural dexterity and thus provide informal training in filing. As one manager commented, "I often ask a girl if she plays the piano, or if she knits, crochets, sews, or does another type of work that would enable her to acquire speed with her fingers."[33]

When filing experts invoked work outside the home to justify women's suitability for filing, they turned to women's repetitive labor in light manufacturing. The rationalization of work that brought women into factories began in the mid-nineteenth-century industries of textiles and papermaking. Judith McGaw argues that in nineteenth-century paper mills, before and after mechanization, women were assigned jobs that were "monotonous and interruptible, requiring neither long training nor initiative."[34] In paper mills, women's work centered on the rag room, where they utilized "manual manipulation and visual discrimination" to sort rags and cut them to standard size.[35] This foreshadowed the information labor of filing at the turn of the twentieth century, when standard-sized paper circulated in the office as correspondence and records. In the office, women used filing cabinets to sort paper at a glance and therefore manipulate information to be used by men; not falsifying it but handling information, moving information, within the office.

Filing, as a feminine task, made dexterity critical to clerical work. Concerns about dexterity had not existed in an office exclusively populated by men. Prior to the filing cabinet, male clerks had filed loose papers in boxes and pigeonholes without any concern about the speed of their fingers, though some men expressed anxiety that clerical work was becoming too repetitive and rote.[36] However, reconceived as part of a technological process, filing (defined as operating a filing cabinet) expressed the dominant economic and material values that changed the tempo of work in the name of efficiency; as machine work, it demanded manual dexterity.

The introduction of women and machines into the office occurred in a period in which "hands and machines began to work together in new ways that challenged previous definitions of 'manual' labor, [as well as] 'craft,' and touch," Rachel Plotnick argues. Outside of the office, push-button technology developed to delegate strength to a machine. The gendered "popular rhetoric of simplicity, effortlessness and no requisite skill on the part of the user" associated with push buttons was also applied in the office, but in the office it was mental activity that was delegated to a range of different machines operated by touch.[37]

In turn-of-the-twentieth-century offices, as the filing cabinet mechanized remembering, so the typewriter mechanized writing. Compared to previous writing tools, a typewriter user was more overtly seen as a machine operator. By fusing the body with the machine, the typewriter broke the continuity between mind, body, and writing.[38] As Gitelman argues, typewriters "challenged the author as agent by offering a newly mechanized, newly gendered, and self-consciously 'managed' imposition between the mind and page."[39] The result was writing composed of words created from standardized and discrete units (typed letters) in contrast to cursive writing. Like the contents of the filing cabinet, it was information defined as "always perfectly precise."[40]

The rethinking of clerical work as a process-oriented mode of (machine) work depended on a new understanding of information.[41] Although in other contexts *data* existed as an alternative label, in the American business world *information* became the common name for a particularly instrumental form of knowledge, something that could be understood with little context.[42] Loose paper stored in folders, along with index cards, punch cards, and the increased use of graphs and tables, signaled the importance of information to the development of the large-scale business enterprises that defined capitalism in the early twentieth century.

Loose paper gave information a material existence as a thing that could be detached and repositioned, reordered and recombined, all in the name of the precision, accuracy, and speed associated with storing paper in filing cabinets. To be clear, this conception of information predates the filing cabinet, but the use of unbound paper, guide cards, and tabbed folders made it easier to comprehend. This was information as a thing that had presence in the world. It was something that was standardized, atomized, and stripped of context. This information, easily grasped, was critical to early twentieth-century capitalism. Efficiency required productivity and planning, which depended on always being able to access information about every aspect of business. This was grounded in the belief that the more precise information was, the greater the certainty in planning—it was a faith in granular certainty.

Misfiling

What if information could not be found? What if papers went missing? As I have argued, if this happened, neither the filing cabinet nor filing systems were at fault. While the filing cabinet promised to independently perform work a person had previously done, it still needed people to operate it. Although rarely stated as such, this acknowledged that the processes of standardization critical to making clerical work machine work could only be partly regularized; partial because the capacity of the technology meant "some actual human being who was much more unpredictable than a machine in aptitudes, skills, and personality" had to be involved.[43] Therefore, misfiling, when identified, drew attention to the person who filed; disembodied hands were reconnected to a body.

As a mode of misuse and error, misfiling is what Victoria Olwell calls a "bodily malfunction." That is, "the cloak of invisibility covering the body drops away . . . the moment that body makes a mistake."[44] Misfiling makes visible a very particular body, that of a young woman—Miss File misfiled. Therefore, in the occasional discussions of misfiling, the limitations of the filing cabinet as a machine were articulated to, and through, the lingering anxiety about the presence of young unmarried women in offices. These became inextricable because both ideas expressed concerns about productivity grounded in the limitation and contradictions inherent in dominant ideas of gender, labor, and machines.

The labor of file clerks was efficient in part because commonsense understandings of gender and sexuality lowered its costs. File clerks were poorly paid, not only because they were women and young, but also because they were unmarried. An "assumed heteronormativity" created an informal marriage bar and a family wage.[45] Women were identified as short-term workers who had to leave their jobs when they (inevitably) got married. Following on from this, it was logical that women be employed in jobs that required limited training and skill, with little opportunity for advancement: jobs like filing. If a woman kept working after marriage, low-level work and low pay continued to be justified on the grounds her husband, as a man, would have a better-paying job that would provide the income necessary to support a family.

However, while young unmarried women supplied cheap labor, they also provided the explanation for misfiling. Age and sexuality trumped gender to offer an explanation for the absence of the innate dexterity and sense of order otherwise invoked to present women as ideal file clerks. From this perspective, unmarried women who worked close to men could be distracted while they thought about potential husbands. Surveys of women office workers did support the belief that marriage was a priority for young women in offices, but it was not clear if it dictated their actions in the office.[46] Advice literature focused on managing female desire, assuming marriage dominated the thoughts of female clerks. However, unwanted sexual advances and harassment from men, while common and a concern for women, were not behaviors to be managed or even publicly discussed.[47] Women had to curb their emotions and the "feminine instinct to attract, to awaken a response" in a space where women were hired to "add to the general attractiveness of the office," as the male manager of an employment service put it (figure 7.6).[48]

In one advice article, Elizabeth McDowall, an experienced female office manager, instructed file clerks to "leave fine clothes, the theatre, pleasant parties, Tom, Dick and Harry, at home." This was necessary because if a woman brought such thoughts into the office, it would break down the teamwork of the senses and mind: "important tasks cannot be accomplished with your hands while unimportant details fill your head. You cannot file 'Amusement' under 'Work.' They are at the extremes of the alphabet."[49]

7.6 From filing cabinet catalog, 1917. Courtesy of the Hagley Museum and Library, Wilmington, Delaware.

Miss File would misfile if she failed to compartmentalize, if she failed to keep her personal concerns and work duties in their proper place and order; an explanatory structure that evoked the act of misfiling.[50] Therefore, it is not surprising that the filing cabinet was offered as a tool to teach young women to better order their lives by controlling their thoughts and desires. McDowall argued that office technologies would teach the "three necessities of efficiency": concentration, accuracy, and good nature. Introducing another office technology, she explained concentration as the need to "control your thoughts as you must your pencil, with a firm grip despite outside disturbance and inward annoyance."[51]

Framed more broadly, filing, as office work, was understood to impart middle-class values: moral and social respectability, education, and upward mobility all anchored in a heteronormative family centered on a male breadwinner and female domesticity. This pedagogical function of a filing cabinet showed the conflation of efficiency and middle-class values. The emerging idea of the middle class was also used to police whiteness in the white-collar world of the office; it also universalized the racial organization of the offices of dominant corporate capitalism as *the office*. White, Anglo-Saxon, middle-class women aimed for positions with responsibility, such as personal secretary or office manager. In contrast, the women whose primary work involved actual filing tended to be immigrant workers or the American-born children of immigrants, whose whiteness and middle-class identity, while more dubious, still gave them access to the office; these were the women who needed training in the manners and norms writers associated with middle-class identity. However, clerical work gave white women, broadly defined, an employment opportunity available to Latina, Black, and Asian women only on a limited basis, usually within their own communities.

According to a former secretary, the main problem in offices was "unbridled individuality running riot all over the place."[52] In the office, the "individuality" of women of dubious class, racial, and ethnic backgrounds marked deviance from acceptable middle-class behavior. At this lower end of the clerical hierarchy, the conflation of middle-class values and efficiency was not equivalent to the collapsing of identity into work that made professions the basis of middle-class identity. Rather, as an aspirational identity imposed on low-level clerical workers, it made the ideal worker a woman whose work was defined by the rationality of the machine she operated; a worker defined by and subsumed within routine to ensure the smooth working of the systems that classified paper and people to constitute the modern office.[53]

Office equipment company Shaw-Walker's signature advertising campaign, "Built Like a Skyscraper," offers a way to restate the argument that the filing cabinet organized information and gender in the office. The company's trademarked image linked masculinity and modernity: a drawing of a man in a suit jumping into an open filing cabinet drawer next to a sketch of New York City's recently completed Woolworth Building, the tallest skyscraper in the world when the campaign began in 1913. This image left visible the steel frame at the top of the building. Therefore, to build a filing cabinet "like a skyscraper" was to construct a steel skeleton strong enough to support drawers weighed down with thousands of bits of paper.

Shaw-Walker's advertisements constructed a series of physical encounters with its filing cabinets. These used male and female bodies to illustrate different aspects of what the company called the "essentials of office equipment": strength, rigidity, easy operation, noiselessness, economy of floor space, maximum capacity, and good design (figure 7.7). In addition to jumping into open drawers, men also performed "handstands" (that look like pull-ups) on open drawers. The latter were used to signify the "rigidity" of the drawer as opposed to the "strength" illustrated by a man jumping into the drawer (other companies made a similar point with photographs of men sitting or standing in the open drawers of a filing cabinet).[54]

The "Built Like a Skyscraper" campaign was not subtle. It does not take much for a scholar familiar with theories of gender representation to argue that this brief exercise routine reflected the male anxiety the arrival of women clerical workers in offices created, particularly for those men who still worked as clerks: the phallic-like skyscraper, the unsheathed tip of the Woolworth Building, the rigid and erect athletic male body, all sought to make explicit that the masculinity of the men who worked in offices was not to be questioned (including those men higher up the hierarchy who thought their way through the day).

However, the image used to show "easy operation" illustrated the gendered division that linked women to a particular form of manual work: machine work that required dexterity, not strength. In contrast to the conflation of strength and masculinity, a female body was used to show how easily a full file drawer (weighing seventy-five pounds) could be opened

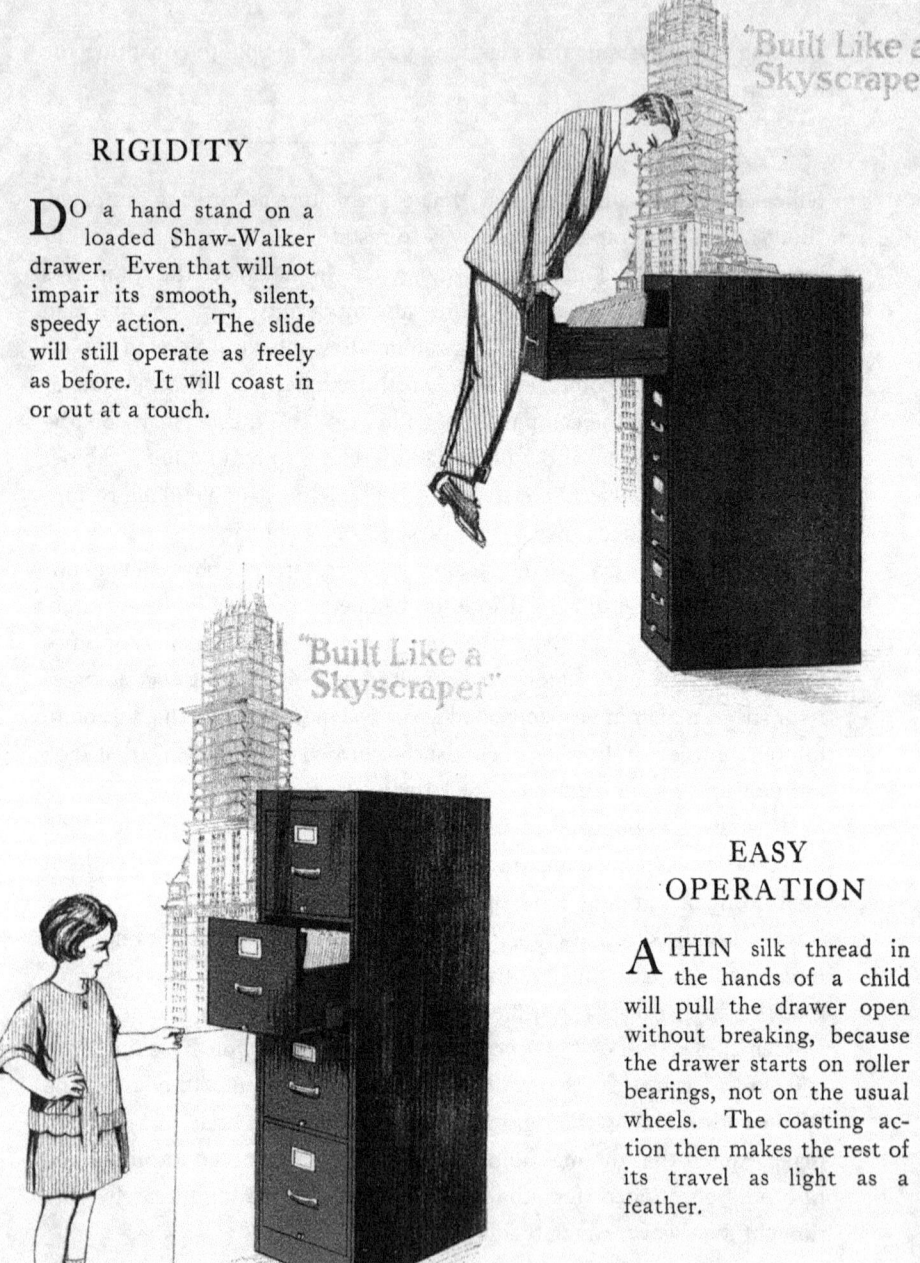

RIGIDITY

DO a hand stand on a loaded Shaw-Walker drawer. Even that will not impair its smooth, silent, speedy action. The slide will still operate as freely as before. It will coast in or out at a touch.

EASY OPERATION

A THIN silk thread in the hands of a child will pull the drawer open without breaking, because the drawer starts on roller bearings, not on the usual wheels. The coasting action then makes the rest of its travel as light as a feather.

7.7 From filing cabinet catalog, 1927. Courtesy of the Hagley Museum and Library, Wilmington, Delaware.

and closed. However, the illustrator did not use just any woman's body to activate the filing cabinet. They drew a young girl, opening a fully loaded file drawer by pulling on a cotton thread, to convey how easy it was to use a filing cabinet; filing was so easy anyone could do it, even a young girl.[55]

In another campaign, Shaw-Walker took up the implication that anyone could operate a filing cabinet by focusing on the interior of the drawer. In an attempt to sell the "ideal system of filing office letters," the company told potential customers, "You, a stranger to the file, can't look long for a letter because everything is in full view.... The names of all the regular correspondents can be read the instant the drawer is pulled out. You don't need to be an expert to find a letter. Simply open the drawer."[56] While you didn't need to be an expert to operate a filing cabinet, the "anyone" who could simply open a drawer and glance inside was a "file girl" (albeit older than the girl who pulled a cotton thread).

If anyone could file, it only required a woman to do it, because a man was needed to do work that a woman couldn't. The "stranger" Shaw-Walker's ad copy celebrated as being able to use a filing cabinet labeled the gendered subjectivity of a deskilled worker, a worker alien to the masculine skills used to define the office in the early twentieth century. As Sharma shows in her critique of McLuhan's media materialism, technologies and their temporal architectures privilege particular bodies and spaces over others.[57] As I have argued, a filing cabinet does some things and not other things. Within a gendered conception of efficiency, it provides a proper place for papers and information; it does this because there is a proper way to use it. That use depends on the materiality of the filing cabinet, on its physicality, on the convergence of a specific object and particular hands.

Notes

1. Library Bureau, "Will Miss File Mis-File?," *The LB File*, April 1920, 20. Library Bureau Papers, Herkimer County Historical Society, Herkimer, New York (hereafter, HCHS).

2. Kwolek-Folland, *Engendering Business*; Hartman Strom, *Beyond the Typewriter*.

3. For an insightful media materialist critique of a different file storage technology that prioritizes ontological questions over social relations of power, see Vismann, *Files*.

4. For a detailed critique of storage, see Robertson, *The Filing Cabinet*. For a different version of this argument that uses the concept of containment, see chapter 6, this volume, on Tupperware.

5. Sharma, "It Changes Space and Time!," 67; see also introduction to this volume.

6. Leffingwell, *Office Management*; Jecale and Parker, "The 'Problem' of the Office."

7. Gitelman *Scripts, Grooves, and Writing Machines*, 189.

8. Wallace, *Filing Methods*, 72.

9. Cramer, *The Filing Department*, 27.

10. American Institute of Filing, *A Course in Correspondence Filing for Home Study*, 13.

11. Immediately prior to the vertical filing cabinet, there were other attempts to store loose paper; index cards and their storage cabinets offered a different strategy for deconstructing the book. See Yates, *Control through Communication*, 31–34; Krajewski, *Paper Machines*.

12. For a broad survey of furniture used to organize information, see Mattern, "Intellectual Furnishing." Mattern also uses "cabinet logic" in the title of a talk but does not develop it as a concept; see Mattern, "'Cabinet Logic.'"

13. McLuhan, *Understanding Media* (1994), 116, 160, 171; Hessen, *The World in a Box*, 151–52; Krajewski, *Paper Machines*, 14–16.

14. Robertson, "Granular Certainty."

15. Library Bureau, "Boston Salesmen's Periodical Meetings 1898–1899," 203–4, HCHS.

16. Brown, *Filing*, 1.

17. Library Bureau, "A Few Letters from Users of the Automatic Index" (Boston: Library Bureau, n.d.), HCHS.

18. Library Bureau, *Filing as Profession for Women*, 31–32.

19. Library Bureau, *Filing as Profession for Women*, 31–32.

20. For an extended critique of bodies, technology, and automation in the twenty-first century, see Atanasoski and Vora, *Surrogate Humanity*.

21. Wallace, *Filing Methods*, 12.

22. Robertson, "Learning to File."

23. McCord, *A Textbook of Filing*, 19.

24. Braverman, *Labor and Monopoly Capital*, 220.

25. Roberts, *The Intangibilities of Form*, 93; Yawman and Erbe Mfg Co., *Vertical Filing Down-to-Date* (Rochester, NY: Yawman and Erbe, 1919–20), 13, National Museum of American History, Smithsonian Libraries' Trade Literature Collection, Washington, DC.

26. Zandy, *Hands*, 181.

27. Yawman and Erbe, *The Executive's Workshop: A Booklet on Efficient Office Management* (Rochester, NY: Yawman and Erbe, 1922), 11–12, Trade Catalog Collection, Hagley Museum and Library, Wilmington, Delaware (hereafter, HML).

28. Gardey, "Culture of Gender, Culture of Technology," 87.

29. McLuhan, *Understanding Media* (1994), 4, 90.

30. This phrase comes from a critique of the gendered labor of typing. See Lupton, *Mechanical Brides*, 43.

31. Bittel, Leong, and von Oertzen, "Paper, Gender, and the History of Knowledge," in *Working with Paper*, 9.

32. Quoted in Light, "When Computers Were Women," 461.

33. Charles L. Pederson, "Three Million Customers and the Filing Problems They Create," *The File*, February 1936, 6, HCHS.

34. McGaw, *Most Wonderful Machine*, 342.

35. McGaw, *Most Wonderful Machine*, 338.

36. Zakim, "Producing Capitalism."

37. Plotnick, *Power Button*, xv, 111.

38. Kittler, *Gramophone, Film, Typewriter*, 183–265.

39. Gitelman, *Scripts, Grooves, and Writing Machines*, 188.

40. Impressions, "The Filing Cabinet," 15.

41. Nunberg, "Farewell to the Information Age."

42. Von Oertzen, "Machineries of Data Power."

43. Liu, "Transcendental Data," 72.

44. Olwell, "The Body Types," 50.

45. Hicks, *Programmed Inequality*, 234.

46. Cavan, "The Girl Who Writes Your Letters."

47. Hartman Strom, *Beyond the Typewriter*, 373.

48. Frances Maule, "Women Are So Personal," *Independent Women*, September 1934, 280; Hartman Strom, *Beyond the Typewriter*, 391.

49. McDowall, "The Requisites of a Good File Clerk," 760.

50. Thank you to an anonymous reviewer of this chapter for pointing out this connection.

51. McDowall, "The Requisites of a Good File Clerk," 758.

52. Maule, "Women Are So Personal," 280.

53. Alan Liu makes a similar argument about late twentieth-century knowledge workers in *The Laws of Cool*, 123.

54. Shaw-Walker, *Built Like a Skyscraper* (Muskegon, MI: Shaw-Walker, 1927), 4–5, HML.

55. For a similar use of young girls in the contemporaneous promotion of electronic push buttons, see Plotnick, *Power Button*, 111.

56. Shaw-Walker, "The Ideal System of Filing Letters (and Finding Them)" (Muskegon, MI: Shaw-Walker, n.d.), HML.

57. Sharma, *In the Meantime*.

8 Computers Made of Paper, Genders Made of Cards

CAIT MCKINNEY

In 1969, Marshall McLuhan published a deck of cards, meant to be used for problem solving. His Distant Early Warning Line Card Deck (DEW deck) referenced the chain of sixty-three Cold War Arctic radar stations built by the Canadian and US governments across Inuit land between 1952 and 1957.[1] This electronic boundary would give joint combat operations a two-hour warning of impending Soviet missiles. McLuhan's cards are illustrated with cartoons, aphorisms, and jokes characteristic of his work. The cards functioned like a Magic 8 Ball: a user facing a decision could pull a card from the deck and read its aphorism as a through-line to pondering their problem. For McLuhan scholar Peter Zhang, "The cards stretch the mind. They put the user in a state of mind conducive to the solving of problems. They do not so much shed light on the situation directly as arouse and lubricate the user's mental apparatus."[2] Like the actual Distant Early Warning Line, this deck staged a prophylactic media problem: how might technologies ward off harm and manifest the future?[3] Though this was the deck's intent, many of the actual aphorisms on the cards ("The stripper puts the audience on by taking them off," "Thanks for the mammories," or "A Japanese wife never speaks irritably to her husband—she merely rearranges the flowers") read more like jokes about gender, race, and sex work uttered behind a Boys Club's closed doors by those with enough power to approach decision making as a card game (figures 8.1–8.3). Women appear but only as objects holding up a theory and function.[4]

Index cards like these are key objects in electronic media's extensions and translations of experience into information systems, but they also have a story to tell about gender that is much richer than the bad jokes on McLuhan's DEW deck.[5] Index cards were often marketed as accessible, tactile entries to information management via turns to their use in domestic contexts. Framed in gendered terms, manual information handling became a soft entry to computing in the 1960s and '70s.

That McLuhan created and published this card deck suggests more than a passing interest in paper cards as a way of designing an information system. For McLuhan, cards formalized a mediated relationship to information—according to McLuhan's son Eric McLuhan, who codesigned the cards, they "provoke lateral thinking."[6] Cards here are vested with immense formal significance as technologies that alter experience. Index cards—a broader category of cards that reference other information—are significant objects in the transition to electronic information management characterizing the mid-twentieth-century period of McLuhan's analysis in *Understanding Media*. Index cards organized recipes in boxes, helped maintain card catalogs, and input information into computers. As Shannon Mattern argues, through their use, display, and storage, index cards helped usher in a twentieth-century computational sensibility that informed how North Americans thought about information, management, and systems.[7] As they were encoded, shuffled, and categorized by hand, index cards provided users with tactile experiences of information as an object to be systematized and managed.

This chapter analyzes how a selection of instructional articles and manuals on indexing with paper cards from this period explained new computing processes to readers. These texts drew on cultural understandings of women's craft and aptitude for domestic organization in order to frame computers as tactile, approachable tools, ready for use by amateurs. I focus on a prefabricated device called the Knitting Needle Computer, which repurposed computer punch cards for manual, hobbyist indexing, and was designed to sort cards with knitting needles. Through devices like this one, gendered labor and gendered experiences with paper cards underwrote

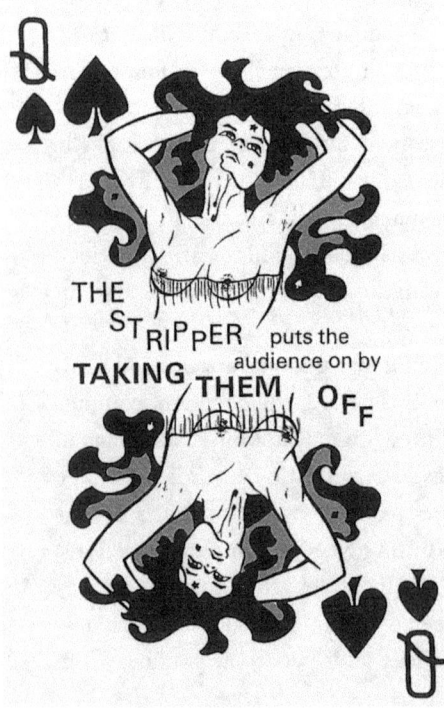

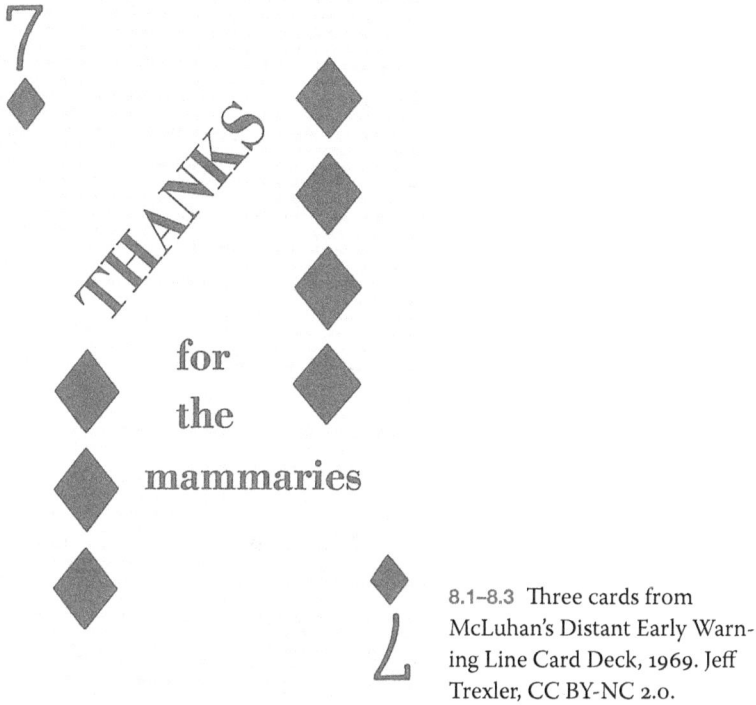

8.1–8.3 Three cards from McLuhan's Distant Early Warning Line Card Deck, 1969. Jeff Trexler, CC BY-NC 2.0.

midcentury efforts to ease information-saturated publics into the ideas and practices of computing.

Here, tools are extensions of man, where paper cards usher information sensibilities part of the way to computing. *Information sensibilities* describes how people understand, manage, and make data actionable using specific techniques and devices, both existing and on the horizon. Information sensibilities are constructed in practice, as the formal dimensions of media meet users and their socially situated techniques, which are always gendered and gendering. As feminist media history recenters craft methods and domestic metaphors like cleaning and sorting as rightly technological labor, the "Strippers," "Japanese wives," and lactating women scorned as objects depicted on McLuhan's cards become active participants in the transition to a computational information sensibility. A feminist analysis of paper cards as precomputational devices shows how gender is entangled with the ways new information sensibilities develop.

Computers Made of Paper | 145

The Knitting Needle Computer

The Knitting Needle Computer reimagined computer punch cards as the raw material for manual information storage and data-matching functions. All one needed to build one of these computers was a hole punch, a deck of cards, a shoebox, and a sorting needle appropriated from the knitting basket. In the instruction manual *Indexes and Indexing* (1959), Robert Collison lays out how to build one of these computers. Aimed primarily at amateur indexers, Collison's manual provided practical instructions on how to manage information using simple tools, like paper index cards. First, he describes the twentieth century in terms that evoke McLuhan's obsessive emphasis on the electronic information age: the 1960s would usher in a "great age of indexing," in which "heroic efforts" would be needed "to provide a key to the growing mass of information which is accumulating so rapidly that no-one can grasp its immensity."[8] Collison's chapter on mechanized indexing features a hypothetical discussion of how "business machines"—early punch-card-operated computers—might be "adapted" "for indexing purposes."[9] Similarly, amateur indexers could adapt computer punch cards for small-scale, manual indexing using knitting needles.

Knitting Needle Computers made small data-matching projects easier by semiautomating how information could be encoded and then retrieved. Take, for example, Collison's illustration, which depicts how to make an index to a book about English churches using this method (figure 8.4). Each church in the book is represented by a card, its name handwritten on the front of that card. Each card is prefabricated with a uniform set of punched-out holes along its edges, giving the Knitting Needle Computer its technical name: an edge-notched card system. Sets of holes are assigned to different information categories chosen by the user or designer of the computer. To encode a card, the user converts a single hole into a notch in the card edge, using a punch. Collison's sample card represents where Tewkesbury Abbey is mentioned in the book: The top edge of the card encodes letters, and "T" for "Tewkesbury" is punched. The bottom edge and the right edge of the card indicate the page number where Tewkesbury Abbey appears in the book: 15 and 7 are punched to indicate page 157. The same method can be used to create other kinds of small databases by changing the information categories the holes represent. For example, a softball fan could create a database of all the players in a league. Holes along the top edge of the card might correspond to "first letter of player's last name," while holes along the right edge of the card can describe "position played" or "batting average."

According to Collison, a batch of matching cards could then be retrieved from the larger stack, by sliding "a knitting needle of slightly smaller diameter than the holes in the cards" through the appropriate hole.[10] Using their knitting needle and a batch of "not more than two hundred" cards ready to be sorted, "the indexer thrusts the knitting needles through the hole denoting the letter [T] and shakes the cards." All of the cards that have had their T hole punched into a notch will not be picked up by the needle and will fall to the table below. The user is left with a pile of cards that share a common notch and data point.

As Collison optimistically explains, "this process is repeated batch by batch and letter by letter until, at the end all the cards will be found to have been sorted *automatically* into the order of the letters of the alphabet."[11] Despite his word choice, little about this process is automatic except for the future computing processes it aspired toward. Edge-notched cards looked like punch cards used to input information into a mainframe computer during this era, but they were designed to work within a cumbersome hand-sorting system.

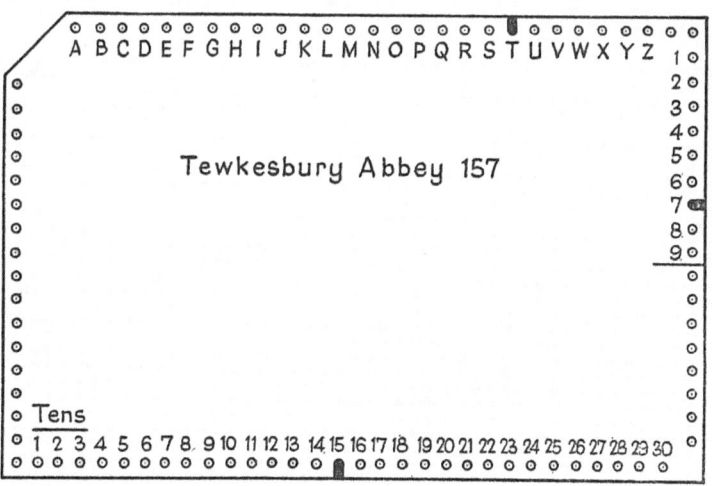

8.4 Illustration of punch card and knitting needle mechanized indexing system (Collison, *Indexes and Indexing*, 144). This example shows that Tewkesbury Abbey, an English church, is mentioned on p. 157 of a given book, and was used to create a subject index for the back of that book.

Like most midcentury indexing manuals written in the shadow of emergent database computing, Collison was teaching readers how to manage information using analog tools, but with an eye to the digital revolution that would soon offer new forms of what he called "mechanized indexing." An ambitious reader of Collison's instructions would not learn how to input data and run-type commands into a computer, but they could design a semiautomated, paper classification system that was conceptually similar to electronic database tools. In other words, edge-notched card users were experiencing something approaching computing, using knitting needles and paper cards.

Edge-notched systems were based on the large-scale, mechanized punch card databases that had been used as early as the 1890s for applications such as national census keeping and Social Security administration.[12] Edge-notched systems were sold to hobbyists as small kits that could be handled and manipulated without expertise, or the help of tabulators and sorting machines. The Knitting Needle Computer provides an example of how emergent computing figured in the imaginations of amateur information managers when actual computers were not available to them. Collison explains that the inaccessibility of computers "need not deter the average indexer from at least considering what measure of mechanization lies within his grasp, and what more—with the coming of mass-produced equipment—may shortly be at his disposal."[13]

Of course, the Knitting Needle Computer was not really a computer at all: it could not manage large volumes of data like an actual computer could; it was not made of metal, semiconductors, or wire; it did not need to be plugged in. The Knitting Needle Computer's distant proximity to actual computing was its point—by being not quite a computer but close enough to one, the machine helped explain computing processes to amateurs in highly tactile, unintimidating terms that they already understood. The device used gendered experiences and understandings of information to do this translation work, bridging paper cards and computers in an information sensibility animated by knitting needles.

Naming this paper card system a computer draws on gendered labor as a form of what Lisa Nakamura has called "flexible capital" for explaining, marketing, and building trust in computers.[14] The Knitting Needle Computer gently ushered potential computer users working in information fields (librarians, indexers, cataloguers, and hobbyists)—into the principles of automated information retrieval, and exemplified how computing could change the way information was imagined, managed, and mediated.

Edge-notched cards were effective at specific, small tasks known as "personal indexing," exemplified by the alphabetizing bibliographic project Collison illustrates above.[15] These tasks are much smaller in scale than the computational possibilities that the Knitting Needle Computer moniker promised. Collison admits that "not more than 200 cards" could be sorted at a time.[16] While indexing manuals tend to dwell on the positive aspects of edge-notched systems, it is easy to imagine the frustration and mess involved in shaking out matching sets of cards from a stack of hundreds. Here, shaking out a haphazard pile of cards on the table or floor is supposed to be productive instead of a total nightmare. The chaos of falling cards and worry that the wrong information might slip through the needle's grasp undetected undermined the system's promise to order and efficiently manage data. The Knitting Needle Computer was bad at robust data management, but succeeded in other pedagogical ways; namely, by providing an exemplary metaphor through which new, potentially intimidating database imaginaries and "bureaucratic machines" could be explained using practical materials that made computing seem accessible and tactile.

This accessibility was produced, in part, by articulating mechanized information management to the gendered practice of knitting. Articulation across disciplines is a common rhetorical tactic for building comfort with new technologies. Geoffrey Bowker calls this process "legitimacy exchange," where experts in one field justify their work through reference to the authority of experts in another field, building a closed system of expertise.[17] The Knitting Needle Computer exemplifies gendered legitimacy exchange, where typically undervalued domestic work is capitalized upon for its craft authenticity in order to build trust in new database computing. In this scenario, "women's work" is understood as properly technological to the extent that it maps onto the tools and processes at play in emergent computing technologies.

Collison's choice of a knitting needle is notable for the tool's status as a familiar household item used in domestic work. There are precedents for adapting these kinds of tools in information management. The first sixteenth-century designs for indexing devices were based on looms used to weave textiles.[18] Paper slips inscribed with information to be ordered were fed through two vertical strings, mounted to a board. The strings represented the vertical warp on a loom while the slips became the horizontal weft, temporarily woven through the strings in lieu of glue that would make reordering difficult.¹⁹ While these card looms borrowed physical design from handicraft, more recent feminist media histories have shown how midcentury women textile makers and their equipment were used to build amateur belief in the accessibility of computerized information management.

In the 1960s—the heyday of edge-notched card systems—women's textile labor was used to shore up the reliability of new computer hardware that the public did not readily understand and trust. Daniela Rosner has explored how NASA built memory for Apollo 11's guidance computer—via its subcontractor Raytheon—by hiring a factory staff of women textile workers near Boston to weave binary programs into "rope-core memory" using copper wire.²⁰ Engineers at NASA touted this "LOL" (Little Old Ladies) computer as fail-safe because it was made using a form of traditionally female labor. Nakamura has shown how the Fairchild Corporation employed Navajo women weavers toward similar ends, drawing on racialized and gendered capital to depict their "handiwork" assembling semiconductors as a reliable foundation for complex computing applications. In publicity materials, Fairchild promoted Navajo women's "natural" characteristics of docility, manual dexterity, and creative cultural handicraft to construct the circuits they built as high quality and reliable, because they were like weavings.²¹

Here, gendered and racialized ideas about care, craft, and skill become public relations strategies for making computers and spaceships seem as comfortable as a quilt made by Grandma. These weavers knew how to weave a program or semiconductor, but this weaving is not recognized as knowledge-based technological work.²² The weavers' gendered capital is flexible enough to bridge the traditional world of textiles with new forms of computing.

Today, applications of textile work to computing are evident within maker cultures that promote the accessibility of coding through turns to knitting. Code Academy, a suite of online tutorials that teaches amateurs how to program, explains that "knitters and other 'yarncrafters' understand what it means to build something one stitch (bit) at a time, and yarncrafting pattern designers (coders) know what it means to code, use an API, design, test, debug, and maintain the source code—even if they don't realize it yet."²³ There are material, technical similarities between making textiles and using computers, but highlighting these similarities always serves a pedagogical purpose more than an experiential or technical one; in this case: you will not fail at coding because it's just like knitting, and anyone can learn to knit. Weaving and knitting are tactile processes that require a great deal of technical skill, but they are crafts performed with accessible tools.[24] This is part of their gendered quality, and part of how they are used to construct a developing information sensibility in which computers are teachable, usable, and handle-able.

Beyond computing, the approachability of indexing with cards by non-professionals during the midcentury was often explained through domestic metaphors that extended into other kinds of household tasks. Indexing manuals describe the commonplace, household "systems designs" of women as prototypical "indexing" in order to cast mediated information management as second nature, and to lend indexing the authenticity and necessity of craft. Writes Collison, "Indexing is largely a matter of setting one's house in order. Nearly everyone does it in private life in some way or other, merely so that they can find things again when they need them. When a housewife makes a separate place for everything in the kitchen she is in fact creating a living index, for not only she, but all her household, will gradually get used to the system she has created and be able to discover things for themselves."[25] Here women workers are conceived as a general type, ideal for the practice of indexing because of experience designing small-scale functional systems—pantries, recipe boxes, domestic schedules. This housewife's kitchen ordering is a mediated systems-design practice that transforms the experience of "all her household." Within these terms we might recast the "Japanese wife" who merely rearranged the flowers confined to McLuhan's DEW deck as an information worker in her own right, whose work on home systems translates and circulates in wider information management cultures.

Indexing's organizing concepts and common materials are articulated to the realm of women's work in order to communicate ease and accessibility. Domestic materials stand in as a basic unit of information, unremarkable, familiar, and therefore easily managed in everyday life. Using the domestic sphere to illustrate how indexing is easy also has the effect of diminishing indexing work: if a woman can index, anyone can.[26] Using an anthropological gaze, the would-be indexer reading this manual is told to notice and observe housewives' information management practices (the reader is by necessity not one of these housewives), and recognize this activity as a naive, secondary class of "craft indexing" that is not apparent to itself as technical work. Makers of ordered pantries and seamless domestic schedules lend expertise to the indexing discipline without status as legitimate participants or potential collaborators in that field.

Edge-Notched Cards in Action

Recipe boxes and pantry systems are forms of personal indexing, a term that describes small-scale projects best suited to management through edge-notched card kits. Because of their small scale and hobbyist application, there are limited records documenting actual use of edge-notched card systems. A 1967 *Guide to Personal Indexes Using Edge-Notched, Uniterm and Peek-a-boo Cards* opens with the general suggestion that these systems are useful "to keep a note of periodical articles, pamphlets and reports . . . found interesting."[27] More specific amateur uses include prefabricated children's fingerprinting kits, character cards for Dungeons and Dragons games, amateur naturalist identification of birds and trees, and dissertation writing or personal research file management.[28] Well-documented edge-notched card databases are limited to high-level projects where indexing work eventually led to publication or public display. Edge-notched cards presented a logical fit for 1960s technotopian countercultural aesthetics in conceptual art and back-to-the-land movements; edge-notched card systems' use in these projects reflected the broader computational ethos of this work as it emphasized access to tools as a means of mastery and resource management.[29]

Experiments in Art and Technology (E.A.T.), a collective founded in 1967 by Bell Telephone engineers Billy Klüver and Fred Waldhauer, and artists Robert Rauschenberg and Robert Whitman, paired engineers and artists in technology-related collaborations. The E.A.T. collective relied on an edge-notched card system to match participants' technical skills, type of desired collaboration, media format, location, and equipment, among other categories (figure 8.5). Pairings were organized by matching information categories instead of subjective, intuition-based decisions about who ought to work together. The insertion of tiny sorting needles in holes marked with data categories like "lasers," "fiberglass," and "giving lectures" ensured that both parties were equally interested in the same materials and activities. While managing collaboration is most often considered a form of gendered, affective labor, the technologies at play in E.A.T.'s system privileged detached efficiency, rationalizing the alchemy of matchmaking through database logics.

The *Whole Earth Catalog* is perhaps the most notable use of an edge-notched card system during the long 1960s. This counterculture-defining document drew on aesthetics similar to E.A.T.'s in order to provide readers with access to tools such as books, recreational equipment, and mechanical

8.5 Job-printed, edge-notched card used in Experiments in Art and Technology, 1968. 20 × 26 cm. Getty Research Institute, Los Angeles (940003).

devices.[30] In this catalog, new computing technologies became just another resource-management device, like gardening equipment or bicycle repair tools. Catalog editor Stewart Brand used an out-of-the-box edge-notched card system manufactured by Indecks to manage entries for the *Whole Earth Catalog*, and also sold the deck within the catalog's pages.

Whole Earth's audience provides a window onto the kinds of users who might have found value in, and access to, edge-notched card systems for personal indexing. Media historian Fred Turner identifies the catalog's readership as home-brew computing enthusiasts, back-to-the-landers, artists, libertarians, and tech-industry hippies, a list in which E.A.T. engineers and artists would easily fit.[31] The Indecks listing in the 1971 catalog explains: "What do you have a lot of? Students, subscribers, notes, books, records, clients, projects? Once you're past 50 or 100 or whatever, it's tough to keep track, time to externalize your store and retrieve system. One handy method *this side of a high-rent computer* is Indecks. . . . [It's] meant the

> **Indecks Information Retrieval System**
>
> What do you have a lot of? Students, subscribers, notes, books, records, clients, projects? Once you're past 50 or 100 of whatever, it's tough to keep track, time to externalize your store and retrieve system. One handy method this side of a high-rent computer is Indecks. It's funky and functional: cards with a lot of holes in the edges, a long blunt needle, and a notcher. Run the needle through a hole in a bunch of cards, lift, and the cards notched at that hole don't rise; they fall out. So you don't have to keep the cards in order. You can sort them by feature, number, alphabetically or whatever: just poke, fan, lift and catch. Indecks is cheaper than the McBee system we used to list.
>
> We've used the McBee cards to manipulate (edit) and keep track of the 3000 or so items in this CATALOG. They've meant the difference between partial and complete insanity.
>
> —SB
> [Suggested by Ernest L. Gayden]
>
> Sorting allows you to retrieve the information that has been Recorded, Coded, and Notched (Steps 1, 2 & 3).
>
> Align the Deck at the clipped corners...
>
> Pass the Sorting Rod through the hole with the number which matches the listed code number of the category you wish to retrieve...
>
> Shake gently...and all cards notched at this hole will drop.
>
> THE CARDS YOU WANT HAVE BEEN RETRIEVED
>
> **Handbook of Mathematical Functions**

8.6 Indecks kit advertised in the *Last Whole Earth Catalog*, 1971.

difference between partial and complete insanity" (figure 8.6).[32] Crucially in this catalog listing, Indecks is not a computer, but does the same thing as one (just more handily) by releasing information retrieval from the confines of human memory through mediated externalization.

Instead of drawing upon comparisons to women's work, E.A.T. and *Whole Earth* both turned to other kinds of gendered metaphors to communicate tactility, simplicity, and usability by artists, engineers, and catalog readers. Like McLuhan's DEW cards, E.A.T. and *Whole Earth* imagined and celebrated forms of white, settler masculinity grounded in using the right tools to master resources, including information. They drew upon accessible craft techniques inherent in edge-notched cards' textures as media, but extended these techniques toward the masculine-coded realms of engineering, conceptual art, and tool cultures. Here, cards pushed information sensibilities toward the horizon of computing, where craft techniques shed their associations with knitting and took on masculine edges—tinkering, coding, shuffling as nearly computational extensions of man toward new information sensibilities.

A third case of edge-notched cards used for a traditionally domestic task challenges divisions between information management and women's work. Librarian Barbara Wheaton used edge-notched cards to create her Cook's Oracle recipe database, beginning in 1962 (the project is ongoing). Wheaton attempted to index every recipe ever published in American and European cookbooks. She adopted an edge-notched system in the 1970s, but later transitioned to a Microsoft Access Computer database when her

Knitting Needle Computer failed to keep up with the project: "my categories kept expanding, and the cards did not."[33] Wheaton's work turns the "indexing is easy because it's like a recipe box" premise on its head, showing that domestic information is just as unwieldy as any other data set, and that managing this information is indeed technological and even computational labor. By using edge-notched cards within the domestic realm normally invoked only for rhetorical purposes, Wheaton's work challenges the gendered division between information indexer and craft indexer. In a twist of irony, Wheaton's is the only project to engage explicitly in the edge-notched card system's failure; the growing deck of cards could not keep up with domestic information purported to be far less complex than engineering, conceptual art, or countercultural infrastructure. In response, Wheaton's recipe box became an Access file, moving on to an actual computer.

Nearly Electronic

The Knitting Needle Computer was nothing like a computer in relation to that era's room-sized, mainframe business machines; it was small, portable, easy for amateurs to operate, had physically limited storage capacities, could not output data by printing or writing to tape, and was resolutely analog. Calling what is essentially a deck of cards a computer nonetheless produces proximities to computing cultures. To some extent, naming these decks computers has the effect of making them into computers by expanding that category and articulating it to existing gendered information sensibilities; computing is demystified as "The Computer" becomes merely a device for externalizing and abstracting memory as information to be managed with technology. Proximities to computing—what I call the Knitting Needle Computer's nearly electronic status—provide one way that publics eased into widespread database cultures. Wheaton's transition from edge-notched cards to an Access database is a case in point. The Knitting Needle Computer figured users as physically capable of, and engaged with, the creation and manipulation of information using nearly electronic machines, and serves as a unique example of what "The Computer" meant within the 1960s public imagination. People did not necessarily understand how these machines worked, but associated them with social and technological progress.[34]

Edge-notched card systems were popular during a transitional stage in how institutions managed large quantities of information. The postwar introduction of mainframe computing allowed information storage and retrieval to become more technologically complex than manual systems such as card catalogs allowed.[35] Using computer databases, information could be stored and sorted quickly, and across multiple categories. By the early 1970s, information technology corporations such as Santa Monica's RAND offered computerized indexing software for institutional use, and by the early 1990s, consumer-grade software such as the Microsoft Access program used by Wheaton became available.[36] During the 1960s, however, computing was the jurisdiction of technologically sophisticated institutions like universities, large corporations, or government agencies. The transition to widespread computing for amateur information management required technological change through the personal computer, but also pedagogical processes: ways of explaining to would-be users what computers could do.

The mass production of edge-notched systems by the mid-twentieth century responded to demand for mechanized systems that could make information retrieval instantaneous. Printed information proliferated in workplaces, libraries, institutions, and other contexts, ushering in an era of bureaucratic, scientific management, systems thinking, and emerging computational understandings of how information might be organized and used.[37] An indexing sensibility is part of this developing "scriptural economy" that media historian Lisa Gitelman attributes to changes in printing methods, the availability of cheap paper, and scholarly subspecialization.[38] Indexes and bibliographies represent a distinct genre of midcentury document, constituting "materials that inventory, describe, catalog, or otherwise facilitate control over other materials."[39]

As a transition period marking both technological change and an emerging information sensibility, this nearly electronic era positioned edge-notched card systems as a stepping-stone for those who could not otherwise access computer databases. Beyond hobbyist use, these systems were recommended for small organizations that needed to manage records collections. Leslie Axelrod makes this recommendation to engineers in his 1962 article "An Information Retrieval System for a Small Research Department." Axelrod writes, "after considering several alternatives, I finally decided on edge-notched cards because they are relatively inexpensive and convenient to manipulate and store."[40] Celebrating cards' simplicity and manipulability, Axelrod justifies his choice against the inaccessibility of computing for some: "the biggest lesson to be learned is that not every IR [Information Retrieval] System requires a digital computer and a full time staff. With only a modest investment in material and time, even a small research organization can have a workable information retrieval system."[41] Edge-notched systems became a manual practice of resistance to digital computing in technical workplaces, promising good-enough information retrieval solutions that were, above all, affordable and usable by existing workers who need not be replaced or reskilled. Here, edge-notched card systems represent resistance to the new working conditions engendered by computing, in which subspecialization and systems administration inserted more layers of bureaucracy and distance between workers, their tools, and their colleagues. The warm, domestic sphere and joyful hobby cultures represented by edge-notched card kits did not match the sterile "digital computer and full time staff" to manage it that these engineers wanted to avoid.

Though hobbyists worked with information from home, they did so within the same scriptural economy as these engineers, drawing on the same techniques, whether as birders or recipe collectors. The small-scale systems described by Axelrod were developed and sold as kits for home users beginning in the early 1950s. A handful of companies mass-produced prefabricated edge-notched systems that amateurs could order by mail and adapt to their own needs (see figure 8.7). The Indecks kit advertised in the *Whole Earth Catalog*, along with the McBee system, are the most widely cited within instructional literature from the period.[42] These companies sold cards, sorting needles, and edge-notching punches, along with starter kits that contained all of these elements in a portable, plastic case that materialized the ready-to-hand tool status of the device. Starter kits also came with illustrated instruction booklets for using the deck, which reflected the product's amateur audience.[43] Needles sold with these sets came in bundles of five and were made specifically for the task of sorting cards. They were thinner and more like the precision-cut needles used in factory-based knitting machines than the thicker, coated metal, wood, or plastic knitting needles used in handicraft.[44] Collison's instructions for creating a DIY edge-notched system suggest that users appropriate actual knitting needles for the task and punch holes to match their size.

The Knitting Needle Computer was resolutely tactile because it placed computing in the hands and actions of its users; computing and needling are made equivalent. Edge-notched systems are further described in computational terms when information is "encoded" on them.[45] Punch encoding is more complex than simpler inscriptive techniques like shorthand because it requires machine sensibilities to be read: the needle instrument deciphers a predetermined punch code to cross-reference multiple cards, potentially across several categories, drawing associations that human memory can't make on its own. An adept edge-notched card user could brandish two

8.7 Indecks information retrieval system, Computer History Museum, Mountain View, California.

needles at once in order to extract cards with two data points in common, for example all the players in a softball league database whose names start with "M" (name category of holes) and play third base (position category of holes).

Knitting Needle Computer users did not just create information; they repaired it, using mending sensibilities also apparent in craft cultures. John Bryan's edge-notched system instructions include advice on performing repair.[46] As Bryan explains, "miscoding" was a common problem caused by "punching out the wrong hole or holes" on cards.[47] "Fortunately, the remedy is simple. Cut a strip of suitable size from another card and glue it in place."[48] Indecks sold prefabricated "Hole Repair Belts" to complement their kits.[49] Just as code could be written with a hole punch, and read with a knitting needle, it could be repaired with a little bit of glue and paper. Mispunching a card becomes an opportunity to demonstrate the easy manipulability of edge-notched cards; code could be rewritten with the simple application of a tiny, needle-blocking piece of paper, cut to size.

Information encoded on cards is parsed using conspicuously simple, gendered imagery. Not only were sorting needles described as "knitting needles," the phrase "peek-a-boo cards" (a game used to amuse babies) was sometimes attributed to these systems to illustrate how cards appeared out of a larger stack when sorted by needle.[50] While the Knitting Needle Computer could not parse large quantities of information, the machine still put into practice several rudimentary database functions including coding, mechanized storage and retrieval, and cross-referencing capabilities. Most importantly, the device made these functions visible and controllable, like reaching for the sugar on the pantry's top shelf. In other words, for computing to seem appealing and within reach to hobbyist information managers, men needed to be guided through these processes gently, not by their actual mothers and wives, but by their proxies: knitting needles and ordered pantries, or the women on McLuhan's cards.[51] These gendered techniques and imaginaries about media are critical to a feminist understanding of how information sensibilities emerge.

Conclusion

The amateur information manager figured by prepackaged card kits and edge-notched indexing instruction manuals enjoys leisure time devoted to bird watching or Dungeons and Dragons, hobbies that suggest lives free from the rigors of domestic work or child care. Knitting needles are tools this hobbyist does not own, but might borrow and repurpose, both literally from their wives, and figuratively through the gendered capital they offer. The Knitting Needle Computer promised this hobbyist accessibility, tactility, and mastery over information, all key components of an emerging information sensibility that included computing, during a period when women were the most common users of actual computers in workplaces. As Mar Hicks has shown, despite the prevalence of women as computer programmers during the midcentury, programming was feminized and cast as merely clerical, a practice of carrying out instructions issued by others using new business machines.[52] Knitting Needle Computer users, on the other hand, were creatives who used small-scale information systems to manage information of their own making.

For our media histories, when a new technology sits close to computing, we might need to look a bit sideways or askance to understand what that technology is doing with this proximity to actual computers; if the Knitting Needle Computer could only store and manage a small quantity of information, often awkwardly, then it served other purposes within the computational imaginary. This tool drew on gendered capital to explain electronic information management in approachable terms, and to encourage amateurs to practice some of the database functions that would become commonplace by the 1980s and 1990s. New technologies and the transformations they bring require explanation. This was McLuhan's focus as a public intellectual in the 1960s. Though his analysis left women on cards and in the margins, the emergent understandings of media he described were bound up with gendered techniques such as knitting. Looking in these margins at minor objects like paper cards, it becomes clear that emergent information sensibilities drew on ideas about gender just as much as they did electricity, computers, and other tools.

Notes

1. Hird, "The DEW Line and Canada's Arctic Waste."
2. McLuhan and Zhang, "The DEW Line Card Deck as a Metagame," 242.
3. Mulvin, "Media Prophylaxis."
4. This point about the function of the figures on McLuhan's cards builds on Armond Towns's analysis of the Black body simultaneously present and excised by the "Western Man" concept undergirding McLuhan's media theories: Towns, "Toward a Black Media Philosophy."
5. , McLuhan, *Understanding Media*, 2001, 63–67.
6. McLuhan and Zhang, "The DEW Line Card Deck as a Metagame."
7. Mattern, "The Spectacle of Data."
8. Collison, *Indexes and Indexing*, 19.
9. Collison, *Indexes and Indexing*, 143.
10. Collison, *Indexes and Indexing*, 144.
11. Collison, *Indexes and Indexing*, 145, emphasis added.
12. For a history of these large-scale systems, see Heide, *Punch-Card Systems and the Early Information Explosion*.
13. Collison, *Indexes and Indexing*, 143.
14. Nakamura, "Indigenous Circuits," 933.
15. See Foskett, *A Guide to Personal Indexes*.
16. Using a different form of measurement, John Bryan suggests selecting a stack of no more than one and a half inches thick. Bryan, "A Multi-purpose Information Retrieval System," 404.
17. Bowker, "How to Be Universal," 116; see also Fred Turner's discussion of legitimacy exchange and closed loops of expertise in *From Counterculture to Cyberculture*, 25.

18. See Krajewski, *Paper Machines*, 13–14.

19. Krajewski, *Paper Machines*, emphasizes the relationship between sorting cards and weaving fibers to provide a media archaeological explanation for how new technologies emerge through the remediation of established practices.

20. Rosner, *Critical Fabulations*. See also Wolfinger, *Moonshot*; Fildes, "Weaving the Way to the Moon."

21. Nakamura, "Indigenous Circuits," 921, 926–27.

22. The talking-head-style documentary cited above (Wolfinger, *Moonshot*) features several male Apollo engineers telling the LOL weavers story according to this narrative strategy.

23. Carroll, "How Knitters Are Human Computers."

24. On craftsmanship, tactility, and skill, see Sennett, *The Craftsman*.

25. Collison, *Indexes and Indexing*, 12.

26. Classification work's construction as easy because women can do it has a longer history in library and information management cultures. See Garrison, "The Tender Technicians," 132. While these examples turn women indexers into abstractions, women made important contributions to the development of indexing systems: some of the earliest indexers were women, including Mary Petherbridge, whose book *The Technique of Indexing* (1904) was a popular early instructional manual. See Archibald, "Indexes, in Praise of."

27. Foskett, *A Guide to Personal Indexes*, 9.

28. Kevin Kelly's blog post on edge-notched card systems as "dead" media includes a lengthy comment section in which readers of the post relate their own uses of edge-notched cards, past and present. See Kelly, "One Dead Media."

29. On this counterculture technological aesthetic, see Turner, *From Counterculture to Cyberculture*.

30. Turner, *From Counterculture to Cyberculture*, 71.

31. Turner, *From Counterculture to Cyberculture*, 71–73.

32. *The Last Whole Earth Catalog*, 320, emphasis added. Kelly's blog post alerted me to this use of Indecks in the catalog.

33. Barbara Wheaton, quoted in Wilson, "The Archive of Eating." In this article, Wheaton says she transitioned to a Microsoft Access database in the 1980s; however, Access was not introduced until 1992.

34. See Peters, *How Not to Network a Nation*, especially chapters 1 and 2.

35. See Bourne and Hahn, *A History of Online Information Services*.

36. See RAND, *Specifications for the RAND Abstract and Index System*; Ware, *RAND and the Information Revolution*.

37. Robertson, "Learning to File."

38. Gitelman, *Paper Knowledge*, 54.

39. Gitelman, *Paper Knowledge*, 58.

40. Axelrod, "An Information Retrieval System," 92.

41. Axelrod, "An Information Retrieval System," 93.

42. Other suppliers included Information Retrieval Systems Inc. of Princeton, NJ. It was also possible, though quite labor intensive, to design one's own cards, as Collison suggests in *Indexes and Indexing*.

43. Indecks Research Deck Needle Sort Punched Card Kit, 1966, Catalog Item #102647065, Computer History Museum, Mountain View, California, http://www.computerhistory.org/collections/catalog/102647065.

44. Bryan, "A Multi-purpose Information Retrieval System," 407.

45. Bryan, "A Multi-purpose Information Retrieval System," 402.

46. Bryan, "A Multi-purpose Information Retrieval System," 406.

47. Bryan, "A Multi-purpose Information Retrieval System," 406.

48. Bryan, "A Multi-purpose Information Retrieval System," 406.

49. *The Last Whole Earth Catalog*, 320.

50. *The Last Whole Earth Catalog*, 402.

51. Mulvin, *Proxies*.

52. Hicks, *Programmed Inequality*.

9 Sky High

Platforms and the Feminist Politics of Visibility

RIANKA SINGH AND
SARAH BANET-WEISER

It is fair to say that, in the past decade, Western media have provided a heightened platform for feminism. Feminist manifestos, hashtag activism, and feminist-themed aspirations have crowded most media platforms, making a specific version of feminist subjectivity and its parent political commitments both hypervisible and normative within popular media. Media platforms such as Twitter, Instagram, and Facebook have enabled a visibility of feminisms that have long struggled for a broader space and place in culture, which often makes it difficult to distinguish between and among them.[1] Popular feminism relies on multiple media platforms both to occupy a position of self-empowerment and to communicate a version of empowerment to users (what Rosalind Gill has called "gendered neoliberalism"[2]). In this chapter, we explore the relationship between the platform and feminist empowerment. Despite a recent focus on the digital platform and feminism's relationship to it, with the #MeToo movement as the most obvious example, there is a history of women's relationship to the platform that extends well beyond the digital. We find it useful to turn to the materialist media theory of both McLuhan's *Understanding Media* to elevate the platform as a medium of communication itself and also *The Mechanical Bride* more specifically.[3] In *the Mechanical Bride*, McLuhan argues that women are transformed into "love machines" where the end goal is "love unlimited" when they use technologies that modify their bodies.[4] We object to the characterization of women as agentless "love machines," but if we were to continue the machine metaphor, we would suggest thinking about how platforms mechanize popular feminist politics.

In "The Politics of Platforms," Tarleton Gillespie offers the following useful typology as a frame through which we understand platforms: *computational*, "an infrastructure that supports the design and use of particular applications," thus referring almost solely to digital platforms; *architectural*, which refers to the physicality of the platform (it "has been broadly used to describe human-built or naturally-formed physical structures, whether generic or dedicated to a specific use: subway and train platforms, Olympic diving platforms, deep-sea oil rig platforms, platform shoes"); *figurative*, where the platform is understood in more conceptual terms, such as a position achieved, or the use of *platform* to designate a starting point for further achievement; and *political*, where the platform indicates a place to articulate one's political views.[5] Gillespie connects the political use of *platform* with its architectural use, pointing out that the physical platform was often used as a way for a politician to make his or her voice heard, above the fray. As he argues, *platform* is "a term that generally implied a kind of neutrality towards use—platforms are typically flat, featureless, and open to all—[and] in this instance specifically carries a political valence, where a position must be taken."[6]

Importantly, Gillespie argues that platforms often draw on all of these meanings, so that "'platform' emerges not simply as indicating a functional shape: it suggests a progressive and egalitarian arrangement, promising to support those who stand upon it."[7] Indeed, platforms are often framed as necessary for a kind of empowerment; they are spaces and places to amplify one's voice, to have a speaking part in a narrative, to display power, even in limited ways. In popular discourse, to be given a platform is synonymous with being given a voice. Of course, as Gillespie points out, well before digital platforms, spaces such as the ancient Greek polis, the soapbox, "hobo" oratory, and political protests gave individuals platforms for them to be seen and their voices to be heard. The construction of a platform as an authorizing, open, empowering space certainly shaped (and continues to shape) the framing of digital media; on social media, as the story goes, users are empowered by digital platforms, which affords them a voice by lowering barriers of entry. Indeed, since at least 2011, when Occupy Wall Street and the Arab Spring gave rise to what was then referred to as "the Twitter revolution," these sites have often been celebrated for their political visibility.[8]

Yet the empowerment of the platform, as it rests on becoming and being visible and noticeable, also means that bodies—often abject or marginalized bodies—are put on display and made vulnerable to a range of surveillance mechanisms. While platforms offer one a kind of spotlight, they also demand that bodies occupy this spotlight in a particular way: there are different ways to be visible, and different goals of visibility as a practice. The visibility that comes with occupying the platform isn't necessarily a solution, as visibility hides as much as it reveals. Visibility, in other words, can be a trap. Astra Taylor, in her work *The People's Platform*, offers a useful critique of a techno-utopian vision of the internet as an equalizing space, refuting the notion that social media sites enable democracy. She argues instead that the internet amplifies offline inequalities: "instead of making our relationships horizontal and bringing prosperity to all, the gap between the most popular and the practically invisible, the haves and the have-nots, has grown."[9] What Taylor and others argue about the democratizing potential of the digital platform is that we need to attend to the limitations of visibility, and how the visibility of some relies on the invisibility of others.

If we take up McLuhan's focus on the medium instead, it becomes easier to both locate and avoid the visibility trap set up by contemporary understandings of digital platforms. McLuhan would not necessarily have been interested in how platforms might enable democratic participation, for example. Rather, he points us toward an understanding of how platforms transmit messages about differential power relations. McLuhan urges us to "turn from the content of messages to study total effect."[10] Indeed, in this chapter we are concerned with the total effect of the platforms that have come to mediate feminist politics. In what follows, we contextualize contemporary feminism's relationship to digital platforms within a longer history of platforms and what these spaces have authorized and enabled. We position feminist digital platforms alongside three other platforms: the witch's gallows, the slave auction block, and the platform shoe. All of these platforms elevate a body, thus putting these bodies on display for evaluation, objectification, and vulnerability. We look to these other platforms as a way of highlighting that the digital platform is overdetermined as an empowering force. And although not networked in the way of the digital, but rather dispersed through time and space, these objects that elevate and amplify those who stand on them are significant to our understanding of contemporary feminism. Following McLuhan's predecessor Harold Adams Innis we consider platforms to be space-biased media.[11] They facilitate the expansion of decentralized power and adapt easily over time. We see this adaptability by tracing earlier iterations of these platforms and recognizing the ongoing effects that they have on sustaining inequality among those who mount them. These other platforms unsettle the assumption that visibility via the platform is always about giving someone a voice.

Gallows

The twenty-first century witnessed a sort of renaissance of the concept of the witch hunt where, like its origins, it also referenced accusations, belief, and gendered dynamics of power. Yet, unlike the witch hunts of the sixteenth century, when women were accused of being witches as a way to control them, and then hung from gallows in public spectacles, the contemporary witch hunt is a twisted reversal, whereby men in positions of privilege, when accused of sexual harassment and assault, have claimed to be victims of a witch hunt. For example, amid the allegations that Harvey Weinstein sexually assaulted numerous women and the subsequent rise of the #MeToo movement, Hollywood director Woody Allen warned of what he called "a witch hunt atmosphere where every guy in an office who winks at a woman is suddenly having to call a lawyer to defend himself."[12] US President Donald Trump routinely accuses women, the media, and Democrats of engaging in a witch hunt over just about everything he is accused of, including sexual assault. Allen and Trump reference witch hunts in these instances as if it is men in positions of power who have to fear violent persecution that thousands of women across the world have been subject to since at least the mid-1400s.[13]

What does this have to do with the platform? Historically, the witch hunt involved the singling out of women who challenged social norms and the status quo, through either behavior or appearance. While men have also historically been the targets of witch hunts, the majority of witch hunts have involved the persecution of women, as Silvia Federici, in *Caliban and the Witch* and *Witches, Witch-Hunting and Women*, elegantly argues.[14] This persecution was a way of ensuring the expectations and identities of women in a newly forging capitalist society, so that they would conform to dominant gendered power relations. Federici posits that "women were the main target of this persecution because it was they who were most severely impoverished by the capitalization of economic life, and because the regulation of women's sexuality and reproductive capacity was a condition for the construction of more stringent social control."[15] Since the witch hunt was about a broader form of social control of women, what made one a witch were vague symbols of difference; it could be one's status as poor, elderly, or nonreligious, or it could be a bodily sign of difference: a mole or birthmark.[16] The gallows from which women were hung (after being accused of being witches) were elevated platforms, the hangings a public spectacle of visibility and violence that was seen as a deterrent and mechanism of control for other women.[17] The gallows themselves are not the source for controlling women; it is the visibility of the bodies who were forced on the platforms, the spectacle of punishment, that worked as a mechanism for control.

That is, the platform of the gallows functioned as a reminder to all women of the potential violence that would occur should they threaten or challenge dominant gender hierarchies and practices. Federici attributes women's persecution as witches as being linked to their threat to power imposed by the church and state, so that the visible hangings helped to maintain and justify that power.[18] As Federici argues, the formation of a fear of witches and their subsequent persecution has always been linked to the fear and persecution of women more broadly. As Federici writes, "The witch hunt instituted a regime of terror on all women, from which emerged the new model of femininity to which women had to conform to be socially accepted in the developing capitalist society: sexless, obedient, submissive, resigned to subordination to the male world, accepting as natural the confinement to a sphere of activities that in capitalism has been completely devalued."[19]

The witch hunt as a way of erasing difference was therefore a system for disciplining women. Putting nonconforming women on trial for witchcraft meant that, as Federici puts it, "At the stakes not only were the bodies of 'witches' destroyed, so was a whole world of social relations that had been the basis of women's social power."[20] The gallows were elevated platforms, but clearly did not indicate a kind of empowerment; on the contrary, the visibility garnered on the platform functioned as disempowerment. McLuhan writes that "the effects of technology do not occur at the level of opinions or concepts but alter sense ratios or patterns of perception steadily and without any resistance."[21] In this sense, it is the case that a platform can and does elevate anybody, even if the effects are different. By taking up McLuhan, we observe that the platform is a technology that puts bodies on display and that this logic alone has significant effects on human experience. Witches' gallows follow this same logic of putting bodies on elevated display and in this instance mediate punishment and violence.

Indeed, it is precisely because the logics of the platform are established but often go unnoticed that it has been so easy in the contemporary moment for powerful men like Trump and Allen to appropriate the concept of the witch hunt. When the bodies of powerful men who are accused of sexual assault occupy a platform (either political or digital), they can then rewrite the history of witch hunting and apply it to their own privileged status. This shift from women being hunted and murdered as witches to powerful men claiming that any accusation against them is a witch hunt demonstrates that the power of the platform might be the platform itself rather than its changing content.

Auction Blocks

Another example of how the platform has figured as a site of violence, persecution, and perverse capitalism is exemplified in the United States in the seventeenth and eighteenth centuries by slave auctions. Auction blocks serve, in ways both similar and different from witches' gallows, as an example of power putting abject bodies on visible display. Black men and women were forced onto a platform, the auction block, so that they were readily visible for sale to slave owners. The visibility of the auction block was a mechanism of evaluating and objectifying Black bodies, literally transforming them into commodities for sale, as mere capacity for labor. The platform itself is merely a form of elevation; the bodies that were forced onto these platforms to be made visible are the materiality of this moment, signifying the manifestation of racist power and control.

In many accounts of slave life, the auction block figures as the location of the traumatic separation of families as people are bought and sold to different slave owners throughout the American South.[22] Anne C. Bailey recounts how auctions were referred to as "the weeping time" because slaves understood that after they climbed onto the block, they would be displaced from their homes and families.[23] The block also indicates the efficient sale of humans; as Bailey explains, the appearance of people on the block was significant to showcasing value.[24] Slave owners evaluated factors such as body composition and general good health (as a way to consider whether the slave would be a good plantation worker). But people were also evaluated for indicators of obedience, like posture and whether or not the slave might be defiant, which could be read as a sign of resistance or likelihood of escape. For both Black slaves and white slave owners, the visibility afforded by the platform (the auction block) was fundamentally about objectification and abjectification of Black people; for the slaves, it was about their bodies forcibly made visible as abject objects, and for the slave owners, the visibility of the auction block gave them a better view in order to evaluate the "objects" for sale.

For example, in his description of the slave auction at the St. Louis Hotel in New Orleans, John Theophilus Kramer describes the elegantly dressed men and women, slave traders, who enter the hall and wait for the auction to begin. One by one, men, women, and children are called up to the auction block, where their names, ages, and skills are read out before the auctioneer. At the auction Kramer attends, 149 people are sold in total. Kramer, who is an abolitionist, describes each sale and makes known his discomfort with the ways in which the people who climb up on the auction block are crudely categorized and sold. For example, he describes three siblings who are put on the auction block together and sold to separate buyers: "I will not attempt to imagine the anguish and horror that my fair female readers would have felt, if they could have witnessed the picture of that poor distressed family the despairing features of those three innocent girls upon that slaughter-bench, like three faultless lambs offered for sacrifice!"[25]

In this example of slave auctions, the platform figures as a technology that amplifies bodies in the name of logistics. As different people for sale mount the slave auction block, their physical attributes are made more visible to buyers needing workers; thus the platform functions as a way to ease financial transactions. The platform in the example of the slave auction block is a technology of moving human capital and objectification.

Platform Shoes: Fall, Pause, Rise

It's Paris Fashion Week, 1993, and designer Vivienne Westwood is debuting her newest pair of platform shoes (figure 9.1). The shoes are bright blue and made of leather fashioned to look like crocodile skin, with blue silk laces. Most notably, though, is the platform sole that measures an unusually high 30.5 centimeters on each shoe. On the catwalk in Paris, the British supermodel Naomi Campbell, at the peak of her career as a runway model, is wearing Westwood's platform shoes. When it is Campbell's turn to walk and show off Westwood's signature piece in the collection, she takes a couple of steps down the runway before her left ankle and then her right buckle in the obviously too high shoes. She crumbles to the ground. Campbell sits on the

9.1 Vivienne Westwood, platform shoes, 1993.

runway for a few seconds, then laughs in embarrassment as people lining the runway lean in to try to catch a glimpse of the once-towering woman taken down by her own shoes.

Platform, or high-heeled, shoes make a woman physically vulnerable and unstable—they elevate a body on an insufficient platform that is typically limited in its capacity to support body weight. Starting in the 1970s, during the resurgence of platform shoes in popular fashion, health concerns related to wearing the shoes began appearing in scientific journals. For example, Dr. Michael Whitehouse wrote to a British medical journal in 1974 warning of what he called "Platform Shoe Syndrome," where he noted the connection between his female patients wearing platform shoes and an increase in knee pain and "tenderness over the patellar ligament."[26] It is obviously difficult to run in platform shoes, making fast escapes from any situation difficult.[27] And, as natural gait will be dangerously altered in platform shoes, ankle sprains are more likely.[28] Driving in a platform shoe will slow braking response time and increase the chances of car accidents.[29] In an article for the *New York Times*, Lauren Stover reported on a burgeoning specialty podiatrist industry where doctors perform foot surgery for women who want to wear high heels more comfortably. In Stover's article, one doctor called these invasive surgeries "Cinderella procedures."[30]

Yet Vivienne Westwood and other shoe designers have successfully sold the idea that the platform shoe is the quintessential expression of femininity, a natural extension of the body, a platform that communicates power, femininity, and sex appeal. The platform shoe, which became a popular staple in women's fashion in the 1970s and made a comeback in the 1990s, has a history that predates these somewhat recent cultural moments. Since at least 220 BC, platform shoes have acted as a way of heightening and thus increasing the visibility of their wearer. The shoe was also designed to alter the gait of the women who wore it to ensure an appearance of femininity. Indeed, the platform shoe has occupied, and continues to occupy, a venerated place in Western cultural imagination: a woman in heels is a woman in power, in control of her body and sexuality. This imagination is animated in popular culture: think Sarah Jessica Parker and her endless discussion of shoes as an independent woman writer in *Sex and the City*, or to films such as *Working Girl*, *Charlie's Angels*, and countless others where a female protagonist, on her way to corporate power and success, or to fight an evil villain, weaponizes her heels as a clear symbol of powerful femininity. Even beyond popular culture, there is a recent academic interest in high-heeled shoes, especially in the field of media studies, despite the historical feminist scholarship that has theorized the platform shoe as an obvious impediment to women's empowerment.[31]

Here, we use the platform of the platform shoe (pun intended) to return to the platform of digital feminism. The affective relations women are expected to have with the platform shoe—empowerment, confidence, self-assurance, sexiness—resonate with the discourse of empowerment of popular feminism that circulates on multiple digital platforms. For example, some modern-day neoliberal popular feminist heroes, such as Sheryl Sandberg, Melinda Gates, Anne-Marie Slaughter, and Michelle Obama, are all proponents of a feminist politics that sees women successfully climbing the corporate ladder as the key to empowerment.[32] It matters here that neoliberal feminism is equated with being high powered: verticality stands as a marker of success. It's no wonder, then, that shoes which will literally raise a woman from the ground are also linked to empowerment: Mike Zundel has argued that heels signify power in the boardroom, and Summer Brennan argues that the very purchasing of shoes is also sometimes presented as a mode of feminist liberation.[33] She writes, "Modern shoe consumerism, especially, is often presented within the politically feminized language of *choice*. A woman's right to choose becomes a 'woman's right to shoes.'"[34] As such, there is a connection between what both popular feminism and high heels signify culturally and politically.

Of course, this connection is complicated—there is certainly not a consensus that popular feminism and high heels signify the same kind of cultural power. For example, Summer Brennan's book *High Heel* grapples with the question of whether high-heeled shoes celebrate a woman's sexuality or make women sexual objects.[35] In the early 1990s, Sandra Bartky was also writing about how high-heeled shoes are part of a disciplinary practice that controls and hinders the movement of women.[36] Even some of McLuhan's observations, although from a notably less feminist perspective, echo this sentiment. Analysing a Phantom Pencil Seams Nylons ad, McLuhan writes of the woman's legs on display, "To the mind of the modern girl, legs, like busts, are power points which she has been taught to tailor, but as parts of the success kit rather than erotically or sensuously. She swings her legs from the hip with masculine drive and confidence. She knows that 'a long-legged gal can go places.' As such, her legs are not intimately associated with her taste or with her unique self but are merely display objects like the grill work on a car. They are date-baited power levers for the management of the male audience."[37]

Platform shoes figure as an apparatus of elevation and visibility, and as a way of structuring a particular kind of femininity in much the same way as the digital platforms on which much popular feminism circulates. McLuhan's analysis of the Phantom Pencil Seams Nylons ad highlights how women's legs are managed by advertisers in order to draw and keep the male gaze. Indeed, McLuhan would consider platform shoes, alongside other garments that restrict a woman's ability to move in the world, as an example of her "mechanization." In *The Mechanical Bride*, he theorizes what he calls "the interfusion of sex and technology."[38] For McLuhan, the connection between sex and technology is twofold. First, there is a masculinist drive to make sex mechanical, and second, man wants to "possess machines in a sexually gratifying way."[39] McLuhan imagines that those objects which alter a woman's natural body are part of man's project to mechanize women.

For example, #MeToo, #TimesUp, and #YesAllWomen are all movements that have relied on the digital platform for reinvigorating a popular feminism.[40] Our interest in platform shoes is not centered around an argument about whether the shoe is empowering or not. We do not think it is useful here to think about shoes as tools for empowerment. This idea of shoes as empowering exists in the first place because of a contemporary white and popular feminist imperative that sees visibility and elevation as vital to feminist liberation.

The platform shoe, and the women who wear them while inhabiting offices on the top floors of office buildings, highlight how a particular popular feminism has an attachment to the platform. This popular feminism is usually white, heterosexual, and dedicated to corporate capitalism. The platform that elevates some women is a requirement for white feminist power to operate and maintain its dominance. Liberating or not, this apparatus of elevation mediates popular feminism. Banet-Weiser explains the link between what she refers to as an economy of visibility and popular feminism when she writes, "In a capitalist, corporate economy of visibility, those feminisms that are most easily commodified and branded are those that become most visible. This means, most of the time, that the popular feminism that is most visible is that which is white, middle-class, cis-gendered, and heterosexual."[41] The platform shoe, when considered as a technology of popular feminism, can only ever be empowering for those that are already poised to be most visible. It therefore doesn't matter if a platform shoe is empowering. What is significant here is that there is a perceived need for a technology, in this case a shoe, as a way of mediating empowerment.

Conclusion

We began this essay with some questions: What are the goals or aims of platformed visibility? It is to empower or objectify? To amplify or make abject? The answers to those questions, we argue, offer a more conjunctural and full understanding of the use of platforms. We have attempted to demonstrate in this short essay the necessity of taking context, medium, and content into account when analyzing the social and cultural function of the platform. Using the contemporary context of an increasingly visible popular feminism, we argue that thinking historically about other, perhaps more material platforms helps us think through the political efficacy of the popular feminist digital platform. Put another way, the differential effects of visibility, historically mediated by material platforms, demands a conjunctural analysis. In an age of amplification, where we celebrate digital platforms for reinvigorating feminism, we must also look at the lessons learned from other ways media require particular kinds of visibility.

Notes

1. Banet-Weiser, *Empowered*.
2. Gill, "Postfeminist Media Culture."
3. McLuhan, *Understanding Media* (1994); McLuhan, *The Mechanical Bride*.
4. McLuhan, *The Mechanical Bride*, 154.
5. Gillespie, "The Politics of 'Platforms,'" 3.
6. Gillespie, "The Politics of 'Platforms,'" 4.
7. Gillespie, "The Politics of 'Platforms,'" 4.
8. Bennet and Segerberg, "Digital Media and the Personalization of Collective Action"; Bennet and Segerberg, *The Logic of Connective Action*.
9. Taylor, *The People's Platform*, 232.
10. McLuhan, *Understanding Media* (1994), 26.
11. Innis, *Empire and Communications*.
12. Chow, "Woody Allen Warns of 'Witch Hunt.'"
13. Cawthorne, *Witch Hunt*.
14. Levack, *Witchcraft, Women and Society*; Federici, *Caliban and the Witch*; Federici, *Witches, Witch-Hunting and Women*.
15. Federici, *Witches, Witch-Hunting and Women*, 2.
16. Barstow, *Witchcraze*, 59; Hill, *The Salem Witch Trials Reader*, 129; Federici, *Caliban and the Witch*; Cawthorne, *Witch Hunt*, 18.
17. For more on this kind of spectacular punishment, see Foucault, *Discipline and Punish*.
18. Federici, *Caliban and the Witch*. In other literature on witch hunts, the sexual nature of the violence done to women accused of being witches was also highlighted. See for example Cawthorne, *Witch Hunt*; Ward, "Witchcraft and Sorcery."
19. Federici, *Witches, Witch-Hunting and Women*, 32.
20. Federici, *Witches, Witch-Hunting and Women*, 33.
21. McLuhan, *Understanding Media* (1994), 18.
22. Kramer, *The Slave Auction*; Randolph, *Sketches of Slave Life*; Bailey, *The Weeping Time*; Jones-Rogers, *They Were Her Property*.
23. Bailey, *The Weeping Time*, 3.
24. Bailey, *The Weeping Time*, 17.
25. Kramer, *The Slave Auction*, 25.
26. Whitehouse, "Platform Shoe Syndrome," 225.
27. Mika et al., "The Influence of High and Low-Heeled Shoes."
28. Furman, "Look Out Below," 2.
29. Warner and Mace, "Effects of Platform Fashion Shoes on Brake Response Time," 143.
30. Stover, "Make Them Fit Please!"
31. Brennan, *High Heel*; Zundel, "High Heels as a Mediating Technology"; Bartky, *Femininity and Domination*.

32. Rottenberg, *The Rise of Neoliberal Feminism*.
33. Zundel, "High Heels as a Mediating Technology"; Brennan, *High Heel*, 5.
34. Brennan, *High Heel*, 147.
35. Brennan, *High Heel*, 147.
36. Bartky, *Femininity and Domination*, 68–69.
37. McLuhan, *The Mechanical Bride*, 94.
38. McLuhan, *The Mechanical Bride*, 94.
39. McLuhan, *The Mechanical Bride*, 94.
40. Banet-Weiser, *Empowered*.
41. Banet-Weiser, *Empowered*, 13.

Part III
Media after McLuhan

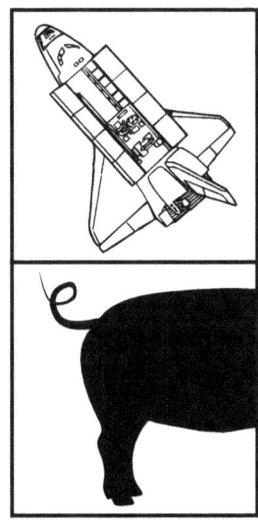

10 Scanning for Black Data

A Conversation with Nasma Ahmed and Ladan Siad

SARAH SHARMA
AND RIANKA SINGH

Nasma Ahmed is the director of the Digital Justice Lab, an initiative that engages diverse communities to build alternative digital futures across Canada. Ladan Siad is a creative technologist whose work focuses on the intersections of technology, transnational blackness, and Black queer trans feminism.

This interview is a continuation of a conversation that Nasma Ahmed and Ladan Siad had at the McLuhan Centre for Culture and Technology in 2017 as part of a Monday Night Seminar on Queer Black Data Justice in the city of Toronto. Ahmed and Siad came together to talk about the complexities they experience as Black folks navigating various technologies in the digital age.

Sarah Sharma (SS) Thank you for the gift of this ongoing conversation over the last few years. We really want to highlight for our readers something that came to the fore during your Monday Night Seminar in 2017 and again in our other conversations and collaborations. We've been struck by your technological understanding of the experience of blackness. It isn't one that I can say I've even encountered in feminist technology studies.

Ladan Siad (LS) Yes, I think we are thinking differently than someone like Donna Haraway—it's not as though she is the only techno-feminist, but you know what I mean. There's a lot that doesn't fully resonate with me when it comes to Haraway, and I want to note that even though she is not the only person talking about technology in a way that is feminist, she stands in for a lot of white feminist takes on media/technology.

Rianka Singh (RS) Can you say more? Where does she fall short for you?

LS On the one hand, I always feel that white feminist takes on media have a really deep void when it comes to anything that is connected with race. So, when they try to think about race, especially around questions of technology, I notice this void is exceptionally deep. I haven't read anything in Haraway that makes me feel like she understands how technology works on my body. I've been left to think that maybe her theorizing makes sense for white women. I think she understands what racism does in the world but then she adds it onto a perspective on technology. It is an afterthought—an addendum—two separate structures. She isn't thinking about blackness as a critical practice or that technology is already tied up in experiences of race.

So, this is why McLuhan has stuck with me—of course he isn't a feminist and we don't read him as a critical race scholar (in fact it is often the opposite), but he is thinking about the technological at a higher level—like way up here. So, if his theory can be drilled down, if he drills down, down, down, and if the logic works all the way down, then it would also work for thinking about race too.

SS Exactly. I guess you all know I'm of the mind that McLuhan has a theory up for grabs—one that didn't account for everything and everyone, but that doesn't mean it can't. In fact, we can. We must or we can drill down.

Nasma Ahmed (NA) That's why I have found McLuhan useful too. He is giving us a power analysis which we can then expand to think through issues of race and gender. I also used to talk about technology as a tool, something to be seized. I used to think of it as a tool, but as you build relationships with technology around you, you realize the larger impact that it has on how you operate in the world. How you communicate, relate to people—it's way more than the physical hardware or the intercommunication that is occurring. I think my understanding when I was kid was actually more nuanced beyond a tool-based approach—I thought of technology as way beyond a tool, but that notion kind of seemed to get pushed out as I started working and studying in the field.

SS Say more!

NA Well, as a kid you understand technology as an expansive universe! You are like, "What is this thing?" I was talking to strangers online, literally just exploring the world on Google dot com. I think that once I started working in the field as a technologist, technology did start to become coded, overdetermined, as just a tool in discourse. I went from being a part of what felt like an expansive universe where I was communicating with people all over the place, and this was shaping a huge part of my identity. It was shaping how I was relating to individuals, how I would use the devices, how I think about my race and my gender. But as I entered university and became a community organizer, I was taught to be "tool-versed" instead. When you are working in community organizing, you do need to be tool-versed. We almost forget the deeper connection with the things we are using and how it relates to and shapes our work.

The only reason I came back to this McLuhan-like power analysis understanding is because I was working with these amazing activists out of Mexico City, and they frame the body as the first technology. I had to remind myself that it doesn't work to just frame technology as a tool, and we have to consider the larger power structures.

LS I feel like Sylvia Wynter and McLuhan in conversation would be more interesting for me than hearing Donna Haraway in conversation with a Black person.[1] For me, reading Sylvia Wynter has informed a lot of my understanding of humanness. I want to figure out how using Wynter's conception of humanness and the exclusion of some bodies as human is a technological concept. I think it's the same thing. Whoever creates technologies thinks of them from a white perspective and then people have to fit in. This is why there is a disjointed way that some people use technology. There isn't a reference for us; instead, it's based on a universal assumption of what a user is. The universal user is a white man. That is a power analysis that comes from Wynter and McLuhan.

When we create different technologies, we are creating a world. We are deciding who gets to be in these worlds too. We then just get conditioned to use dominant technologies, like Apple products for example. This is just the same as what whiteness feels like to me. We are conditioned to operate in an already designed world that was not designed with us in mind.

SS Sylvia Wynter and McLuhan could be thought of in the context of refusal too. When you were saying why Haraway doesn't work for you, this might also extend to white feminist forms of refusal that are about disconnection and about starting over. This isn't a perspective that I think a lot of raced people would adopt. There isn't a reset. Is there a different mode of refusal that you see, one that is more generative?

LS Yes, exactly. Refusal needs to be generative. For me, we need to use Arthur Jafa, Sadiya Hartman, and Tina Campt to think about refusal.[2] These aren't people always explicitly talking about technology, but they are the people I turn to in order to think about technology. What they are offering is a formulation for talking about blackness and technology.

NA In terms of refusal, I think about the recent conversations about facial recognition technologies. There are these questions about who gets read as human and who is scannable and accurately scanned. There is a whole other question about if we should be accurately scanned though. In these cases, I don't just think about refusal, I think about absolute shutdown. We don't need a restart. The technology should not exist at all. Because often these technologies get built for a specific kind of human, it becomes increasingly difficult for our refusal to be a shutdown because these technologies work so well for some people. I don't really think there's any need to diversify facial recognition technologies, for example. We aren't asking to be viewed as human by facial recognition firms. Some people *are* asking for it, and that can be difficult and contentious. Some people do want to be legible to the white man, to be viewed as human; to be seen through a technology can be a validation of our existence. But then it gets used for policing and for surveillance. I think you have to shut that shit down. So, what does it mean for refusal to not be a restart, to not be invested in making the machine better? I mean, then there is also of course another conservation around who gets to have the power to ask for a shutdown.

It is still just really interesting to see that folks want to be viewed as human by a technology. I remember with Snapchat filters a few years ago, some Black people were mad because the filters didn't always recognize their faces. That's fair; it's a human thing to want to be seen. But the problem is not just that the infrastructure isn't meant for us, it's that it isn't *good* for us. How do we deal with this contention? This is where refusal gets interesting for me. We don't need the white feminist perspective, but it is true that some things need to be shut down.

SS Is this also a distinction between thinking of tech in terms of representation versus how you are thinking about it as culture?

LS [laughs] Visibility is a trap.

NA The prison industrial complex is a good example of this. Across the US, there is an end to cash bail. The end of cash bail brings in new forms of e-incarceration and other forms of technological tools being used to oppress people. We have to think about how technology is a way to further oppress. You can still punish through the use of technology. We don't always see these connections right away because of this discourse of technology being a tool. We miss the power analysis. In a struggle for representation, we constantly ask for diversification of data sets, the diversification of tools that should hear us and see us better, but that isn't necessarily what will help us moving forward. It's a scam. The career pipeline is a scam! Representation is a scam too!

LS By thinking of technology as a tool, we focus on what different technologies can do for us, and that means tech gets separated from its political and social implications. Then the power analysis can get lost too.

NA I think this comes from a place of fear. We fear the role tech plays in our lives sometimes and what this says about us. It's scary to think about how unavoidable technology is and that we can't just avoid it by not using tools. So, it's maybe easier to think from a tools perspective. When I work with folks who are organizing around the livability of a city, they want to avoid thinking about technology. The same folks will fight oil and gas companies, real estate companies. But for some reason, dealing with the technology sector is different. The power game is the same though, even if it's more hidden and the mediation is less recognizable. The invisibility and the distance make it a lot easier for people to try not to think about the power dynamics of technology or technology as the structure where all this is happening.

Similarly, it is the way of dealing with technology that becomes individualistic. It's like there is an understanding that if you change your settings on social media, or limit your use, you will avoid the wider implications. It is not an individual practice though, and it is not about a one-on-one relationship to the technology! I guess, shout out to the technology sector for invisibilizing their materials and their power and hold [laughs]. But then again, maybe we are just tired. It's like, shit, now the cloud is coming for me too. So, then we just choose to get into easier conversations, like about representation.

Sarah, can I ask you something too? Why are people so drawn to media representation or better representations as where to locate the problem? Is it fear?

SS I'm not saying representation doesn't matter, but a key issue is when it matters. If it is the end political goal though, then we have lost. Similarly, describing texts' ideological underpinnings does not seem to do justice either to capturing the inextricable relationship between the technological form and the production and maintenance of difference and inequality. In some cases, the focus on representation can be reduced to just asking for entry into capitalist and therefore misogynistic and racist circuits.

LS Sometimes I think representation doesn't work at all as a politics because in order to be seen or become legible we have to take on whiteness. Diversity is capitalist when it gets justified as being more efficient and working better. Like diversity seems to mean being 50 percent white still. If you have representation, then you have a better product. The goal of representation seems to be like a handshake to make a better world. Yet, a better world is whatever is decided on under capitalism. That quite often feels to me then that my role as a Black person is to make a better world for white people.

NA I'm often left wondering if representation is all we think we can get. It is posed as the best we are going to get; i.e., more Black folks working in technology. But it's not as if those Black folks are CEOs. More Black folks in the machine then? Is that all that we can get? It's funny because people understand the tech sector as the place where there is the most room to make change. I do think there is an opportunity to make better policy, for example, because in some cases the policy just does not exist. But I don't think diversity of hiring is what will really change much. But this capitalist structure makes it difficult to imagine alternatives.

SS Yes, I guess you're answering the question you asked me! When you locate the power structure as being more technological, the possibilities for imagination and creativity can be seized differently. If the end game is representation, to me that is a misunderstanding of where technological power exists.

NA Exactly. I often get stuck in a representation conversation, but this can end up obscuring questions about how technological power operates on particular communities. I think our attention needs to shift so that it is easier for people to locate power in relation to themselves. Power is so often exercised through the technological, and this has significant effects, usually on people of color or other folks living on the margins.

A good example of this is the incoming investments in Toronto from technology firms. For example, Toronto has received 150 million dollars in investments from big tech. And there are rumors of Amazon HQ coming here too. That is scary. People see that and they are excited about jobs and development in the area. I see the potential for displacement because it's already happening in places like Silicon Valley. I remember visiting Oakland and watching Silicon Valley evolve into what it is now. Where the Uber building is now, there used to be a Sears building. When the Sears shut down, it was a predominantly Black neighborhood, and we wondered who was going to buy the land. We understood that its ownership could cause a significant shift for some communities living in Oakland. We found out Uber was moving in. Once the announcement happened, within six months my favorite Black hair shop across the street from the old Sears building shut down. A real estate developer found out that Uber was moving in and made the lease more expensive. The shops around the area also shut down, and it was a perfect opportunity for developers to charge more rent. You know what happened? Uber decided they didn't want the building anymore! They tried to sell it, but the Black hair shop is gone! All the little shops all shut down and got replaced. I provide this example because we see this impact of technology in various ways. The actual city shifts. We are going to see that in Toronto too. What is unfortunate is that while there is excitement for economic development, not everybody is going to benefit. The population of Black folks in San Francisco declined to 5 percent. The income for Black folks is not actually rising at all. So when I think about the intersection of my blackness and my Muslimness in the work that I do, it is beyond a technology being used in a certain way, and it is beyond the possibility that some people that look like me might get a job at Amazon HQ. Technological power impacts us in ways we don't see right away; it is slow and we have experienced it before. Being able to identify and make this form of power known could be more liberating than the conversations we are having about representation.

RS Do you see this misunderstanding of where technological power exists play out in the spaces you are working in too?

LS I'm currently part of an incubator program in New York. There are designers, researchers, technologists who work within art, technology, new media who are all part of this group. You get a year to be in the program with space and some guidance. There aren't really that many critical conversations about technology actually happening there. Instead, again technology is being treated as a tool. What seems to be valorized are projects that are mostly product based.

For example, there's a person who is interested in talking about sex in space. She is trying to patent a mechanism that would give people a way to have sex in space because right now people aren't having sex in space. So, she's anticipating that when people eventually live in space, they will obviously need to have sex. There are all these things that come with trying to make space livable. Her pitch comes from this very white feminist perspective where she is saying we must consult women to make this mechanism. She wants to be on the frontier of negotiating sex in space.

But doesn't she actually need to be talking to sex workers? We haven't figured out sex on Earth, and now she wants to talk about sex in space. If you really want to talk about people who have progressive views about negotiating sex, then it's the sex workers you have to talk to. You know what's going to happen? Sex workers are going to be taken to space.

We had this whole conversation, and I eventually ended up telling her this whole idea felt really racialized because her understanding of the future is one where women will be brought to space to have sex with the men who are there. This becomes a race question, because who do we think that Elon Musk is going to want to have in space with him? There are questions about desirability. My Black ass isn't going to be the one called to space. Space exploration just feels like it is dominated by white men. They are going to decide who gets to come to space with them. This idea of developing technologies for space was so obviously [an] example of a white feminist framing of space and of the future. I don't necessarily think innovative products are the route to saving the world. It has to be more radical to that.

RS Could you explain how your relationship with technology is connected to your identity as a Black person?

LS I remember when I first came across this quote by artist and cinematographer Arthur Jafa: "When we came, we were not human beings, we were things.... We were the first technology. We are the technology that drove the American industrial engine. Our relationship to technology is very particular."[3]

It instantly fascinated me and I wanted to be able to understand it more. I felt the statement viscerally and intrinsically and I wanted to ground that statement for myself. I Googled "Black people as technology" to see what would come up. The first things to come up were about Black innovators of technology or the flip side—how certain technologies discriminate against Black folks. I wasn't finding what I was looking for, and nor did I know exactly what I was looking for. I wanted to know what this quote meant to me.

This quote seemed to explain what I had long been encountering—structures and systems of power that were meant to actively classify and control me and my family—things like immigration, the welfare system, and the institutions of education in Toronto. Upon reflection, I had learned to maneuver through institutional space in a way that translated almost exactly how I was maneuvering through digital spaces.

RS Can you speak more about the context that makes you think differently about technology?

LS Well, I think that sometimes people's less critical or tool-based thinking about technology is because they have not had to maneuver through particular spaces. Having particular ways in which social controls come to bear on your life means you can identify control mechanisms, and I can see technology as one of them.

So being on welfare and being a refugee in Canada and feeling like I've been in limbo for sixteen years has a lot to do with how I've learned how to maneuver in the world. You understand what you have and what can be done with what you have.

This is sort of what makes some people feel like they are technology. For example, I think of myself as a scanner. I have to get a lay of the land, identify all the land mines, and figure out how to get through them all and come out not just surviving, but trying to thrive. I think it is also part of being a Black, queer trans person. You navigate these spaces differently not knowing how people are going to perceive you. You are always in constant negotiation. You are the technology because you are always scanning. It's like, "Where am I? How am I going to do this? What should I change?" We are the technology because of that.

NA Yeah, sometimes technology can feel like one of these land mines too. Sometimes I operate on social media as if I am white, as if I don't see the land mines. It is a different way of being online. You can absolve yourself of so much responsibility. When I'm operating as if I'm white, I am not tempering my responses. Sometimes I wish I had the confidence of a white man. I operate like this sometimes, but then I have to pull back. I have to think about my career.

LS A white person on the internet doesn't have to think so much about the web of how the world actually works. They tweet as if there isn't going to be any repercussions!

SS Part of it is an investment in gender in a particular way. You are invested in uplifting white womanhood, just like white manhood gets historically uplifted. We just don't give a fuck about creating some bridge to lift white women up to the same level as their male counterparts. This analysis of gender does not connect with me. White women cannot use intersectionality! I have arguments all the time about this too.

NA It's a power analysis—how many times will we have to say this?

SS Yes, this is just the thing! Intersectionality is not just available for you to list your identity categories.

LS Sometimes this happens with white queers too. There is still an investment in whiteness, and we can't talk about the same things because we aren't invested in the same thing. You want me to check my race at the door to help build a future not made for me.

SS Let's return to Tina Campt.[4] I'm interested in hearing more about how you are thinking with her. Black feminists writing on refusal are still talking about the technological; they just don't say they are. When I say technology is intersectional, I am thinking with Black feminists and saying that if we locate the technological as part of these other intersections, this could do so much for deepening our analysis. I am not suggesting that we need to understand our technologies better necessarily. I think the technological can be added to Crenshaw's roads.[5] This isn't to make intersectionality available to everyone. But it seems like white feminists use technology as their road—this is the route they feel they can take. But instead we have to take the technological as being a road like economic power is, or other forms of power. It's at the intersection.

NA Exactly. This is what I love about Simone Browne's work.[6] She shows us how the technological operates as power.

When I was younger, I thought I was going to go into immigration law. I was obsessed with migration and my family's history of migration and the connection between migration and labor, so I thought I was going to go to school and that was all I was going to do. The summer before university and throughout my first year, I worked at a health technology company. I ended up taking a computer science class (I did not like it). It was interesting that technology was being used as a tool, and I thought there had to be an intersection with the other things I care about. At the time, I was also a community organizer and was working with youth in Scarborough, and I thought there had to be a connection. Part of that connection was working with nonprofits. A nonprofit would be like, "Hey, our website doesn't function, our website is getting hacked, or xyz," and I had the technical knowledge, so I would give support. I ended up helping build websites for organizations or set up WordPress sites or helped protect shelters dealing with hacking, for example. I just went with it and realized this is what I am interested in.

I am interested in supporting communities and organizations and navigating this relationship with technology. It first started as a practical demand. They needed something, so why not help lend that support? Eventually I started thinking about policy alongside my experiences with different digital technologies. As I was working with folks in the US, I was starting to connect my ideas of liberation and community justice and what it means to make place and space and merge it with technology. Folks in the US were mapping eviction or finding ways to surveil the police, and I was learning these histories and practices and realized I could use technology as a way of resisting forms of oppression or creating new ways of existing in the world or in the future world. The reason I bring the background of not being interested in technology is because when these ideas were opened up, especially by amazing women of color in the US—in Detroit, in LA, in San Francisco—and learning about their resistance, I saw the connection to our everyday lives that I didn't see before. What continues to ground me to this weird space that I can't explain to my mom or to anyone outside of the space is that as technology continues to impact our lives, there is something possible in regards to how we resist and how we exist beyond the current infrastructure that is available. This is where I find technology fascinating. There are possibilities. If white men can do it, we can do it too. We can actually do it better. I see myself in this in-between where I am not trying to persuade people to care about digital issues but to point to how it intersects with their lives and forecast the ways in which it will, so we can resist and create new ways of being. It's not constant resistance; it's just noticing that technology will always impact our lives and be used as a control mechanism. That is why I am interested in technology and in scholars who think about the future that is grounded in indigeneity and blackness and the ways we think about labor and capital. No matter what, my focus is always liberation. To imagine a future where things work out for us.

LS A lot of Black feminists are still talking about technology even when they aren't doing it explicitly. If you are writing about how Black feminists maneuver particular spaces, and what we lose in our navigating, that's just the same as talking in more technological terms about data loss.

NA Thinking with prison abolitionists, for example, is so important when you are developing approaches to the technological. They tell us to shut shit down.

LS I'm trying to think about technology more as a culture too. That's why people are going to have different experiences with the technology they are using too. I remember when we didn't have a computer at my house and then when we did. This means people have a different relationship with technology. Some people feel more embedded in it. Their technology says something about them, and they are okay with it. There is also a generation of folks who want to go back to some pure sense of technology, like when less people were making connections and networking. I think there are also good people who want to transform technology as it is now and not go back to a time when we weren't so interconnected. So, I wonder what my relationship to technology says about me and how it reflects the culture I am in. I think this gets reflected in how I organize around tech, what I make with it, what I use.

As a Black person, living in a Black culture, what does this mean? Maybe it's that the way we use technology is the same way we think about a jazz musician. We are always improvising. It's like, meme culture is Black culture. It's technological improvisation. Like, Black Twitter! That's technological improvisation.

SS What do you think white people don't understand about Black Twitter?

LA It's because they aren't in the culture! They just *cannot*. It's the same as not understanding Black culture. I think this is why I sometimes don't want to speak to white people about anything. I have to explain context and history around almost anything. It's exhausting. This happens even in simple conversations about, you know, public transportation.

NA There is also a subtlety in how meme culture and Black culture, like Black Twitter, operates. It's so subtle in its humor. It takes a lot of processing if you are not a part of the context. The fact that I'm dying from a hotep Squidward meme is because I have an understanding about the cultural relevance of hotep memes. This is a subtlety that is hard to capture. This is what is so great about Black Twitter. I think it's supposed to be hard. There shouldn't be an easy translation. There's something about this subtlety that we don't have to talk about. It's between us, and it's in our own silos. This is like our own safety net, and it's how we survive in our comedy and our humor.

Notes

1. See, for instance, Wynter, "The Ceremony Must Be Found"; Haraway, *Simians, Cyborgs, and Women.*
2. Campt, "Black Visuality and the Practice of Refusal."
3. Brown, "'Black People Figured Out How to Make Culture in Freefall.'"
4. Campt, "Black Visuality and the Practice of Refusal."
5. Crenshaw, "Mapping the Margins."
6. Browne, *Dark Matters.*

11 3D Printing and Digital Colonialism

A Conversation with Morehshin Allahyari

SARAH SHARMA
AND RIANKA SINGH

Sarah Sharma (SS) We are curious to know more about your medium of choice, and where you see the political potential of 3D printing? Can you tell us about how and when you encountered 3D printing as the media that you would use to make your feminist intervention into masculine tech culture of the art world?

Morehshin Allahyari (MA) Three-D animation and 3D-produced simulation are directly born and shaped out of two fields: the military and the gaming industry. The tech and entertainment worlds are, as you know, dominated by white and masculine figures. This also includes places like Silicon Valley and a lot of other tech and corporate spaces that work with 3D animation and simulation software. These are the spaces that also work with machines like 3D printers and scanners.

Two thousand thirteen was the beginning of a sudden hype around 3D fabrication and 3D scanning technologies. But so much of the creative and cultural products that were being produced in these tech spaces really felt banal and boring to me. You could see the obsession with technology for technology's sake in the very objects that were being produced. I saw a potential in these tools that seemed to be largely undiscovered.

In 2012, I was just out of grad school, and I got accepted to a technology residency program in Dallas. SculptCAD was run by Nancy Hairston. I didn't know a thing about 3D printing machines when I got there, but I had studied 3D animation in the past and I knew the software that gave me the skill set to create 3D models or animation. But other than that, I was not familiar with the machinery of 3D technology.

I haven't thought about this in a long time, but your question brings me back to the first time I walked into this space. There was Nancy! This badass woman who was running all this tech stuff. This is a really good example of the longing for representation—wanting to see some kind of representation of yourself in the spaces you find yourself in. Up to that point, I had only been in tech places populated by white men—university, galleries, coworking spaces alike. Watching Nancy both be in charge of the space but also her knowledge about 3D software and machines was so inspiring that I felt not just that I wanted to but could do this work. This was the beginning of my interest in doing 3D printing work.

During that residency at SculptCAD, I started to work on my project *Dark Matter*.[1] In this project I created a selection or kind of a sculptural mash-up of objects or things that were forbidden or unwelcome in Iran politically and culturally. At this point I was thinking about 3D printing as a machine that allows us to document and build an archive—in this case, objects that could be built to leave a historical trace. I had a humorous mash-up of a dog wearing a dildo with a satellite dish or a Barbie with a VHS tape for a torso or a pig with a gun on its back. All of these things are of course forbidden or unwelcome in Iran for religious or political reasons. Through this mash-up I was creating new possibilities for both rethinking about these objects and for documenting them. This way of thinking about 3D printing and 3D scanning continued in my practice. I was really fascinated by the technology that was not really being used. I encountered the 3D printer as a very poetic machine. It was a machine

11.1 Morehshin Allahyari, *3-D Printed Dog, Dildo, Satellite Dish*, 2014.

that seemed to figure within the cultural imaginary as a technology to reproduce and replicate but really it was a departure for creating disobedient systems to match with different situations and circumstances.

So that's sort of the beginning of my journey to fab labs and maker spaces which continued becoming more important in my work when I started an art residency at Autodesk. Autodesk is a space that creates software for 3D automation, modeling, and gaming. Being in this space in San Francisco, the so-called heart of all it all, was really important because once again I found myself in a space that was very white and very masculine. Everyday people would pass by me in the lab and have no idea what I was working on. They really had no idea what I was doing. They were just giving me money and access—which was kind of amazing!

SS Did they ask what you were up to?

MA [laughs] Not really. Not at the beginning. I was just doing my thing. Even in the residency there were seventeen of us, and a lot of other residents were architects and designers. They all seemed to be much more connected to each other. This is when I had just started working on

11.2 Morehshin Allahyari, *Lamassu*, from *Material Speculation: ISIS*, 2016.

Material Speculation: ISIS and developing ideas around the poetics of 3D printing things that had been destroyed.[2] I was also thinking about the practical aspects of 3D printing the artifacts that had been destroyed in Iraq by ISIS and trying to reconstruct these objects. Once I started working on the project and getting press, then people started to stop and ask.

I have to say that compared to a lot of other technology fields like robotics or AI, at the moment, it is more common to see women working in fab labs. But I've had this fear that the same thing that seemed to happen with coding in the '80s, where women were getting pushed out because they felt isolated because of the masculine culture, and they were not being promoted, etc., will be repeated also in the fab labs eventually.

Every time I walk into maker spaces and see women or femmes, I am so happy to see them, but I am always simultaneously worried that it is temporary and they too will meet their fate of being pushed out of this pocket of tech culture.

SS Your feminist approach to technology and 3D printing is definitely dual. On the one hand, you are addressing the actual spaces and the people that occupy these spaces you yourself have worked in and will continue to work in, but you also have a feminist approach to the actual medium, to the technology you are working with. I'd love to get further into this with you and ask you not only what a feminist theory of 3D printing looks like, but also what is feminist about 3D printing?

MA I think about this often in my own work, especially in terms of the question of technology being gendered. If technology is already gendered, what does this mean for my practice, and if not, how does my use of 3D printing make it gendered in a different way? One thing I have always felt is important in my approach to technology is that it also relates to my gender, where I grew up, and my relationship to the technological tools around me. When I say I am interested in the poetics of technology, I am thinking about how we can find both emotional and poetic ways of activating them anew. This is of course not to equate femininity with emotion. But I feel that there are so many examples of men using technology that either just calls on philosophical jargon where they position their use as abstract or conceptual, or we see a banal and a one-on-one relationship with technology. Then I see women, and especially women of color, use technology in a much more complex way. Of course, a lot of that is because we have to work so much harder to have access to use the tools and to have access to spaces to use the tools. So, once we do have that access, how can we take it for granted?

Growing up in Iran, there was also a culture that made computers feel really masculine. My father bought me my first computer when I was fourteen. Before this happened, I would go to his office to use his computer. I remember he told me when he bought the computer that there aren't that many people who know how to use a computer in a way that is useful or meaningful but that he thought I could do it. When my father said that, I felt so empowered. He had a teacher come to our house to show me how to do basic computing functions like open files or delete things. When you don't grow up with computers around, this is not as intuitive. Having some figure, in this case my father, who saw my interest in the tool and was able to help me have access to it in a way that was not common meant I was determined to use it in a meaningful way. Even when I would go online as a teenager, I would go to Yahoo chat rooms and I would go to book and literature pages. All of these things really shaped my relationship to technology. I would say not having easy access also shaped my relationship to it. Once it is easily accessible or it is simply part of our environment, as said by McLuhan, we don't notice it. The way he wrote about how no one realizes the light bulb is a technology until it starts to break down has resonances here. But it isn't the breakdown or just noticing the media that life unfolds within but rather, for my approach, it is that we also lose sight of its potential and poetics. When access is hard, we form a radically different relationship to it. This is the crux of that feminist approach. And for me, it was defining in this very way.

Rianka Singh (RS) Let's shift to the politics of care implicit to your work in the context of 3D printing and scanning.

MA Care is something I've been thinking and writing about in relation to my research over the last three to four years on the use of 3D printers and 3D scanners by Western institutions and digital archaeology spaces in Eurocentric countries and North American countries. One thing that I've come to realize is that there is a really specific language that is used in explaining the mission of these spaces. A lot of these spaces are archaeology spaces, and they do projects where they go to the Global South and 3D scan historical and cultural sites. Their claim is that they will save cultural heritage that we all share. They are especially interested in sites that are destroyed by conflict. For example, sites destroyed by ISIS in Syria. This language of a shared and universal cultural heritage that is being heroically saved is presented in two ways. I use terms of *alignment* and *becoming an ally* to describe them. Alignment is the idea that we share space and it is being saved. This uses wording that sounds like care and has been used for years. It's wording that is used to colonize. The idea is really "That is not yours—it's for all of us, so we get to own it with you." The other term, becoming an ally, is a more top-down approach. We hear that our culture is cared about, and there is care for the things that are destroyed so someone will come and save it for us. The questions that remain with these *proposals of caring* are about, what is being taken away and what is being given back?

I connect this with the concept of *violent care*. The term was originally used by Thom van Dooren, who talks about endangered crows in

Hawaii.³ He sees how choices are made to save a species of crows by killing the other animals who are preying on them. Through these acts of interfering in a natural process, what takes place is an act of violent care. I use this as a way to connect to the point of how cultural heritage work connects with 3D scanning and printers to interrupt cycles in a way that is violent. Another way that this violence is displayed is that those who are doing the saving also remove themselves as part of the problem. ISIS takes pride in destruction. They are bold, direct. In their showcase of destruction, violence is presented as an eventful crisis; an explosive, sudden kind of violence. You see it and it immediately shocks you, while, for example, the US military hides, deletes, unarchives its violence and war crimes from public; or justifies it as a work that needs to happen for the safety of its people. Alongside this, those having access to platforms choose to participate in this kind of invisible violence. They and those speaking about ISIS violence remove themselves from that picture, pointing fingers at what's obvious. For example, after ISIS['s] destruction of Palmyra's 1,800-year-old Arch, a project launched in London and then in New York as the result of major collaborations between the UK-based Institute for Digital Archaeology, UNESCO, and Dubai's Museum of the Future. In a video documentation of its ceremony, as a white fabric gets pulled down to unveil the reconstructed site of Palmyra, Boris Johnson, the former mayor of London, stands there to tell the audience, "No one should have the power to delete such monuments from our historical record. This is an arch of triumph and in many ways a triumph of technology and determination. We're here in a spirit of defiance, defiance of the barbarians who destroyed the original as they have destroyed so many other relics in Syria and the Middle East."

People in the audience applaud. Then they take turns to take selfies with the new Palmyra, and they perhaps go back to their safe homes, never thinking back at what it was that was wrong with that image: how ISIS formed in [the] first place as a result of [the] US and Europe invasion of the Middle East. This violence that sits side by side to that so-called barbarian violence, the one that is equally real and destructive, is once again deferred, delayed. Has gone invisible. Pushed into some background, into some corner in some political maneuver of the bad and the good. So the violence I am talking about here is not just about how these figures remove themselves from a cycle they had been part of for centuries, but also a kind of violence that is about reclaiming.

ISIS reclaims the objects through destruction, through creating absence. The Western governments and tech companies reclaim it after destruction, through a new kind of presence; and we fail to see the violence of that presence in the way we see the violence of the absence.

SS Your work seems to develop with this trifecta of violence, tech, and care all the way through. I can even see this at play when you are talking about where your work is situated within the white male domination of the field. You then see the political possibility of a poetics and care tied to this power dynamic with the technology. It's amazing to see the coherency of all your work as it also provides new theoretical frameworks for thinking about media and technology.

RS Yes, can you touch more on this relationship between violence and technology in your work? How does gender fit into the frame here?

MA Let's be blunt. Historically, white men are *the* colonizers, right? This same image we see throughout history of the colonizing lands and cultures extends to tech spaces. But now colonizers are using new tech to colonize new spaces. One thing that is interesting to me is the idea of white men positioning themselves as heroes of tech. This superman figure is born out of a white survivalist attitude where they are in the center of these spaces and the crisis but then get to become the heroes.

SS It's almost as if they are the mechanical solution themselves?

MA Exactly. We see this figure in Western cinema and literature and then in real-world examples of men being saviors. When you look back at the master-savage relationship, it's the same thing. The white men are educating. This extends to my critique of tech spaces where men go to other countries and become allies. The help comes in the form of teaching people how to scan cultural heritage, for example. At the same time, other people are asked to do the work of scanning and then the data are taken from them. The data get secured so that the Western "saviors" are the only ones who have access to them.

It's crazy because when you hear the interviews or the TED talks that these people give, they have no shame about any of this work. There is no pausing and questioning the work. At the end of the day, these same people then end up collaborating with spaces like Google Arts and Culture Institute, etc. To me, there seems to be a comfort in traveling around the world and taking from other people and cultures without reflecting on what this taking means, whether it's their knowledge, traditions, or historical artifacts. There is also always a no-questions-asked type of celebration of what the white man does while, if the same thing is done by women of color, they are going to be questioned or not taken seriously on the validity of their project.

SS Do you have examples of this from your own practice?

MA I always say that my "favorite" examples seem to happen in Germany. In 2016 I was in Berlin and doing a talk at a conference on Sci-Art. There were tons of people from all around the world who do a lot of this work on conservation and scanning at historical sites.

This was the first time I used the term *digital colonialism*. I was talking about how I was noticing a problem in the work being done at cultural heritage sites. This was in a space that was 80 percent men and 99.9 percent white. On the same night, people who did a project called Project Mosul won an award for doing amazing work and saving the cultural heritage of Mosul. The project was one where they tried to reconstruct artifacts destroyed in Mosul by crowdsourcing images. I was working on my project of reconstructing artifacts at the same time, and I knew their project would not work as they were claiming or promising because I understood the actual circumstance of somewhere like Iraq that has been at war for over thirty years. There have not been tourists or functional museum staff and funding at Mosul, and so there are not enough images to do reconstruction work from still images. If you look at their website now (four years later), it's a bunch of half-put-together 3D models of the destroyed artifacts. That night it felt isolating to be doing the work I do. These two men from Australia and the US winning an award that seemed to me like a fraud/unreal mission while once again, what I had raised as a colonial concern was pushed in some corner and undiscussed through the end of the conference. This stuff happens all the time.

SS Related to your term *digital colonialism*, it is clear you don't really separate the digital from other material forms or lived reality in terms of colonialism. But is there a different psychic weight to digital colonialism?

MA Digital colonialism is a framework for critically examining the tendency for information technologies to be deployed in ways that reproduce colonial power relations. I think the reason this kind of framing about digital colonialism has been helpful is because it is doing something with using digital technologies that is different than material or object-based colonialism. We all understand the history of colonialism much more tangibly. We see it in when we walk into many historical museums based in the Western countries, for example. But when I give talks on digital colonialism in different venues, especially at universities, I get the same reaction. Every time I give this talk, I see a light bulb go on in the students or other audience members, where they finally see and understand what I mean when I say digital colonialism and cultural heritage. What I've been trying to do with my research on digital colonialism is to use more traditional examples like this as frameworks to make sense of the issues that come with new tools and technologies like 3D scanners and 3D printers, and to apply these historical colonial examples to what's happening now, at this very moment. I like to emphasize that I don't have all the answers for these questions. What I certainly know is that we have to explore these issues beyond what's positive and simple at first sight. This is a position I am committed to holding and exploring and that I try to use in many of my lectures in relation to digital colonialism.

Also, I think it helps to not take technologies that are new and exciting as neutral or nonpolitical or nongendered. This is something that has to be repeated over and over, both in popular culture but also in critical studies of media. So, connecting all of these points together to talk about this notion of digital colonialism and all that it involves, again like the idea of becoming an ally or being a white savior and all of these other layers, can be framed under this term *digital colonialism*. I think it really helps with understanding colonialism in a different way. Sometimes people ask me why I wouldn't just use already established terms like *postcolonialism* or *electro-colonialism*. (And I mean, guess which demographic asks these questions?) I think digital colonialism is different from these existing terms that are more specific to other instances that are not necessarily what I am trying to get at. Digital colonialism is more focused and more specific about certain phenomena.

Younger students in fields related to digital technology who are using tools like 3D scanners and 3D printers have not thought about all of the political aspects of the technologies they are using. Obviously digital colonialism isn't just about these tools, but in my research, I have focused more on these specific tools. You can think about digital colonialism in so many ways. One of my personal favorite examples is that three years ago I bought a gift for my mom's birthday on Amazon, and when I added a personal note to the gift message box in Farsi, and hit "save," it gave me an error that these characters are unknown and so my message can't be saved. Farsi and Arabic (which share similar characters) are spoken by 500-plus million people around the world. Imagine that this many people around the world are forced to use English for something this simple (sending a personal note with their gift) if they want to use a service like Amazon, and because of the domination of English as the international language of the world. This is what I call another example of digital colonialism. And there are so many other versions of this, from the whitewash filters that are popular on social media to the way Google Maps operates.

RS After being one of the students who sat in one of your talks in Toronto and did have this light bulb moment you're talking about, I'm curious if there are feminist media and technology scholars that you engage with in your practice. Who are you thinking with? I've seen you reference Donna Haraway.

MA Studying Haraway or Braidotti or other feminist theory hasn't been directly connected to my digital colonialism work because I think someone like Haraway is also still critiqued for her thoughts on cyborg universality. Similarly, the idea of staying with the trouble still comes from a Global North, Western, white feminist-centric perspective. So I think that while I really love and have been inspired by so many things in Haraway's thinking (especially how she uses storytelling and fabulation as a framework to her research and writing), I also think that for me there is a gap when it comes to reading and learning from women not based in the Global North and Western countries and specifically in relationship to technology.

SS Who do you feel a connection with, then, at this level? Or do you feel that you're going it alone, in a way?

MA I do think there is a serious lack when it comes to theories of technology and women of color with focus on South West Asia / North Africa (SWANA). There are a lot of scholars, thinkers, and writers of race, gender, futurity, and technology that I am inspired by every day, for example, Sara Ahmed, Audre Lorde, Octavia Butler, Simone Browne, and Ruha Benjamin; also, younger, more contemporary female, queer friends and colleagues with whom I feel like we are building new worlds and platforms.

In the past years, I specifically have worked with and been in the same panels and activist spaces with writers and theorists such as Rasheedah Philips and Nora Khan; but as I mentioned, when it comes to more specific new media theories that focus on SWANA, then I feel a sense of isolation. Not to say that I am the only one writing and thinking about technology and the Middle East and feminism in this way, but I do long for a bigger community of us to build and work together. I know this is changing and going to change. So, all I can hope is that I will be a part of being this force and bringing this change.

SS Well, you are also on the front lines here, not just as an artist but also as a technologist. We want to capture you here because you are doing media theory in a completely novel way and important way. I wanted to turn back to this and engage with you further on media theory a bit. We have a question on McLuhan and automation, and you can get to it any way you want.

In *Understanding Media*, McLuhan wrote a chapter on automation. He was responding to discussions that were happening as early as 1963 about automation and the future of work. For McLuhan, automation is made possible by what he was calling electric technology, and the introduction of these new technologies in the information age would change the way people think, work, and produce things. McLuhan wrote, "Automation is not an extension of the mechanical principles of fragmentation and separation of operations. It is rather the invasion of the electrical world by the instantaneous character of electricity. That is why those involved in automation insist that it is a way of thinking, as much as it is a way of doing."[4]

We've been thinking about how 3D printing has been almost like an epistemological framework for you. It's almost like you have a 3D lens that you see the world through. I was wondering if you think 3D printing reveals the political to you in a way that would be impossible with another medium?

MA Obviously, the most important thing is that it is the first technology that does what it does in terms of going from digital to physical in an additive process. I should mention that the technology of 3D printing has been around for over thirty years, but it wasn't always accessible or user friendly as it is now. So, the fact that this one machine became a tool that is easy to have in my studio or in a fab lab and you can buy an okay version of it for like three hundred dollars is a big deal. As an artist who does 3D work, whose work before this was all screen based with some installations, this machine allowed my work to exist differently in a physical space. The 3D scanner does the reverse, which is to take the physical and bring it into digital. Both processes were not possible as easily as they are now without access to these tools.

So I think going back between physical and digital spaces in this way and being able to rethink our relationship with the machine and the material, and the politics of these things, is something that I was fascinated by. From the very beginning, when I did the *Dark Matter* series, I fell in love when I started thinking about what it would mean to have this machine in a place like Iran or other countries and spaces where there is censorship. You can just print something you are not allowed to have or [that] is hard to buy.

The naughty example is a dildo. You know what I mean? You can't just walk into a store and buy that in Iran. You cannot order it on Amazon either. But you could have a machine and print something that is completely forbidden and functional! The fact that I could have access to this thing felt really crazy. I could just print something in my studio, and nobody will ever know. Not just the dildo example, but there are all sorts of objects you can create that weren't possible before.

I borrow the term *disobedient objects* in defining some of the work I do or the work of many artists, designers, activists in our *3D Additivist Cookbook*. The term *disobedient object* is the title of a book by Catherine Flood and Gavin Grindon in which they define this concept as "how objects can change the world by out-designing authority."[5] The book includes items from protest movements over the past three decades from around the globe. I really loved this framework and was curious, what would the creation of disobedient objects through the use of a 3D printer look like?

SS Other than the dildo, are there other disobedient objects you've made? Something that captures you. I'm thinking about how weird it would be to center this on the dildo after you've just finished talking about masculinity invading the spaces you are working in.

MA Yes. A full circle! I would say all the figures that I've created and refigured in my *She Who Sees the Unknown* series are disobedient figures with disobedient monstrous stories.[6] That's actually the premise of my most recent project: a long-term research-based work that focuses on 3D scanning, 3D printing, and storytelling to re-create monstrous female/queer figures of Middle Eastern origin, using the traditions and myths associated with them to explore the catastrophes of colonialism, patriarchism, and environmental degradation. I see a strong connection between this notion of building disobedient objects and embracing monstrosity as a position to turn around the demonization of the other, the immigrant, the woman of color (who is often too angry and therefore monstrous!), etc. So each of the five jinn figures that I've worked on in the last three years of this research (Huma, Aisha Qandisha, Ya'jooj Ma'jooj, the Laughing Snake, and Kabous) are refigured (a term I have also coined and developed as part of this project) through a complex multimedia process. I should also mention that these chosen mythical stories and figures are largely forgotten and unknown. Even growing up in Iran, we never read or heard about any of these stories, while our school education and mythical books are full of male superheroes. I often wondered what happened to the female superheroes. To give Huma, and Aisha, and the rest of these jinn figures bodies, literal physical bodies through the use of 3D software and machines, is also an act of doing something with history, leaving a kind of mark and trace behind. It's an act of reimagining the possibilities of the future and through the reimagination of the past, which is what I think I am best at doing and making.

I want to also add that both *The 3D Additivist Manifesto* and *The 3D Additivist Cookbook* were also really important for building theories and frameworks, and allowing new ways of thinking that are able to unlock something in the technology that has yet to be unlocked.

SS You are invested in altering, in feminist ways, the way we produce things, even in these examples you are giving. Your sense in the power of the technological is pretty strong, but you are still cognizant that there are useful ways to use it. This isn't an argument that a lot of people make. You return to it as a tool and seem to alter what the meaning of a tool is through a feminist lens.

MA I think in learning and exploring technology and art, I have always appreciated the kind of work that does something magical with and to the technology, something poetic, while also keeping it all grounded and practical. And when I say magical, I mean witchcraft, divination, I mean literally showing us something, revealing or reversing in and with a technological tool in a way that we had never thought about. Often this characteristic gets framed as groundbreaking or chilling. Literally pushing through and holding the hand of the audience in seeing something

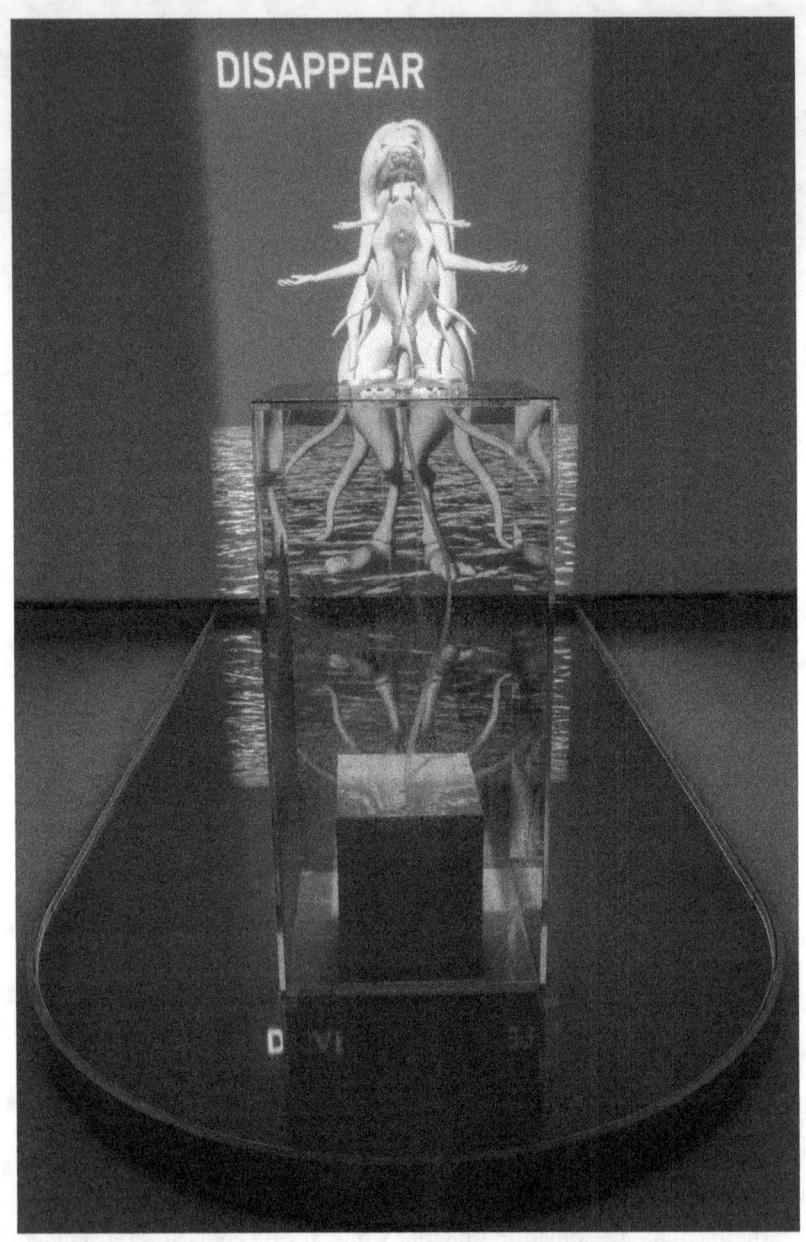

11.3 Morehshin Allahyari, *Aisha*, from *She Who Sees the Unknown*, 2019.

new with me is what I constantly want and think about when making new work. But I also want to keep a balance between that very aspect of the work to something practical. Whether it's putting an activist hat on and putting together discussion panels or reading rooms or changing my role to more of a historian and archaeologist by re-creating an object that is destroyed. I think my work tends to do all these things at once. I want to make work that is connected to real-world problems, but it's also fictional. This means that my work does not just reflect my relationship with technology as a tool but is about how technology shapes and builds the world I am reflecting on. I am gaining knowledge of the unknown by making it known and knowable, whether by building archives or seeing the figure of the hybrid queer jinn as the better replacement of the cyborg. Because jinn, unlike the cyborg, can "see the unknown." And if you can see the unknown, you can conquer many worlds. That's how I like to imagine it all.

Notes

1. Allahyari, *Dark Matter*.
2. Allahyari, *Material Speculation*.
3. Van Dooren, *The Wake of Crows*.
4. McLuhan, *Understanding Media* (1994), 349.
5. Flood and Grindon, *Disobedient Objects*.
6. Allahyari, *She Who Sees the Unknown*.

12 Toward a Media Theory of the Digital Bundle

A Conversation with Jennifer Wemigwans

SARAH SHARMA

Sarah Sharma (SS) Your work breaks new ground by bringing an Indigenous cultural approach to understanding how digital technologies can foster collaborative connections among First Nations communities globally. Your work suggests that an Indigenous cultural resurgence can utilize the digital, not in terms of being connected or networking, but rather in terms of how Indigenous Knowledge [IK] might consider the digital as a new realm. I've always thought of you as a new media theorist because of how your work is attuned to the way that digital protocols and what you consider to be Western and colonizing internet media logics are in tension with IK protocols.

Jennifer Wemigwans (JW) In many ways I've had a difficult time finding Western internet theory useful to my work. Likewise, media studies work concerned with identity related to other media forms, whether TV or film, did not really speak to my concerns with Indigenous values or Indigenous futures, for that matter. I did not write *A Digital Bundle* or create Four Directions Teachings.com as a resource to just represent or transmit Indigenous Knowledge so that it could become a commodity, so that it would be appropriated or consumed.[1] Rather, I wanted to bring forth Indigenous Knowledge as a genre itself. Indigenous Knowledge can exist in the digital realm in carefully constructed ways that adhere to the protocols of their respective communities.

SS Yes, in *A Digital Bundle* you often refer to your website as an Indigenous artifact. Can you speak more about that and how that might be related to digital media or even understood as a media artifact?

JW Four Directions Teachings.com can also be understood as an Indigenous artifact or more specifically a medium with its own Indigenous message to understand, if we want to be more specific here. I've always been interested in McLuhan's theory of tactility, and this website is a tactile artifact. It isn't a website that one enters and reads as a linear text, nor is it a website that one enters and then has Indigenous Knowledge transmitted to them. It goes beyond Western ideas of what knowledge transmission is. In fact, many non-Indigenous visitors to the site do not possess the skills to read and engage with the site as a digital bundle. This knowledge and experience is something that Indigenous visitors to the site know intuitively and acknowledge through their interaction with the site. The ability to engage this tactile Indigenous artifact is an example of Indigenous Knowledge. This website is a medium that is imbued with knowledge protocols including how this knowledge is shared or allowed to be shared. Initially, when I was applying to Indigenous arts councils for Four Directions Teachings.com, it never got funded because it always divided the jury. Half of the Indigenous arts council would say, "This is audacious and who does she think she is?" And the other half would say, "This is really innovative and shows a lot of promise." But it always divided the jury, so it never got funded. Why I'm saying that is because people were, rightly so, like . . . "How can we put Indigenous Knowledge on the internet? That's never been done. How can we do that?" And when we started, I didn't know how to do it. It's not like I did the proposal and had the interface design in my head. I had a concept, but I had to go listen to the teachings, sit, much like this process, and sit, talk, have those many cups of tea . . . do the transcriptions, sit with those transcriptions, really try to figure out what the pieces are that can be used for this medium. So I would do my research by taking part in a long process with my team that involved intensive discussion, deep listening, and working with the Knowledge Keepers to ensure that their teachings were not being taken out of context.

Indigenous intellectual property is not the same as Western intellectual property. There are different protocols around sharing traditional knowledge that must be respected. First, you must practice deep listening to understand the teaching. I explained to the Elders that I could not post the entire teaching because it needed to be placed within a parameter that fits the medium of the technology. In this case, I knew that each teaching had to be about thirty or forty minutes in duration. The edited version was shared with each Elder to make sure that it was not taken out of context and that the meaning of the teaching was intact. It was also understood that each Elder and Knowledge Keeper chose what teachings they would share. I did not impose a theme or request specific teachings, because this request was not for me but for a public digital online space. The interface design for each teaching was also shared with the Elders for their feedback, direction, and of course consent. That was my process, but once in community, each Elder had their own very specific protocol that I adhere to. I speak about some of these cultural protocols in the book and their cultural significance. The most important takeaway to understand is that these protocols are governed by natural laws that are deeply spiritual and community specific.

By respecting these protocols and also realizing that these protocols are also medium specific, in this case the digital, IK can be created in a way to withstand the Western audience's tendency to just consume our teachings. It is deliberately designed to stand up to colonial erasure.

SS There is a tension in your work between resurgence and refusal. I know you don't want to call yourself a new media theorist because it seems to go against the grain of the generous work you do and would also go against Indigenous values, but your media theory is also important for the politics of refusal. How do you work this out?

JW I have a responsibility to refuse the structure and paradigms of the university that would turn Indigenous Knowledge into a commodity. I do not want to brand myself or my research. Rather, I want to articulate that there are other ways of working and being in the world that support Indigenous epistemologies and paradigms. As an academic, you have to make choices about where you put your energies because there are so many demands from your students, the academy, and the research process. Right now, I don't have a Twitter account. I'm not on social media. I feel hesitant to do that because I see it as playing into structures that the university demands to make me into a commodity, and to make my work a commodity. And I don't want to do that. Almost every step of the way, no matter what I teach, read, write, or when I speak, I ask myself what my politics are, what are my ethics for doing the thing I am doing.

SS What has made you feel like you are on the right track?

JW Victor Masayesva Jr., who is a well-regarded artist and Hopi Knowledge Keeper, contacted me to come and work with the Timekeepers, who have been meeting across North and South America. I was so surprised and honored because we have never met. He approached me because of the work I do and the way the work is done. He verified with me that I see myself as a helper and that this is the kind of work I do, and it was so humbling because it is the way that people validate you through the community. They look at what you do, not what you say [laughter]. So they see that, oh, you see yourself as a helper, and that is a good thing because our Elders and Knowledge Keepers want people who can help them and not just take from them and exploit them.

SS Or a theorist, even? And I guess there's no official title of Media Theory Helper to be found within media studies!

JW Yeah, like that! We're not trying to claim a status of power in this way. We're just trying to say that we're making solid decisions, but we're trying to make decisions on older, different models. I've definitely thought about my approach as offering a model, but I don't say a new model, I'd say another model. Not a new theory, then, but another theory. And then reception matters within the fields you are working in outside of your communities.

SS Can you speak a little more about this, especially given the impetus to decolonize media studies, decolonize the university, decolonize education?

JW Decolonize is a complicated term because it comes out of an international discourse of world conquest and imperialism. I would like to know what Elders and Knowledge Keepers think about that term. What are the words or concepts that they would use to think about "decolonize" as a process? It may be that is not the best term/concept to capture the presence and difference of Indigenous Knowledge. For example, many non-Indigenous people do not understand Four Directions Teachings .com because they cannot comprehend the symbolic presence of this site. They have no referent for the words, images, or even the circular interface used because they are derived from Indigenous philosophies and worldviews. As a result, I often see when I talk to non-Indigenous people who have visited the site that they think what they see on the site are folk stories. Only those people who have some experience and understanding in Indigenous worldviews can begin to appreciate the site as an introduction to Indigenous Knowledge.

SS Is it also a different way of approaching the technology in the first place?

JW Yes. The internet is more than just a repository or a placeholder for knowledge. I understand that there have been critiques of cyberspace and what types of space it is and the disciplinary conversations between geography and media, but this is not at all how I think of the digital realm in terms of Indigenous Knowledge.

Four Directions Teachings.com is a tactile artifact that, like McLuhan's notion, integrates all the senses. Where the work goes beyond McLuhan's notion of tactile is through the demonstration of relationships and relationality. From an Indigenous perspective, the site accomplishes this work through the design interface of the four directions. Within Indigenous epistemologies, the teachings of the four directions are central and key to philosophical understandings of the universe and human beings' roles and responsibilities. Indigenous visitors to the site are able to read the relationships of the four directions and understand that the direction and placement of each quadrant has significant meaning for each teaching. They also appreciate that each Elder's biography locates that Elder within their community and tells the reader how they are or have become acknowledged and accepted as an Elder.

Non-Indigenous visitors to the site don't recognize that these people are Elders, Knowledge Keepers, or that the stories being shared are teachings. They don't recognize the importance of the interface design and how the circle represents a holistic model that is rooted in the teachings of the four directions. They seem unable to grasp that part of the teaching is the interface design that shows the relationships of each direction and hence the impact and flow of relationality from each of the four directions. Non-Indigenous reception of the site seems completely unable to grasp that it is not linear; it is not text based. It is like when McLuhan argued that the potential of the electronic universe was that it did not have to be linear.

So, the circle, the medicine wheel, the tepee, they are signifiers, but they are particular to diverse Indigenous nations and to the Elders and Knowledge Keepers that teach them. And just as Western people have talked about theory and signifiers—so do Indigenous people. But we have our own set of signifiers, and our own set of theories and models as demonstrated and presented on [the] Four Directions Teachings.com site.

SS Let's return to your idea that the internet is not just a repository. This example is important because you are showing us how the formal properties of the internet are bound to a colonial imagination. In many ways the design of this culture's dominant technologies is at odds with Indigenous values and IK protocols.

JW Yes, the idea of a digital bundle is there to counter these colonizing logics of the internet—its history of development and how it is experienced today. If we go back to the idea of a genre or a new artifact, a digital bundle is a very unique space on the internet because it is a knowledge bundle. Indigenous communities cherish and take care of knowledge bundles because it is understood that knowledge bundles are imbued with spirit and therefore are living entities that must be cared for. They are not things such as books but are items or collections that have been brought to life through ceremony and through the protocols of their communities. A digital bundle exists within the parameters of Indigenous philosophy and values and therefore cannot utilize Western internet theory because those technical concepts and conceptions do not apply.

It does not take up the common discourse around technology. A digital bundle is not a portal; it is not an interface. It is experiential, but not for the sake of experience. It is not about entering another realm, like an Indigenous realm.

SS A digital bundle cannot be captured and consumed. It is designed to resist appropriation.

JW A lot of Indigenous people who are responding to my book say to me, "You work in media? Thank you. This has clarified for me the understanding between creating something that actually comes from community, that is about knowledge." It is really important to me to make a distinction between an artist's piece or an information piece versus a digital bundle.

Working with Indigenous values and processes is very different, especially if you position yourself as a helper. It is understood that in the role of a helper, you accept that your role is not interpretation or transmission but facilitator—you're facilitating this knowledge that is coming from a very specific Knowledge Keeper or Elder. This model and practice are very different from the Western roles of producer, director, or even artist. Unfortunately, the media arts world works against this helper approach, even though it is at the heart of Indigenous practices. Instead, there is an impetus to attach oneself to the Western model of what art is, what media is, and to create art or the art world. It's about celebrity and about caches of little bits of power. And it's just so sad because Indigenous people are often forced to take up a whole Western theory of art and Western theory of media.

Working as a helper reinvigorates Indigenous collaborative models of community creation. For example, in the research I'm undertaking now for Indigenous Timekeepers, the Elders and Knowledge Keepers I'm working with understand that what we are creating are knowledge bundles and that these bundles will be created through utilizing new technologies. We are all open to the process and have acknowledged that we will have to take great care and time to work with these technologies to ensure that they are respectful and appropriate to the task at hand.

SS Can you elaborate more on this point, or maybe with an example of how a particular media form or practice has been extended within the Indigenous media arts community in a way that is contradictory to IK protocols?

JW Media festival programmers working in both traditional film and new media like VR [virtual reality] seem to have no interest in content that is faced through those media in ways that reflect IK directly from Knowledge Keepers. They almost always prefer to hand pick specific artists to demonstrate their personal vision through the media in ways that are highly individualized and idiosyncratic. This has its place, of course, but it is not the same as IK as a bundle shared through the protocols of those who hold that knowledge.

So, for example, VR offers a spectacular opportunity for expressing Indigenous Knowledge. However, to date, I have not seen one (VR) project that incorporates Indigenous Knowledge. People like Victor Masayesva and other Knowledge Keepers and Elders who I talk to about this truly get what it means to say the medium is the message.

VR can radically alter the social experience of time and space, what is considered near or far; how this is even defined gives a new possibility, a different time and space and sense of relationality that could be symbiotic to Indigenous ways of knowing. It also offers something different than what the website medium of Four Directions Teachings .com is doing. We can understand them both as technologies that can extend IK and must be shaped by a different set of knowledge protocols. VR enables us to visually and symbolically represent the knowledge and orally share it. These are important features. You cannot do that with print. And I do not mean VR is immersive. To say so is exactly to take the colonizing view of the experience and stay there.

On the website, you can see the relationships between the four quadrants. You see how one quadrant is the opposite [of] the other quadrant, and that means something. For example, there is a medicine wheel teaching that depicts the four stages of life. The beginning is the child in the east; the youth stage is positioned in the south; the adult stage of life resides in the west; and the elder, the final stage of life, is in the north. When this life stage teaching is shared, Elders will note the diametrical positioning of the adult in the west to the child in the east. This relationship demonstrates that the child is dependent upon the adult, just as the Elder in the north being diametrically opposite to the youth in the south demonstrates that Elders need to guide the youth. These signifiers denote the relationships that are needed and depended upon for each life stage. This reading of the life stage teaching is overly simplistic and is not mine to share. I use it here to merely demonstrate the position and relationships that exist in each quadrant and how meaning is derived from the spatial understanding and directionality of these relationships.

This paradigm is significant in all teachings. You have to see the relationship of the whole together, and you see that in the circle. You don't see that in print. So, there's significant signifiers, symbols that Indigenous Knowledge Keepers are sharing. And Indigenous people who are open to that kind of knowledge and thinking recognize that. So now think about VR. This is where it starts to get really exciting for people like me who want to do this, and why I get so disappointed and frustrated when the exploration of these technologies is controlled through non-Indigenous processes, agencies, and ideas.

It's that these teachings, from sitting in many, many longhouses and many lodges—I understand that the teachings are relational. And this is something that we hear in modern, postmodern theory: everything's relational, relational this or that . . . okay, whatever—I'm not talking about your relational, I'm talking about relationality in terms of Indigenous values. So, when we say relational, it doesn't just mean things are multiple yet tied to one another, it means you see where you are positioned. Where are you standing? And how are you in relationship to everything around you? What does VR provide? It can provide that experience where you can begin to give people a sense of what it means to be in the center of understanding. For example, it means you can be in the center of the medicine wheel. What does it mean to be in the center of understanding and learn how the stars impact the planet? How could we actually show that story and have you positioned there, seeing where you stand, and what your positionality is? What does it mean when you're in VR and you turn and you face the west? Or you turn and you face the east? Or the south? So, what does it mean in VR when you look up to the sky, and a teaching comes to you from that sky world? Or you look down at your feet, and there is a teaching there of the earth? This is the promise of VR. What is exciting is that if we could have this opportunity, we could actually put people through an experience of approaching a teaching where—maybe, just maybe—it might stimulate some comprehension of what relational means, where they might have some understanding of what it means to actually be in relation, tied to the cosmos and tied to these energies, and that these four directions have significant meaning. In VR we can actually turn our bodies towards them; of course this can never replace or even come close to the real thing, but it can bring us to the doorway of understanding why we need to be under the stars again, why we need to be in real relation with everything around us, and in ceremony. While VR can never, ever be a ceremony, it can help us begin to understand the importance of the ideas and ways kept alive through our ceremonies. So, this is where it was so exciting!

SS And what are you seeing in the exploration of Indigenous content, for example?

JW It can be sad for me, and very flat. You can show a certain cultural experience, but that just becomes a commodified immersive experience. You just enter into a virtual world that is attached to Western ideas of participation and immersion.

SS It is interesting because your idea of the digital bundle takes much of its argumentative force from both resisting Western models of digital experience.

JW Yes, the danger is to work with VR in ways that are wed to linear narratives—print, text, experiential, immersion based, similar perhaps to how McLuhan imagined what happens when one doesn't understand the electronic potential of a new media mindset, when they approach it through print. That is the colonizing mindset of linear progress!

When I saw the immersive VR cultural experience playing out in a linear storyline, I was like, "Yeah, okay, whatever . . . you could do that with a documentary" [laughter]. You're not using that medium, and you are not challenging the potentials of this medium outside the colonizing framework. This medium could position the body in such a way as to actually utilize direction within the profound meanings of Indigenous paradigms. Why aren't we doing that? This is the potential of VR, that is the message—it can determine a new understanding of directionality and orientation. We must utilize direction. And for Indigenous epistemologies, that's huge. Huge!

I've also seen VR as an invitation to a celestial universe. And I loved that we were in space, great—a lot of people utilize space, because it's fun to think you're out in the universe. But, without anything concrete, with no utilization of direction or actual Indigenous Knowledge or philosophy, there was no symbolic interface design incorporating Indigenous understanding. It was just mixing up Indigenous symbols with little teacups and stuff floating around in space. So, I was just like, "Wow, is, this is just like an acid trip, right?" I just felt really disappointed . . . and this was something that if I was invited to, I would experiment and play too, but within the bounds of testing out VR space on Indigenous Knowledge. We need to think about what that medium can actually offer in terms of our own Indigenous Knowledge and philosophy.

VR from an Indigenous perspective, rooted in Indigenous ideas and worldviews, is a tremendous opportunity, because I think it would actually maybe help non-Indigenous people—for once—experience a teaching, or understand some of these concepts that are so highly symbolic, and that are so rich. That they come from such a different conception of thinking. That they might actually be able to understand a little bit of it. But non-Indigenous people might also get to experience the fact that there are things they just cannot grasp, and they need to respect that. When I'm hopeful, I think of VR as offering that kind [of] window on experience of knowledge that resists the colonial gaze or tendency to be so sure in one's knowledge of an other, another. With VR we have a chance to look at the technical specificities and how they intersect with Indigenous Knowledge and then rethink the technology.

SS What made you turn to media studies in the first place?

JW I started looking at new media after I left the world of documentary. I was developing *Hollywood Indians* for the CBC *Passionate Eye*, when they greenlighted the project on the stipulation that I codirect the feature with a white male director of their choosing. I protested and argued for an Indigenous director pairing. They presented me with an ultimatum: pick someone from their list or walk away. I chose to walk. And that's when I said, "You know what? I've got to look at other media, other media forms that will let me do what I need to do. Because I cannot work this way, and I cannot work with the dictates of an industry where commissioning editors are basically bullies." To make a long story short, I refused to work on it with a white senior man. There's documentary, the media form, and then there's the industry. And so that's when I left documentary.

It's kind of bittersweet. Because now, post–Truth and Reconciliation Commission, I have heard from producers and directors in the documentary field that this simply would not happen today. When I graduated with an MFA in film and video from York University, there were no TRC Calls to Action. So, the struggle to work in a good way within Indigenous storytelling was to battle with commissioning editors who had very limited worldviews and perspectives on what constituted good storytelling.

And that's when I started to look at new media, and called my production company Invert Media, dedicated to turn[ing] the mainstream—or what Sandy Grande calls "whitestream"—media on their heads.[2] Shake them up. See what can actually be created. That's what brought me into new media. I needed somewhere where I could work where commissioning editors weren't going to dictate and control the vision and content! I remember the constant arguing and justifying of storylines that were original and respectful. So that was very frustrating. You can imagine you could never have made a project like Four Directions Teachings with a commissioning editor.

SS Let's return again, then, to the impetus in our shared field to decolonize the digital.

JW Decolonizing the digital is also about having staying power. What you produce and put out there should be able to resist being colonized! Why? Because, as our Elders would say, it is informed by spirit and gifted through our cultural teachings. That's what I think. I think to myself, if you're really creating something that is shared as a teaching, then it should last, and have value that is not just part of a particular trend. If it dies within a few years because it's off-trend, what does this say about Indigenous values and Indigenous life? Why should cyberspace be another graveyard for us?

But on the good side, I think there are other artists now that I'm connecting with who are thinking more around those other lines of wanting to push back against Western concepts of media studies, Western concepts of artistry, and being an artist. The work of people like Maria Hupfield and Jason Lujan of the Native Art Department International is so refreshing because they are really thinking in terms of another way of being and existing. So that gives me hope. Vanessa Dion Fletcher embraces Maria beautifully when she writes, "Her performances, sculptures and installations reference different spans and scales of times. The projects specifically reflect her resistance to the Western tendency to essentialize Native artists and treat them as interchangeable producers of exotic cultural experiences. She values expansive exchange over isolation, and inclusion over hierarchy.[3]"

SS What does contemporary media studies do for you?

JW I learn a lot from deep listening and reflection, but I am not always sure how it fits with the work I am doing. The work that really inspires me tends to come from the periphery of mainstream or whitestream theorizing, like Marisa Duarte's *Network Sovereignty* and the connections she makes between land, Indigenous governance, and information.[4] I also really appreciate the contributions of *Algorithms of Oppression: How Search Engines Reinforce Racism* by Safiya Umoja Noble, and Martin Nakata's "Indigenous Knowledge and the Cultural Interface" was very insightful and helpful.[5] People like Margaret Noori on Indigenous language online and Kim Christenson's work on Murkutu, and Joanne Waitoa on Maori knowledge on Facebook.[6] And then of course there are all the brilliant Indigenous writers out there whose work, while not media studies–focused, is a wealth of contribution to thinking about Indigenous Knowledge online.

SS Well, I know you're listening to it, because you come over and listen to it almost every Monday at the McLuhan Centre! [laughter].

JW And I am reading it, but I'm not finding it useful for my thinking. I have a deep appreciation for the work, like I said ... when people are doing the research that is showing how these spaces are colonized, how this technology is colonized. McLuhan used colonizing language but acknowledged that the technology was colonizing. Thinking about artificial intelligence, and who is creating it, who are the authors. Almost everything I listen to, I consider in terms of the cunning tactics of colonization and how they appear in cyberspace while asking myself constantly, how do we start putting Indigenous Knowledge and work on the internet so we're not erased in that space? So, when you had a night on content moderators with Sarah T. Roberts, that really broke my heart. I was just like, "Wow!" So I really deeply appreciate all of that work and what I think it does; it helps me to just start to think even more deeply from different angles about what knowledge is coming from Elders, and Knowledge Keepers, and Indigenous value systems. So, on your night about cancel culture, I think of what could be an alternative. When I think of the platforming of hate or the way digital Islamophobia plays out, I think of the multiplicity of the internet to produce different experiences for different communities—none of which are uniform—and think about what it means to rely on the internet and the digital for Indigenous Knowledge. I think of that and not about how Indigenous people use their internet for empowerment or as a tool they can readily pick up—we have to understand the colonizing crevices and practices, and my work has been to think about what digital protocols intersect with Indigenous protocols—which ones are okay and are about sustenance and making time and space.

And also that we are not contributing to the colonization. The internet is a colonized space. And those theorists are proving it with their work. So, when I sit there I'm just like ... yeah! Good, good that you're doing this research, good that you're proving that point that we all knew from the start, that the internet was a colonized space. We have to think about, where do we want to be in those spaces? And that's why, again with social media, I love all the critiques that are coming out on social media too, like with Twitter, and Facebook, and how they operate. And that's why I don't post, and I don't publish through those spaces. I would rather see Indigenous people create their own sites for engagement like that.

SS Can you say more about that?

JW I think those social media sites could be configured according to Indigenous values and Indigenous ways of thinking. I mean, I'm not in the world of social media, but I appreciate how Instagram was playing with the idea of likes for a while, by not having them. I think that's kind of important.... Is there a different way to show appreciation for somebody that isn't all about trying to create a fan base? And so, I would really question, how do we do social media where it's not creating a fan base? How do we create social media that is really respectful?

I have to refuse branding, I have to refuse participating in colonizing media practices, using the tools of the colonizers, desiring a fan base, likes, etc. I think there is something profound about Indigenous principles that state, "Be careful what you put out there. Be careful how you judge others. Be careful what you say." So how could we create a social media presence that adopted those Indigenous values? One of them might be maybe the reaction of silence. How do you implement silence in social media, as opposed to cancel? What do our communities do? We don't cancel people. We do employ silence. Thinking back to that Monday Night Seminar you held as a town hall on cancel culture at the McLuhan Centre with Sarah Hagi, Christine Shaw, Elisha Lim, and Beverly Bain, it was Beverly who pointed out that there is a difference between call-out culture and cancel culture, and canceling in this way might be at odds with reparative forms of justice for Black people. And so silence is a different kind of approach. I wonder about that. And then I wonder, what could that look like? And some of these things, you don't know what they look like until you actually are part of the process of building it, and creating it.

I look to other theorists and artists and see and understand what they're talking about in terms of those frameworks, and then I walk away and think about that in terms of, how do I apply Indigenous content knowing that these are the challenges? So that's what I try doing. So when I'm thinking about those kinds of things ... and thinking also about ... you know, why people would be like ... at the time web 2.0 was the big thing, like, let's all create content, let's all comment on content—and I was like, that would go against the value systems of the Indigenous Elders and Knowledge Keepers. It could humiliate, denigrate.... It's just not something you do. So, you have to think, when do you employ those things?

Currently I have been sought out by young Indigenous designers to consult with them on Indigenous interface design. I always say to them [that] they need to think about what it is that you're actually doing with the artifacts that you're working with. Are you in ceremony with those pieces? Are they alive? Do they feel alive? Are you enacting any ritual? What part of that ritual or ceremony is important to know as a practice? But it remains offline. So, to shift online, what is it online in terms of what you're trying to convey within Indigenous philosophy or practice? Because right now, they're just archiving, like so many other archives. So, what can you do to challenge your thinking? That was an initial roundtable discussion, and so now they're saying, "Well, we want you to come and consult!" And I'm saying, "I don't know if I have time to do that," because then that means really sitting with this. It takes time to think of these design interfaces, and to really think about what is the content, right? It doesn't even fit within the framework of consulting!

SS What's your dream scenario for the *Digital Bundle* and the future of your work?

JW I dream of an Indigenous Knowledge media center—where we could deliberate and experiment on what constitutes an Indigenous media artifact, replete with new terminology that doesn't rely on Western media terminology. And if it does, it rethinks these terms like connection, networks, public spheres, portals, in terms of IK. I mean, isn't this really what "the medium is the message" is about—if you understand it, then you can change it? This would be a media center that would not host and house representational media but create those digital bundles. It is an involved process that would involve lots of people, cups of tea, deliberation, and of course many Indigenous people outside the academy.

It is about inversion. And we can change it, and we don't have to listen to the mostly white males who are creating the technology, or imposing their value system and worldview inside the technology.

And that's where I think like ... I'm just astounded that ... surely, other people are thinking that—who are Indigenous and working with media—that for an Indigenous person to be medium specific isn't just acknowledging the formal properties of the medium for a Western audience to digest, but rather it should align with Indigenous Knowledge. I don't know. It was just so evident to me with the new technologies that they're so robust that we can actually represent relationships. They're so robust that we can actually give a take on what it might mean to be inside a medicine wheel. What could we learn? These are powerful metaphors that represent Indigenous Knowledge and philosophy, that people don't really understand. Take connection. The only times we as Indigenous people have the true understanding of the connection to everything that exists is when we're in ceremony, when we're in the sweat lodge. And you're in there, and all of a sudden, the universe becomes present. And you're in that universe. We can give some sense of that with VR. I'm not saying create immersive ceremonial spaces to simply enter, because ceremony can never be virtual, of course. But I'm saying we can create that glimmer of that knowledge, and that paradigm, one that's so radically different than what is on currently on offer.

SS You're very much saying that the colonized internet does not have to be your internet.

JW Yeah, and that . . . we even have to think in this everyday existence. In this space that we are right now. What predominantly exists in this space, and what people know, is not the space I know. It's not the space that I interact with, right? So, when I think about the Black Lives Matter movement and the George Floyd protests, it was like . . . for the first time, so many people are understanding now that the police are violent. They didn't understand that before. There was a huge disconnect. If you think about your everyday person, they think that the police are there to serve and protect. It's like there are these levels of being and existing even in this world that we engage in, that we're constantly seeing that it isn't the way it seems. This is where Indigenous Knowledge comes in. It isn't handed to you. You have to figure it out.

And this pandemic isn't helping, because with the Timekeepers project, I can't get out to communities. And I really, really do not see how Zooming and talking to people on the phone is going to help. It's not going to help. I have to put everything on hold until it's safe to meet with communities. So that's really problematic.

But I do feel that there is that sense of urgency that this work needs to get done, because this is the need that the Knowledge Keepers have expressed—that we have to put this knowledge out there for the benefit of our communities and for the little brother. They call everyone else who's not Indigenous little brother [laughter]. Little brother, because they're not very good about thinking about being responsible. They're irresponsible.

Notes

1. Jennifer Wemigwans, Four Directions Teachings (website), http://fourdirectionsteachings.com; Wemigwans, *A Digital Bundle*.
2. Grande, "Whitestream Feminism and the Colonialist Project," 329–46.
3. Fletcher, "The Strength of Water," n.p.
4. Duarte, *Network Sovereignty*.
5. Noble, *Algorithms of Opression*; Nakata, "Indigenous Knowledge and the Cultural Interface."
6. Noori, "Waasechibiiwaabikoonsing Nd'anami'aami"; Christenson, "Does Information Really Want to Be Free?"; Waitoa, Scheyvens, and Warren, "E-Whanaungatanga."

Afterword

After McLuhan

WENDY HUI KYONG CHUN

This book has examined, imagined, and created what remains "after McLuhan." Moving from Black geographies to knitting needle computers, from Shipbo artisans to 3D printers, from Black data to filing cabinets, these chapters extend, distend, and displace the aphorism "the medium is the message." Ranging from love letters to interviews, from media archaeologies to personal journeys, they remake, understandably, the form of the scholarly collection. They reveal movements and media that McLuhan, so focused on the plight of the "enslaved" "Narcissus"—that is, "Western Man"—unfortunately did not acknowledge, such as slave ships and underground railroads (chapter 1 of this volume). They take McLuhan to the literal curb (chapter 2) to explore what contains (chapter 6) and sustains (chapter 5). They weave and spin outside the Eurocentric mirror (chapters 4 and 12); they follow the wires (chapter 3) and miss files (chapter 7). They punch through indices (chapter 8) and stand on platforms (chapter 9). They shelter by refusing (chapter 10) and by fabricating (chapter 11).

An afterword to this book seems both appropriate and repetitive. Arguably, this whole book serves as an afterword: a text that comes after, that proffers a second coming—albeit one not recognizable to the strangers who barge through the McLuhan Centre, claiming to know or be "the One." This book makes it clear that after is not less—and to come after is to change what remains in store for the future.

To underscore the stakes of this intervention, I turn to Gayatri Spivak's reading of the story of Echo.[1] Spivak's writing is key, both to understand the force of this book's wary embrace of McLuhan and to uncover echoes in McLuhan's Narcissus. Ovid entangles Narcissus's tale within Tiresias and Echo's, and thus places it within an "asymmetrical frame of transgression, punishment and dubious reward."[2] Echo is a talkative nymph whom Jupiter commands to distract Juno, while he dallies with other nymphs. Once this ruse is revealed, Juno punishes Echo by taking away her ability to form her own speech: Echo becomes an echo, condemned to repeat the words of others. One day while hiding in the woods, Echo falls in love with Narcissus, and lures him to her by echoing back parts of his questions. Running out, she embraces him. He rejects her and later, after being cursed by another rejected would-be lover, Narcissus falls in love with his reflection in a pond. Echo, who by this point has been reduced to only a voice—or more properly, remains only as a voice—takes pity on him and repeats back his dying words.

In *Understanding Media*, McLuhan diagnoses "Western Man" as Narcissus. Narcissus, McLuhan notes, stems from the Greek word *narcosis*—and it is this coupling of mistaken "slavish" self-love and numbness that McLuhan embraces. He asserts, "The youth Narcissus mistook his own reflection in the water for another person. This extension of himself by mirror numbed his perceptions until he became the servomechanism of his own extended or repeated image. The nymph Echo tried to win his love with fragments of his own speech, but in vain. He was numb. He had adapted to his extension of himself and had become a closed system."[3] This myth brings out the violence and darkness often overlooked in McLuhan's vision of media as "the extensions of Man." According to McLuhan, each extension causes a radical shift in the ratio of our sense perceptions, which our whole body reacts to violently. Because these extensions irritate Man, he seeks to amputate them—and thus make them a counterirritant. For example, the wheel, which extends the foot, "brings about a new intensity of action by its amplification of a separate or isolated function (the feet in rotation). Such amplification is bearable by the nervous system only through numbness or blocking of perception."[4] Once amputated, Man, like Narcissus, embraces his mirror image, and self-knowledge becomes impossible. This violent self-amputation threatens to spread infection everywhere, for this desperate pursuit of a numbing pleasure takes place with "complete disregard for antiseptics."[5] All is not lost, however: instead of amputation, we can become "immune" to the pain via artists or computers, who can "free" us by adapting our sense ratios so we can survive. Understanding, that is, can provide comfort and thus free us from both the irritant pain and the traumatic pursuit of pleasure.[6]

This reading—like the other critical engagements with Narcissus Spivak discusses—excludes Echo, who nonetheless seeks to break through the text. Spivak argues that critical theory—when it ignores Echo—locks itself into a destructive and unethical "self-knowledge." To make this point, Spivak rereads Freud's and Lacan's "narcissus complexes," which both view Narcissus as "primitive" man/child, incapable of entering the Oedipal complex/the symbolic. By doing so, they miss the ways in which the Narcissus-Echo pair reveals "a punishment that is finally a dubious reward quite outside the borders of the self. . . . Echo in Ovid is staged as the instrument of possibility of a truth not dependent upon intention, a reward uncoupled from, and indeed set free from, the recipient."[7] To make this point, Spivak rereads the part in Narcissus's tale, in which Echo responds to his question, "Why do you fly from me?" Ovid glosses over her response; instead, Spivak elaborates on Echo's response—as the truncated "fly from me" (a command)—to discover the difference her echo introduces: "Fly from me—I cannot answer you or I am not your proper respondent: a deferment independent of, indeed the opposite of, the sender's intention. A difference and a deferment together are, strictly speaking—but can one be strict about this?—*différance*."[8] Echo's punishment becomes dubious reward, for repetition always enables difference. Further, by becoming reduced to a voice, Echo remains: she becomes writing.[9]

Further, through her deconstructive embrace, which seeks to disrupt self-knowledge, Echo instantiates ethics and relation. Ethics, Spivak stresses, "are not a problem of knowledge but a call of relationship." More importantly, the call and problem are "in a deconstructive embrace: Narcissus and Echo. If we see ourselves only as subjects (or 'selves') of a knowledge that cannot relate and see the 'self' as writing, our unavoidable ethical decisions will be caught in the more empirical, less philosophical 'night of non-knowledge.' . . . If we move to Echo as the (un)intending subject of ethics, we are allowed to understand the mysterious responsibility of ethics, that its subject cannot comprehend."[10] The deconstructive embrace, which Narcissus flees, inserts Echo in order to make punishment a dubious reward. It echoes "the brothers in a self-knowledge that 'kills.'"[11]

Spivak's call to insert Echo pens McLuhan to a feminist embrace, which reaches toward the Echoes in *Understanding Media*. Who is McLuhan—the artist who offers understanding as comfort—if not Echo? Before he drops Echo, McLuhan writes, "Echo tried to win his love with fragments of his own speech but in vain."[12]

McLuhan moves so quickly away from Echo because he is obsessed with Western Man as a "slave" or "servomechanism." The history of slavery is central to McLuhan's dark narrative—and to the history of computing more broadly. McLuhan used Roman slavery to understand media. Equating slaves, staples, and media, he argued that dependency on these resources fundamentally altered that society. Via Carl Jung, he claimed, "Every Roman was surrounded by slaves. The slave and his psychology flooded ancient Italy, and every Roman became inwardly, and of course unwittingly, a slave. Because living constantly in the atmosphere of slaves, he became infected through the unconscious with their psychology. No one can shield himself from such an influence."[13] Media = staples = slaves was so dangerous, McLuhan argued, because slavish specialization sought to make slaves "indispensable to their masters." Thus, the tragedy of slavery was not the deprivation of a slave's liberty, but rather the "enslavement" of the masters. Indeed, he concluded "The Medium Is the Message" by emphasizing "our" current "enslavement." Describing the gradual specialization of Greek farming, he wrote, "The armies of technologically specialized slaves working the land blighted the social existence of the independent yeomen and small farmers, and led to the strange world of the Roman towns and cities crowded with rootless parasites." By the late twentieth century things were far worse, he contended, because "the specialism of mechanized industry and market organization has faced Western man with the challenge of manufacture by mono-fracture, or the tackling of all things and operations one-bit at-a-time."[14]

McLuhan's analysis is reprehensible at best. Not only does it dehumanize slaves by equating them with media (some humans are "men" and others their extensions), it disregards their experiences. Tellingly, McLuhan prefaces *Understanding Media* by explaining how electronic media have imploded society, bringing together social and political functions and heightening "human awareness of responsibility to an intense degree. It is this implosive factor that alters the position of the Negro, the teen-ager, and some other groups. They can no longer be *contained*, in the political sense of limited association. They are now *involved* in our lives, as we in theirs, thanks to electric media."[15]

These passages not only reveal the biases inherent to his conception of media as "the extensions of man," they also highlight the encounters that did not happen. Addressing the realities of slavery and discrimination would have been key to solving the apocalypse McLuhan foresaw. As Orlando Patterson has argued, freedom as a value emerged not from masters but rather the desires of the slaves.[16] It is no accident that popular cultural imaginary turns to the civil rights and decolonization movements to imagine human revolution—and that it is obsessed with technological punishment and revenge.

Crucially, it is because technologies are treated as slaves that the "coming singularity" is so feared. According to many scientists, technologists, and science fiction writers, AI = the Apocalypse. This fear, however, is intimately intertwined with its alleged promise to equip humans with docile machine-servants and thus spread the perks of the 1 percent—chauffeurs, personal assistants, expert advisors—to the 95 percent. It is because we live in a society in which equality seems so impossible to imagine that the "coming singularity" seems inevitable. As Fredric Jameson has relayed, "Someone once said that it is easier to imagine the end of the world than to imagine the end of capitalism. We can now revise that and witness the attempt to imagine capitalism by way of imagining the end of the world." As Jennifer Rhee has argued in *The Robotic Imaginary: The Human and the Price of Dehumanized Labor*, the enduring power of profoundly raced and gendered robots within the cultural imagination, as well as within STEM, is linked to the history of slavery.[17]

To move beyond the apocalypse, we need to rethink our relation to slavery, and in particular race-based slavery, which is central to the history and contemporary situation of the United States. It is no accident that McLuhan uses the American South to elucidate the consequences of specialization (without directly addressing the history of US race-based slavery). We need to be attentive to the foundational roles of race, gender, and class—and resistance—in technology and our analyses of them.

And this is why the book you hold in your hands is so central. It offers an afterward—an escape from an apocalyptic future—by modeling different logics and understandings of how we inscribe history and the future together. Through its embrace and opening of McLuhan, it offers a way to "understand" that refuses the calls to imitation which haunt antifeminist—Narcissistic—mirrors/guardians of McLuhan. Asking what Echo as ethical instantiation offers "the worldwide collectivity of conscientized feminists of color from bourgeois origins or in passive capitalist relations," Spivak argues that Echo undoes "every act of cultural narcissism."[18] "National identity debates in the South and 'liberal' multiculturalism in the North" want us to engage in a losing game of narcissistic imitation. They call on us to "love-your-own-face, love-your-own-culture, remain-fixed-in-cultural-difference, simulate what is really pathogenic repression in the form of questioning the European universalist superego."[19] Taking up Echo's position can offer both a "Why do you fly from me?" toward the subaltern, who cannot speak, but also might enable the feminist to "ventriloquize the 'fly from me' toward that Narcissus-face, both the self-knowing Ovidian and the deluded Freudian."[20] Further, the deconstructive embrace enables the emergence of "something relating to the need of a uniform civil code for men and women, not personal codes that keep women minors; something that would make it impossible for patterns of transgression and reward to be asymmetrically gendered, in the calculus of the law."[21]

These chapters that you will have read fly from McLuhan. They emphasize the importance of the difference that opens through writing. They move us beyond and through questions of repetition to the forces of movement and media. I thus conclude by echoing their concluding calls to us:

> To think about the technological as a form of power means also to rethink what might be designed and what sorts of new and better social worlds could be newly determined by feminist techno-logics (Sharma, introduction).

> Whether those movements entail Black Lives Matter Global Network protesters blocking freeway traffic or the efforts of youth climate activists like Isra Hirsi and Greta Thunberg, alternative conceptions of movement and media connect to rethinking and re-creating humanness (Towns, chapter 1).

> Perhaps the new crosswalk portent in tomorrow's city is not the small child with the power to stop a cement truck, but the sidewalk protester, placard in hand, with the power to stop a tech behemoth, or a militarized police force, from remaking the city in its own optimized image (Mattern, chapter 2).

> Rewiring these machineries is messy and complex work but involves, at the very least, a more earnest consideration of the material technologies that tether us to our masculinized media (Taylor, chapter 3).

Embracing not knowing as a political media engagement is not an easy proposition, but it also offers the space for much-needed ontological and epistemological creativity (Langlois, chapter 4).

Thank you for keeping my baby alive. That's all I really wanted to say. Warm regards, Mommy Martel (Martel, chapter 5).

These and other efforts to deploy the heuristic of containment, we conclude, can be incredibly productive for scholars of media and technology who seek to better understand the sociopolitical stakes of ever more pervasive, oft-invisible, systems that capture, enclose, and repurpose the worlds we inhabit (Duffy and Packer, chapter 6).

Within a gendered conception of efficiency, it [the filing cabinet] provides a proper place for papers and information; it does this because there is a proper way to use it. That use depends on the materiality of the filing cabinet, on its physicality, on the convergence of a specific object and particular hands (Robertson, chapter 7).

Looking in these margins at minor objects like paper cards, it becomes clear that emergent information sensibilities drew on ideas about gender just as much as they did electricity, computers, and other tools (McKinney, chapter 8).

In an age of amplification, where we celebrate digital platforms for reinvigorating feminism, we must also look at the lessons learned from other ways media require particular kinds of visibility (Singh and Banet-Weiser, chapter 9).

I have to explain context and history around almost anything. It's exhausting. This happens even in simple conversations about, you know, public transportation. . . . This is what is so great about Black Twitter. I think it's supposed to be hard. There shouldn't be an easy translation. There's something about this subtlety that we don't have to talk about. It's between us, and it's in our own silos. This is like our own safety net, and it's how we survive in our comedy and our humor (Ahmed and Siad, chapter 10).

Because jinn, unlike the cyborg, can "see the unknown." And if you can see the unknown, you can conquer many worlds. That's how I like to imagine it all (Allahyari, chapter 11).

But I do feel that there is that sense of urgency that this work needs to get done, because this is the need that the Knowledge Keepers have expressed—that we have to put this knowledge out there for the benefit of our communities and for the little brother (Wemigwans, chapter 12).

Notes

1. Spivak, "Echo."
2. Spivak, "Echo," 23.
3. McLuhan, *Understanding Media* (1994), 41.
4. McLuhan, *Understanding Media* (1994), 42.
5. McLuhan, *Understanding Media* (1994), 63.
6. McLuhan, *Understanding Media* (1994), 43.
7. Spivak, "Echo," 23–24.
8. Spivak, "Echo," 26.
9. Spivak, "Echo," 26.
10. Spivak, "Echo," 32.
11. Spivak, "Echo," 33.
12. Spivak argues that Echo's position is that of the analyst, who strategically repeats certain questions to provoke knowledge.
13. McLuhan, *Understanding Media* (1994), 21. This passage follows a stunning one in which he argues that "the pathos and humor of the American South are embedded in such an economy of limited staples. For a society configured by reliance on a few commodities accepts them as a social bond quite as much as the metropolis does the press. Cotton and oil, like radio and TV, become 'fixed charges' on the entire psychic life of the community."
14. McLuhan, *Understanding Media* (1994), 18.
15. McLuhan, *Understanding Media* (1994), 5.
16. Patterson, *Freedom*.
17. Jameson, "Future City," 76; Rhee, *The Robotic Imaginary*. For more on the AI apocalypse and its relation to discriminatory algorithms, see Chun, *Discriminating Data*.
18. Spivak, "Echo," 27.
19. Spivak, "Echo," 28.
20. Spivak, "Echo," 28.
21. Spivak, "Echo," 29–30.

Bibliography

Ahmed, Sara. "Affective Economies." *Social Text* 22, no. 2 (2004): 117–39.
Ahmed, Sara. *The Promise of Happiness*. Durham, NC: Duke University Press, 2010.
Allahyari, Morehshin. *Dark Matter (First Series)*. 2014. 3D printed sculptural objects. http://www.morehshin.com/dark-matter-first-series/.
Allahyari, Morehshin. *Material Speculation: ISIS*. 2015–16. Digital fabrication and 3D printed objects. http://www.morehshin.com/material-speculation-isis/.
Allahyari, Morehshin. *She Who Sees the Unknown*. 2016. Multimedia project. http://shewhoseestheunknown.com.
Allen, Woody, dir. *Annie Hall*. United Artists, 1977.
Amazon Staff. "Introducing Amazon Sidewalk." *Amazon Blog*, September 27, 2019. https://blog.aboutamazon.com/devices/introducing-amazon-sidewalk.
American Institute of Filing. *A Course in Correspondence Filing for Home Study*. Boston: Library Bureau, 1921.
Andrejevic, Mark. "Surveillance in the Digital Enclosure." *Communication Review* 10, no. 4 (2007): 295–317.
Angus, Ian. "The Materiality of Expression: Harold Innis' Communication Theory and the Discursive Turn in the Human Sciences." *Canadian Journal of Communication* 23, no. 1 (1998): 1–9.
Archibald, Sasha. "Indexes, In Praise of." *Cabinet* 52 (2013–14): 57–63.
Aristarkhova, Irena. "Ectogenesis and Mother as Machine." *Body and Society*, 11, no. 1 (2005): 43–59.
Atanasoski, Neda, and Kalindi Vora. *Surrogate Humanity: Race, Robots and the Politics of Technological Futures*. Durham, NC: Duke University Press, 2019.
Axelrod, Leslie R. "An Information Retrieval System for a Small Research Department." *IRE Transactions on Engineering Management* 9, no. 2 (1962): 92–95.
Bailey, Anne C. *The Weeping Time: Memory and the Largest Slave Auction in American History*. Cambridge: Cambridge University Press, 2017.
Baker, Jeffrey P. "The Incubator and the Medical Discovery of the Premature Infant." *Journal of Perinatology* 5 (2000): 321–28.
Baker, Jeffrey P. *The Machine in the Nursery: Incubator Technology and the Origins of Newborn Intensive Care*. Baltimore, MD: Johns Hopkins University Press, 1996.

Balsamo, Anne. *Technologies of the Gendered Body: Reading Cyborg Bodies*. Durham, NC: Duke University Press, 1996.

Banet-Weiser, Sarah. *Empowered: Popular Feminism and Popular Misogyny*. Durham, NC: Duke University Press, 2018.

Barad, Karen. *Meeting the Universe Halfway: Quantum Physics and the Entanglement of Matter and Meaning*. Durham, NC: Duke University Press, 2007.

Barstow, Anne Llewellyn. *Witchcraze: A New History of the European Witch Hunts*. London: Pandora, 1994.

Barth, Brian. "Curb Control." *American Planning Association*, June 2019. https://www.planning.org/planning/2019/jun/curbcontrol/.

Barthes, Roland. *Camera Lucida: Reflections on Photography*. New York: Macmillan, 1979.

Bartky, Sandra Lee. *Femininity and Domination: Studies in the Phenomenology of Oppression*. New York: Routledge, 1990.

Bates, Beth. *Pullman Porters and the Rise of Protest Politics in Black America, 1925–1945*. Chapel Hill: University of North Carolina Press, 2010.

Baudrillard, Jean. *The Spirit of Terrorism and Requiem for the Twin Towers*. New York: Verso, 2002.

Bax, Christina E. "Entrepreneur Brownie Wise: Selling Tupperware to America's Women in the 1950s." *Journal of Women's History* 22, no. 2 (2010): 171–80.

Beckert, Sven, and Seth Rockman. *Slavery's Capitalism: A New History of American Economic Development*. Philadelphia: University of Pennsylvania Press, 2018.

Beebeejuan, Yasminah. "Gender, Urban Space, and the Right to Everyday Life." *Journal of Urban Affairs* 39, no. 3 (2017): 323–34.

Belaunde, L. E. "Diseños materiales e inmateriales: La patrimonialización del kené shipibo-konibo y de la ayahuasca en el Perú." *Mundo Amazónico* 3 (2012): 123–46.

Benjamin, Ruha. *Captivating Technology: Race, Carceral Technoscience and Liberatory Imagination in Everyday Life*. Durham, NC: Duke University Press, 2019.

Ben-Joseph, Eran. "Changing the Residential Street Scene: Adapting the Shared Street (Woonerf) Concept to the Suburban Environment." *Journal of the American Planning Association* 61, no. 4 (1996): 504–15.

Bennet, Lance W., and Alexandra Segerberg. "Digital Media and the Personalization of Collective Action: Social Technology and the Organization of Protests against the Global Economic Crisis." *Information, Communication and Society* 14, no. 6 (2011): 770–99.

Bennet, Lance W., and Alexandra Segerberg. *The Logic of Connective Action: Digital Media and the Personalization of Contentious Politics*. Cambridge: Cambridge University Press, 2013.

Berland, Jody. "McLuhan and Posthumanism: Extending the Techno-Animal Embrace." *Canadian Journal of Communications* 44, no. 4 (2019): 567–84.

Berland, Jody. *Virtual Menageries: Animals as Mediators in Network Cultures*. Cambridge, MA: MIT Press, 2020.

Berlant, Lauren. "America, 'Fat,' the Fetus." *boundary 2* 21, no. 3 (1994): 45–195.

Bexte, Peter, and Martina Leeker, eds. *Ein Medium namens McLuhan*. Lüneberg, Germany: Meson, 2020.

Bittel, Carla, Elaine Leong, and Christine von Oertzen, eds. *Working with Paper: Gendered Practices in the History of Knowledge*. Pittsburgh: University of Pittsburgh Press, 2019.

Bivens, Rena, and Oliver L. Haimson. "Baking Gender into Social Media Design: How Platforms Shape Categories for Users and Advertisers." *Social Media + Society*, October 2016.

Bollmer, Grant. *Inhuman Networks: Social Media and the Archeology of Connection*. New York: Bloomsbury, 2016.

Bollmer, Grant. *Materialist Media History: An Introduction*. New York: Bloomsbury, 2019.

Boulding, Kenneth E. *The Organizational Revolution: A Study in the Ethics of Economic Organization*. New York: Harper and Brothers, 1953.

Bourne, Charles P., and Trudi Bellardo Hahn. *A History of Online Information Services, 1963–1976*. Cambridge, MA: MIT Press, 2003.

Bowker, Geoffrey. "How to Be Universal: Some Cybernetic Strategies, 1943–70." *Social Studies of Science* 23 (1993): 107–27.

Brabec de Mori, Bernd. "The Magic of Song, the Invention of Tradition and the Structuring of Time among the Shipibo, Peruvian Amazon." In *Yearbook of the Phonogrammarchiv at the Austrian Academy of Sciences*, vol. 2, edited by G. Lechleitner and C. Liebl, 169–92. 2011.

Brabec de Mori, Bernd, Mori Silvano, and Laida de Brabec. "La corona de la inspiración: Los diseños geométricos de los shipibo-konibo y sus relaciones con cosmovisión y música." *Indiana* 26 (2009): 105–34.

Brabec de Mori, Bernd, Mori Silvano, and Laida de Brabec. "Shipibo-Konibo Art and Healing Concepts: A Critical View on the Aesthetic Therapy." *Viennese Ethnomedicine Newsletter* 11 (2009): 18–26.

Brady, Jeff. "Teen Climate Activist Greta Thunberg Arrives in New York after Sailing the Atlantic." NPR, August 28, 2019. https://www.npr.org/2019/08/28/754818342/teen-climate-activist-greta-thunberg-arrives-in-new-york-after-sailing-the-atlan.

Braidotti, Rosi. *Nomadic Subjects: Embodiment and Sexual Difference in Contemporary Feminist Theory*, 2nd ed. New York: Columbia University Press, 2011.

Braithwaite, Phoebe. "Smart Home Tech Is Being Turned into a Tool for Domestic Abuse." *Wired*, June 22, 2018. https://www.wired.co.uk/article/internet-of-things-smart-home-domestic-abuse.

Braverman, Harry. *Labor and Monopoly Capital: The Degradation of Work in the Twentieth Century*, 25th anniv. ed. New York: Monthly Review Press, 1998.

Brennan, Summer. *High Heel*. New York: Bloomsbury, 2019.

Brock, Andre. *Distributed Blackness: African American Cybercultures*. New York: NYU Press, 2020.

Brown, H. S. *Filing: Theory and Practice*. New York: Hubbard, 1933.

Brown, Kate. "'Black People Figured Out How to Make Culture in Freefall': Arthur Jafa on the Creative Power of Melancholy." *Artnet*, February 21, 2018. https://news.artnet.com/art-world/arthur-jafa-julia-stoschek-collection-1227422.

Browne, Simone. *Dark Matters: On the Surveillance of Blackness*. Durham, NC: Duke University Press, 2015.

Bryan, John. "A Multi-purpose Information Retrieval System Based on Edge-Notched Cards." *Bioscience* 16, no. 6 (1966): 402–7.

Bryce, Jo, and Jason Rutter. "The Gendering of Computer Gaming: Experience and Space." In *Leisure Cultures: Investigations in Sport, Media and Technology*, edited by Scott Fleming and Ian Jones. Leisure Studies Association, 2003.

Burawoy, Michael. "Karl Marx and the Satanic Mills: Factory Politics under Early Capitalism in England, the United States, and Russia." *American Journal of Sociology* 90, no. 2 (September 1984): 247–82.

Burroughs, William S., and Allen Ginsberg. *The Yage Letters*, 3rd ed. San Francisco: City Lights, 2001.

Buxton, William J., and Thierry Bardini. "Tracing Innis and McLuhan." *Canadian Journal of Communication* 37 (2012): 551–60.

Campt, Tina. "Black Visuality and the Practice of Refusal." *Women and Performance: A Journal of Feminist Theory* 29, no. 1 (2019): 79–87. https://www.womenandperformance.org/ampersand/29-1/campt.

Canales, Katie. "The WHO Is Recommending Video Games as an Effective Way to Stop the Spread of COVID-19, One Year after Adding 'Gaming Disorder' to Its List of Addictive Behaviors." *Business Insider*, April 1, 2020. https://www.businessinsider.com/who-video-games-coronavirus-pandemic-mental-health-disorder-2020-4.

Carey, James W. *Communication as Culture*. New York: Routledge, 2009.

Carroll, M. K. "How Knitters Are Human Computers." *Code Academy Blog*. May 24, 2013. https://www.codecademy.com/resources/blog/how-knitters-are-human-computers/.

Castronovo, Val, Tam Gray, Daniel S. Levy, Ellin Martens, Michele Orecklin, Alice Park, Julie Rawe, Chris Taylor, Owen Thomas, and Josh Tyrangiel. "One of the Best Last Lists of the Century." *Time*, December 27, 1999. http://content.time.com/time/subscriber/article/0,33009,992982,00.html.

Cavan, Ruth Shonle. *Business Girls: A Study of Their Interests and Problems*. Chicago: Religious Education Association, 1929.

Cavan, Ruth Shonle. "The Girl Who Writes Your Letters." *Survey*, July 15, 1929, 438.

Cavell, Richard. "McLuhan and Spatial Communication." *Western Journal of Communication* 63, no. 3 (1991): 348–63.

Cavell, Richard. *McLuhan in Space: A Cultural Geography*. Toronto: University of Toronto Press, 2002.

Cavell, Richard. *Remediating McLuhan*. Amsterdam: Amsterdam University Press, 2017.

Cawthorne, Nigel. *Witch Hunt: A History of Persecution.* Auckland, New Zealand: Castle, 2004.

Chambers, Deborah. "'Wii Play as a Family': The Rise in Family-Centered Video Gaming." *Leisure Studies* 31, no. 1 (2012): 69–82.

Chang, Emily. *Brotopia: Breaking Up the Boys' Club of Silicon Valley.* New York: Portfolio, 2018.

Chow, Andrew R. "Woody Allen Warns of 'Witch Hunt' over Weinstein, Then Tries to Clarify." *New York Times*, October 15, 2017. https://www.nytimes.com/2017/10/15/movies/woody-allen-harvey-weinstein-witch-hunt.html.

Christenson, Kimberly. "Does Information Really Want to Be Free? Indigenous Knowledge and the Politics of Open Access." *International Journal of Communication* 6 (2012): 2870–93.

Chun, Wendy Hui Kyong. *Discriminating Data: Correlation, Neighborhoods and the New Politics of Recognition.* Cambridge, MA: MIT Press, 2021.

Chun, Wendy Hui Kyong. "Race and/as Technology, or How to Do Things to Race." In *Race after the Internet*, edited by Lisa Nakamura and Peter Chow-White, 38–60. London: Routledge, 2013.

Cimpanu, Catalin. "Akamai to Slow Down Video Game Downloads during COVID-19 Outbreak." *ZDNet*, March 24, 2020. https://www.zdnet.com/article/akamai-to-slow-down-video-game-downloads-during-covid-19-outbreak/.

Clarke, Adele E., Laura Mamo, Jennifer Ruth Fosket, Jennifer R. Fishman, and Janet K. Shim. *Biomedicalization, Technoscience, Health, and Illness in the U.S.* Durham, NC: Duke University Press, 2010.

Clarke, Alison J. *Tupperware: The Promise of Plastic in 1950s America.* Washington, DC: Smithsonian Institution Press, 1999.

Clough, Patricia. *The Affective Turn: Theorizing the Social.* Durham, NC: Duke University Press, 2007.

Cohen, Lizabeth. *A Consumers' Republic: The Politics of Mass Consumption in Postwar America.* New York: Vintage, 2003.

Coleman, Beth. "Race as Technology." *Camera Obscura* 24, no. 1.70 (2009): 177–207.

Collison, Robert L. *Indexes and Indexing.* London: Ernest Benn, 1959.

Cope, Edward A. *Filing Systems, Their Principles and Their Application to Modern Office Requirements.* London: Sir Isaac Pitman and Sons, 1913.

Costanza-Chock, Sasha. *Design Justice: Community-Led Practices to Build the Worlds We Need.* Cambridge, MA: MIT Press, 2020.

Cowan, Ruth Schwartz. *More Work for Mother: The Ironies of Household Technology from the Open Hearth to the Microwave.* New York: Basic Books, 1983.

Cramer, J. A. *The Filing Department.* New York: Bankers', 1917.

Crawford, Amy. "Bringing Up Baby . . . Downtown." *Sidewalk Labs*, July 27, 2018. https://www.sidewalklabs.com/blog/bringing-up-baby-downtown/.

Crenshaw, Kimberle. "Mapping the Margins: Intersectionality, Identity Politics, and Violence against Women of Color." *Stanford Law Review* 43, no. 6 (1991): 1241–99.

Cubitt, Sean. *The Practice of Light: A Genealogy of Visual Technologies from Prints to Pixels*. Cambridge, MA: MIT Press, 2014.

Datta, Ayona. "Gendering the Smart City: A Subaltern Curation Network on Gender-Based Violence (GBV) in India." UK Research and Innovation, 2019. https://gtr.ukri.org/projects?ref=AH%2FR003866%2F1.

Daub, Adrian. *What Tech Calls Thinking: An Inquiry into the Intellectual Bedrock of Silicon Valley*. New York: FSG Originals, 2020.

Davies, Sharyn G., Judy McGregor, Judith Pringle, and Lynne Giddings. "Rationalizing Pay Inequity: Women Engineers, Pervasive Patriarchy and the Neoliberal Chimera." *Journal of Gender Studies* 27, no. 6 (2018): 623–36.

Davis, Jenny. *How Artifacts Afford: The Power and Politics of Everyday Things*. Cambridge, MA: MIT Press, 2020.

Del Valle, Gaby. "New Yorkers Condemn Bezos at an Anti-Amazon HQ2 Rally in Queens." *Vox*, November 15, 2018. https://www.vox.com/the-goods/2018/11/15/18096181/long-island-city-amazon-hq2-protest.

Derrida, Jacques. "Heidegger's Hand (Geschlecht II)." In *Deconstruction and Philosophy: The Texts of Jacques Derrida*, edited by John Sallis. Chicago: University of Chicago Press, 1989.

Doctoroff, Daniel L. "Reimagining Cities from the Internet Up." *Sidewalk Talk*, November 30, 2016. https://medium.com/sidewalk-talk/reimagining-cities-from-the-internet-up-5923d6be63ba#.ubj2h5kdb.

Duarte, Marisa Elena. *Network Sovereignty: Building the Internet across Indian Country*. Seattle: University of Washington Press, 2017.

Duffy, Brooke Erin, and Urzula Pruchniewska. "Gender and Self-Enterprise in the Social Media Age: A Digital Double Bind." *Information, Communication and Society* 20, no. 6 (2017): 843–59.

Duneir, Mitchell. *Sidewalk*. New York: Farrar, Straus & Giroux, 1999.

Earle, Sarah, Carol Komaromy, and Linda Layne, eds. *Understanding Reproductive Loss: Perspectives on Life, Death and Infertility*. New York: Routledge, 2012.

Edelman, Lee. *No Future: Queer Theory and the Death Drive*. Durham, NC: Duke University Press, 2004.

Edwards, Paul. *Closed World: Computers and the Politics of Discourse in Cold War America*. Cambridge, MA: MIT Press, 1995.

Emre, Merve. "On Reproduction." Forum, *Boston Review* 7, no. 44 (2018).

Enns, Anthony. "Review of *Remediating McLuhan*." *Leonardo*, August 2017.

Erickson, Ethel. "The Employment of Women in Offices." *Women's Bureau Bulletin* 120. Washington, DC: Government Printing Office, 1934.

Ernst, Wolfgang. "Media Archaeography: Method and Machine versus History and Narrative of Media." In *Media Archaeology*, edited by Erkki Huhtamo and Jussi Parikka, 239–55. Berkeley: University of California Press, 2011.

Ettachfini, Leila. "Isra Hirsi Is 16, Unbothered, and Saving the Planet." *Vice*, September 18, 2019. https://www.vice.com/amp/en_us/article/a357wp/isra-hirsi-ilhan-omar-daughter-climate-strike-profile.

Eubanks, Virginia. *Automating Inequality: How High-Tech Tools Profile, Police and Punish the Poor.* New York: Macmillan, 2018.

Farokhmanesh, Megan. "Sony Is Now Slowing Down PlayStation Downloads in the US." *The Verge*, March 27, 2020. https://www.theverge.com/2020/3/27/21196835/sony-slow-playstation-downloads-us-internet-speed-isps-usage-coronavirus.

Federici, Silvia. *Caliban and the Witch: Women, the Body and Primitive Accumulation.* New York: Autonomedia, 2003.

Federici, Silvia. *Revolution at Point Zero: Housework, Reproduction, and Feminist Struggle (Common Notions).* San Francisco: PM Press, 2012.

Federici, Silvia. *Witches, Witch-Hunting and Women.* New York: Common Notions, 2018.

Federman, Mark, and Derrick de Kerckhove. *McLuhan for Managers: New Tools for New Thinking.* Toronto: Viking Canada, 2003.

Feldman, Nancy. "Evolving Communities: Aspects of Shipibo and Andean Art, Textiles, and Practice in Contemporary Peru." *Fieldiana Anthropology*, new ser., no. 45 (2016): 51–59.

Feldman, Nancy. "Shipibo-Conibo Textiles 2010–2018: Artists of the Amazon Culturally Engaged." In *The Social Fabric: Deep Local to Pan Global, Proceedings of the Textile Society of America 16th Biennial Symposium.* Lincoln: University of Nebraska, 2018. https://digitalcommons.unl.edu/tsaconf/1082.

Fernández-Abascal, Guillermo, and Urtzi Grau. "Learning to Live Together." *E-flux Architecture*, February 19, 2019. https://www.e-flux.com/architecture/becoming-digital/248074/learning-to-live-together/.

Fildes, Jonathan. "Weaving the Way to the Moon." *BBC News*, July 15, 2009. http://news.bbc.co.uk/2/hi/8148730.stm.

Firestone, Shulamith. *The Dialectic of Sex.* New York: Bantam, 1970.

Fletcher, Vanessa Dion. "The Strength of Water." *Art in America*, October 19, 2017. https://www.artnews.com/art-in-america/features/the-strength-of-water-63303/.

Flood, Catherine, and Gavin Grindon. *Disobedient Objects.* London: V&A, 2014.

Flynn, Bernadette. "Geography of the Digital Hearth." *Information, Communication and Society* 6, no. 4 (2003): 551–76.

Foskett, A. C. *A Guide to Personal Indexes Using Edge-Notched, Uniterm and Peek-a-boo Cards*, 2nd ed. New Haven, CT: Archon, 1970.

Foucault, Michel. *Discipline and Punish.* New York: Random House, 1997.

Franklin, Sarah. "Staying with the Manifesto: An Interview with Donna Haraway." *Theory, Culture and Society* 34, no. 4 (July 2017): 49–63.

Frankopan, Peter. *The Silk Roads: A New History of the World.* New York: Penguin Random House, 2017.

Friedman, Elisabeth J. *Interpreting the Internet: Feminist and Queer Counterpublics in Latin America.* Oakland: University of California Press, 2017.

Frost, Robert L. "Labor and Technological Innovation in French Electrical Power." *Technology and Culture* 29, no. 4 (1988): 865–87.

Furman, Phyllis. "Look Out Below—Platform Shoes Return." *Crain's New York Business* 8–17–2 (1992): 2.

Galison, Peter. "The Future of Scenarios: State Science Fiction." In *The Subject of Rosi Braidotti: Politics and Concepts*, edited by Bolette Blaagaard and Iris van der Tuin, 38–46. New York: Bloomsbury Academic, 2014.

Gardey, Delphine. "Culture of Gender, Culture of Technology: The Gendering of Things in France's Office Spaces between 1890 and 1930." In *Cultures of Technology*, edited by Helga Nowotny. New York: Berghan, 2006.

Garrison, Dee. "The Tender Technicians: The Feminization of Public Librarianship." *Journal of Social History* 6, no. 2 (1972–73): 131–59.

Genosko, Gary, ed. *Marshall McLuhan: Critical Evaluations in Cultural Theory*. New York: Routledge, 2005.

Gill, Rosalind. "Postfeminist Media Culture: Elements of a Sensibility." *European Journal of Cultural Studies* 10, no. 2 (May 2007): 147–66.

Gillespie, Tarleton. "The Politics of 'Platforms.'" *New Media and Society* 12, no. 3 (May 2010): 347–64.

Gilroy, Paul. *The Black Atlantic: Modernity and Double-Consciousness*. Cambridge, MA: Harvard University Press, 1993.

Ging, Deborah. "Alphas, Betas, and Incels: Theorizing the Masculinities of the Manosphere." *Men and Masculinities*, May 10, 2017.

Gitelman, Lisa. *Paper Knowledge: Toward a Media History of Documents*. Durham, NC: Duke University Press, 2014.

Gitelman, Lisa. *Scripts, Grooves, and Writing Machines: Representing Technology in the Edison Era*. Stanford, CA: Stanford University Press, 1999.

Goodman, David. "Amazon Pulls Out of Planned New York City Headquarters." *New York Times*, February 14, 2019. https://www.nytimes.com/2019/02/14/nyregion/amazon-hq2-queens.html.

Graham, Stephen. *Disrupted Cities: When Infrastructures Fail*. New York: Routledge, 2010.

Grande, Sandy. "Whitestream Feminism and the Colonialist Project: A Review of Contemporary Feminist Pedagogy and Praxis." *Educational Theory* 53 (2003): 329–46.

Greene, Gina. "The 'Cradle of Glass': Incubators for Infants in Late Nineteenth-Century France." *Journal of Women's History* 22, no. 4 (2010): 64–89.

Greene, Shane. "Getting over the Andes: The Geo-Eco-Politics of Indigenous Movements in Peru's Twenty-First Century Inca Empire." *Journal of Latin American Studies* 38, no. 2 (2006): 327–54.

Gregg, Melissa. *Counterproductive: Time Management in the Knowledge Economy*. Durham, NC: Duke University Press, 2018.

Gregg, Melissa, and Tamara Kneese. "Clock." In *The Oxford Handbook of Media, Technology and Organizational Studies*, edited by Timon Beyes, Robin Holt, and Claus Pias. New York: Oxford University Press, 2019.

Gross, Terry. "Pandemic Makes Evident 'Grotesque' Gender Inequality in Household Work." *Fresh Air*, NPR, May 21, 2020. https://www.npr.org/2020/05

/21/860091230/pandemic-makes-evident-grotesque-gender-inequality-in-household-work.

Guariglia, Matthew. "Amazon's Ring Is a Perfect Storm of Privacy Threats." *Electronic Frontier Foundation*, August 8, 2019. https://www.eff.org/deeplinks/2019/08/amazons-ring-perfect-storm-privacy-threats.

Guins, Raiford. "Themed Issue: Marshall McLuhan's Understanding Media: The Extensions of Man @ 50." *Journal of Visual Culture* 13, no. 1 (2014).

Hall, Rachel. *The Transparent Traveler: The Performance and Culture of Airport Security*. Durham, NC: Duke University Press, 2015.

Hamilton, Matt. "Protesters with Black Lives Matter Shut Down 405 Freeway in Inglewood." *Los Angeles Times*, July 10, 2016. https://www.latimes.com/local/lanow/la-me-ln-protest-inglewood-20160710-snap-story.html.

Hamilton, Patricia. "The 'Good' Attached Mother: An Analysis of Postmaternal and Postracial Thinking in Birth and Breastfeeding Policy in Neoliberal Britain." *Australian Feminist Studies* 31, no. 90 (2016): 410–31.

Hamraie, Aimi. *Building Access: Universal Design and the Politics of Disability*. Minneapolis: University of Minnesota Press, 2017.

Hanke, Bob. "McLuhan, Virilio and Electric Speed in the Age of Digital Reproduction." In *Marshall McLuhan: Critical Evaluations in Cultural Theory*, vol. 3, edited by Gary Genosko, 121–56. New York: Routledge, 2005.

Haraway, Donna. *Simians, Cyborgs, and Women: The Reinvention of Nature*. New York: Routledge, 1991.

Hartman Strom, Sharon. *Beyond the Typewriter: Gender, Class, and the Origins of Modern American Office Work, 1900–1930*. Urbana: University of Illinois Press, 1992.

Harvey, Alison. *Gender, Age, and Digital Games in the Domestic Context*. New York: Routledge, 2015.

Hayden, Dolores. "What Would a Nonsexist City Be Like? Speculations on Housing, Urban Design, and Human Work." In *Gender and Planning: A Reader*, edited by Susan S. Fainstein and Lisa Servon, 47–64. New Brunswick, NJ: Rutgers University Press, 2005.

Heide, Lars. *Punch-Card Systems and the Early Information Explosion*. Baltimore, MD: Johns Hopkins University Press, 2009.

Henkin, David. *City Reading: Written Words and Public Spaces in Antebellum New York*. Chicago: University of Chicago Press, 2000.

Hessen, Ankete. *The World in a Box: The Story of an Eighteenth-Century Picture Encyclopedia*. Chicago: University of Chicago Press, 2002.

Hester, Helen. *Xenofeminism*. Cambridge, UK: Polity Press, 2018.

Hicks, Mar. "A Feature, Not a Bug." *Technology Stories*, December 4, 2017. http://www.technologystories.org/a-feature-not-a-bug/.

Hicks, Mar. *Programmed Inequality: How Britain Discarded Women Technologists and Lost Its Edge in Computing*. Cambridge, MA: MIT Press, 2017.

Hill, Frances. *The Salem Witch Trials Reader*. Boston: Da Capo, 1996.

Hird, Myra. "The DEW Line and Canada's Arctic Waste: Legacy and Futurity." *Northern Review* 42 (2016): 23–45. https://doi.org/10.22584/nr42.2016.003.

Hobart, Julia Hi'ilei Kawehipuaakahaopulan, and Tamara Kneese. "Radical Care: Survival Strategies for Uncertain Times." *Social Text* 38, no. 1, 142 (2020): 1–16.

Hochman, Brian. *Savage Preservation: The Ethnographic Origins of Media Technology*. Minneapolis: University of Minnesota Press, 2014.

Hochschild, Arlie Russell. *The Second Shift: Working Parents and the Revolution at Home*. New York: Viking, 1989.

Hoff, Timothy. "Deskilling and Adaptation among Primary Care Physicians Using Two Work Innovations." *Health Care Management Review* 36, no. 4 (2011): 338–48.

Hui, Yuk. *The Question Concerning Technology in China: An Essay in Cosmotechnics*. Cambridge, MA: MIT Press, 2016.

Huws, Ursula. "The Reproduction of Difference: Gender and the Global Division of Labour." *Work Organisation, Labour and Globalisation* 6, no. 1 (2012): 1–10.

Impressions. "The Filing Cabinet." *Steel Filings*, June 1918, 15.

Innis, Harold Adams. *The Bias of Communication*. 1951. Reprint, Toronto: University of Toronto Press, 2008.

Innis, Harold Adams. *Empire and Communications*. Oxford: Clarendon, 1950.

Jacobs, Jane. *The Death and Life of Great American Cities*. New York: Vintage, 1961.

James, Selma. "Women's Unwaged Work: The Heart of the Informal Sector." *Women: A Cultural Review* 2, no. 3 (1991): 267–71.

Jameson, Fredric. "Future City." *New Left Review* 21 (2003): 65–80.

Jecale, Ingrid, and Lee Parker. "The 'Problem' of the Office: Scientific Management, Governmentality, and the Strategy of Efficiency." *Business History* 55, no. 7 (2013): 1074–99.

Jhally, Sut. "Communications and the Materialist Conception of History." *Continuum* 7, no. 1 (1993): 161–82.

Jones-Rogers, Stephanie. *They Were Her Property: White Women as Slave Owners in the American South*. New Haven, CT: Yale University Press, 2019.

Jordanova, Ludmilla. *Sexual Vision*. London: Macmillan, 1989.

Keightley, Keir. "'Turn It Down' She Shrieked: Gender, Domestic Space, and High Fidelity, 1948–1959." *Popular Music* 15, no. 2 (1996): 149–77.

Kelly, Kevin. "One Dead Media." *The Technium*, June 18, 2008. http://kk.org/thetechnium/one-dead-media/.

Keyes, Os. "The Misgendering Machines: Trans/HCI Implications of Automatic Gender Recognition." *Proceedings of the ACM on Human-Computer Interaction* 2, issue CSCW (2018).

Kim, Annette. *Sidewalk City: Remapping Public Space in Ho Chi Minh City*. Chicago: University of Chicago Press, 2015.

Kin, Elizabeth. "NYC Agrees to Make All Sidewalk Curbs Accessible to the Disabled." *Gothamist*, March 21, 2019. https://gothamist.com/news/nyc-agrees-to-make-all-sidewalk-curbs-accessible-to-the-disabled.

Kite-Powell, Jennifer. "Are Curbs the Next Frontier in Urban Mobility?" *Forbes*, April 29, 2019. https://www.forbes.com/sites/jenniferhicks/2019/04/29/are-curbs-the-next-frontier-in-urban-mobility/.

Kittler, Friedrich. *Discourse Networks: 1800/1900*. Stanford, CA: Stanford University Press, 1990.

Kittler, Friedrich. *Optical Media*. Cambridge, UK: Polity Press, 2010.

Krajewski, Markus. *Paper Machines: About Cards and Catalogs, 1548–1929*. Cambridge, MA: MIT Press, 2011.

Kramer, John Theophilus. *The Slave Auction*. Boston: R. F. Wallcut, 1859.

Kramer, Michael R., and Carol R. Hogue. "What Causes Racial Disparities in Very Preterm Birth? A Biosocial Perspective." *Epidemiologic Reviews* 31, no. 1 (2009): 84–98.

Krämer, Sybille. "The Cultural Techniques of Time Axis Manipulation: On Friedrich Kittler's Conception of Media." *Theory, Culture and Society* 23, no. 7–8 (2006): 93–109.

Krämer, Sybille. *Medium, Messenger, Transmission: An Approach to Media Philosophy*. Translated by Anthony Enns. Amsterdam: Amsterdam University Press, 2016.

Kroker, Arthur. *Technology and the Canadian Mind: Innis, McLuhan*. Montreal: Grant New World Perspective, 1984.

Kwolek-Folland, Angel. *Engendering Business: Men and Women in the Corporate Office, 1870–1930*. Baltimore, MD: Johns Hopkins University Press, 1994.

Lantos, John D., and William L. Meadow. *Neonatal Bioethics: The Moral Challenges of Medical Innovation*. Baltimore, MD: Johns Hopkins University Press, 2006.

Latour, Bruno. "Technology Is Society Made Durable." *Sociological Review* 38, no. 1 (May 1990): 103–31.

Laurence, Peter L. *Becoming Jane Jacobs*. Philadelphia: University of Pennsylvania Press, 2019.

Law, John. "Introduction: Monsters, Machines and Sociotechnical Relations." *Sociological Review* 38, no. 1 (May 1990): 1–23.

Layne, Linda L. "'He Was a Real Baby with Baby Things': A Material Culture Analysis of Personhood, Parenthood and Pregnancy Loss." *Journal of Material Culture* 5, no. 3 (2000): 321–45.

Le Corbusier. *Toward an Architecture*. Los Angeles: Getty Research Institute Publication Program, 1927.

Leffingwell, William Henry. *Office Management: Principles and Practice*. Chicago: A.W. Shaw, 1925.

Levack, Brian P. *Witchcraft, Women and Society*. New York: Garland, 1992.

Levinson, Paul. *Digital McLuhan: A Guide to the Information Millennium*. New York: Routledge, 1999.

Lewis, Sophie. "Cyborg Uterine Geography: Complicating 'Care' and Social Reproduction." *Dialogues in Human Geography* 8, no. 3 (2018): 300–316.
Lewis, Sophie. *Full Surrogacy Now: Feminism against Family*. New York: Verso, 2019.
Lewis, Sophie. "Mothering." Forum, *Boston Review* 7, no. 43 (2018).
Lewis, Sophie. "Wages for Womb-Work, Polymaternalism, Critical Firestonianism." *E-flux*, November 6, 2019. https://www.e-flux.com/program/297764/e-flux-lectures-sophie-lewis-wages-for-womb-work-polymaternalism-critical-firestonianism/.
Library Bureau. *Filing as Profession for Women*. Boston: Library Bureau, n.d.
Light, Jennifer. "When Computers Were Women." *Technology and Culture* 40, no. 3 (1999): 455–83.
Liu, Alan. *The Laws of Cool: Knowledge Work and Culture*. Chicago: University of Chicago Press, 2004.
Liu, Alan. "Transcendental Data: Toward a Cultural History and Aesthetics of the New Encoded Discourse." *Critical Inquiry* 31, no. 1 (2004): 49–84.
Logan, Robert. *Understanding New Media: Extending Marshall McLuhan*. New York: Peter Lang, 2010.
Lorinc, John. "A Mess on the Sidewalk." *The Baffler* 44 (March 2019). https://thebaffler.com/salvos/a-mess-on-the-sidewalk-lorinc.
Loukaitou-Sideris, Anastasia, and Renia Ehrenfeucht. *Sidewalks: Conflict and Negotiation over Public Space*. Cambridge, MA: MIT Press, 2009.
Lupton, Ellen. *Mechanical Brides: Women and Machines from Home to Office*. New York: Cooper Hewitt National Museum of Design, Smithsonian Institute, and Princeton Architectural Press, 1993.
Mackenzie, Adrian. *Wirelessness: Radical Empiricism in Networked Cultures*. Cambridge, MA: MIT Press, 2019.
Marchessault, Janine. *Marshall McLuhan: Cosmic Media*. London: Sage, 2005.
Marchessault, Janine. "Mechanical Brides and Mama's Boys: Gender and Technology in Early McLuhan." In *Marshall McLuhan: Critical Evaluations in Cultural Theory*, vol. 3, edited by Gary Genosko, 161–80. New York: Routledge, 2005.
Marvin, Carolyn. *When Old Technologies Were New: Thinking about Electric Communication in the Late Nineteenth Century*. New York: Oxford University Press, 1988.
Mattern, Shannon. "'Cabinet Logic': A History, Critique and Consultation on Media Furniture." IKKM talk, Bauhaus University, Weimar, Germany, January 20, 2016.
Mattern, Shannon. "A City Is Not a Computer." *Places Journal*, February 2017. https://placesjournal.org/article/a-city-is-not-a-computer/.
Mattern, Shannon. *Code and Clay, Data and Dirt: 5000 Years of Urban Media*. Minneapolis: University of Minnesota Press, 2017.
Mattern, Shannon. "Intellectual Furnishing: The Physical and Conceptual Architectures of Our Knowledge Institutions." *WordsinSpace*, February 2014. https://wordsinspace.net/shannon/2014/02/26/7542/.

Mattern, Shannon. "Mapping's Intelligent Agents." *Places Journal*, September 2017. https://placesjournal.org/article/mappings-intelligent-agents/.

Mattern, Shannon. "Small, Moving, Intelligent Parts." *WordsinSpace*, June 28, 2016.

Mattern, Shannon. "The Spectacle of Data: A Century of Fairs, Fiches, and Fantasies." *Theory, Culture and Society*, October 2020. https://doi.org/10.1177/0263276420958052.

Maule, Frances. "Women Are So Personal." *Independent Women*, September 1934, 280.

McCord, James N. *A Textbook of Filing*. New York: D. Appleton, 1920.

McCutcheon, Mark. *The Medium Is the Monster: Canadian Adaptations of Frankenstein and the Discourse of Technology*. Calgary, AB: Athabasca University Press, 2018.

McDowall, Elizabeth King. "The Requisites of a Good File Clerk." *Filing*, March 1921, 760.

McGaw, Judith A. *Most Wonderful Machine: Mechanization and Social Change in Berkshire Paper Making, 1801–1885*. Princeton, NJ: Princeton University Press, 1987.

McKittrick, Katherine. *Demonic Grounds: Black Women and the Cartographies of Struggle*. Durham, NC: Duke University Press, 2006.

McKittrick, Katherine. "Freedom Is a Secret." In *Black Geographies and the Politics of Place*, edited by Katherine McKittrick and Clyde Woods, 97–114. Toronto: Between the Lines, 2007.

McKittrick, Katherine. "Mathematics Black Life." *Black Scholar* 42, no. 2 (2014): 16–28.

McKittrick, Katherine. "Plantation Futures." *Small Axe: A Caribbean Journal of Criticism* 17, no. 3-42 (2013): 1–15.

McLeod Rogers, Jaqueline. "City as Techno-human Sensorium: McLuhan, Tyrwhitt and Jacobs." Talk presented at For Whom the Media Matters, Toronto, 2018.

McLeod Rogers, Jaqueline. *McLuhan's Techno-sensorium City: Coming to Our Senses in a Programmed Environment*. Lanham, MD: Lexington, 2020.

McLeod Rogers, Jaqueline, Tracey Whalen, and Catherine G. Taylor. *Finding McLuhan: The Mind, the Man, the Message*. Regina, MB: University of Regina Press, 2015.

McLuhan, Eric, and Marshall McLuhan. *Theories of Communication*. New York: Peter Lang, 2005.

McLuhan, Eric, and Peter Zhang. "The DEW Line Card Deck as a Metagame: A Review of General Semantics." *Et Cetera* 72, no. 3 (2015).

McLuhan, Marshall. "Education in the Electronic Age." *Interchange* 1, (1970): 1–12. https://doi.org/10.1007/BF02214876.

McLuhan, Marshall. *The Gutenberg Galaxy: The Making of Typographic Man*. Toronto: University of Toronto Press, 1962.

McLuhan, Marshall. *The Mechanical Bride: Folklore of the Industrial Man*. Berkeley, CA: Gingko, 1951.

McLuhan, Marshall. *Understanding Media: The Extensions of Man*. 1964. Reprint, Cambridge, MA: MIT Press, 1994.

McLuhan, Marshall. *Understanding Media: The Extensions of Man*. Berkeley, CA: Gingko Press, 2003.

McLuhan, Marshall. *Understanding Media: The Extensions of Man*. Oxford, UK: Taylor and Francis, 2001.

McShane, Clay. "Transforming the Use of Urban Space: A Look at the Revolution in Street Pavements, 1880–1924." *Journal of Urban History* 5, no. 3 (1979): 279–307.

Mika, Anna, Lukasz Oleksy, Renata Kielnar, and Marta Swierczek. "The Influence of High and Low-Heeled Shoes on Balance in Young Women." *Acta of Bioengineering and Biomechanics* 18, no. 3 (2016): 97–103.

Miller, Tyrus. "Rethinking the Digital Hand." *Crosspollenblog*, October 18, 2013. https://crosspollenblog.wordpress.com/2013/10/18/rethinking-the-digital-hand/.

Mitchell, Lisa. *Baby's First Picture: Ultrasound and the Politics of Fetal Subjects*. Toronto: University of Toronto Press, 2001.

Mock, Brentin. "The Toxic Intersection of Racism and Public Space." *CityLab*, May 26, 2020. https://www.bloomberg.com/news/articles/2020-05-26/amy-cooper-exposes-green-space-s-race-problem.

Mulvin, Dylan. *Proxies: The Cultural Work of Standing In*. Cambridge, MA: MIT Press, 2021.

Mulvin, Dylan. "Media Prophylaxis: Night Modes and the Politics of Preventing Harm." *Information and Culture: A Journal of History* 53, no. 2 (2018): 175–202.

Mumford, Lewis. "An Appraisal of Lewis Mumford's 'Technics and Civilization' (1934)." *Daedalus* 88, no. 3 (1959): 527–36.

Nadel, Alan. *Containment Culture: American Narratives, Postmodernism, and the Atomic Age*. Durham, NC: Duke University Press, 1995.

Nakamura, Lisa. "Indigenous Circuits: Navajo Women and the Racialization of Early Electronic Manufacture." *American Quarterly* 66, no. 4 (2014): 919–41.

Nakata, Martin. "Indigenous Knowledge and the Cultural Interface: Underlying Issues at the Intersection of Knowledge and Information Systems." *IFLA Journal* 28, no. 5–6 (October 2002): 281–91.

Newman, Karen. *Fetal Positions: Individualism, Science, Visuality*. Stanford, CA: Stanford University Press, 1996.

Ng, Willa. "Four Principles for the Future of City Streets." *Sidewalk Talk*, April 26, 2019. https://medium.com/sidewalk-talk/street-design-principles-fe35106e0f92.

Ng, Willa. "The Importance of Coding the Curb." *Sidewalk Labs*, August 22, 2016. https://www.sidewalklabs.com/blog/the-importance-of-coding-the-curb/.

Noble, Safiya Umoja. *Algorithms of Oppression: How Search Engines Reinforce Racism*. New York: New York University Press, 2018.

Noble, Safiya U., and Brendesha Tynes. *The Intersectional Internet: Race, Sex, and Culture Online.* New York: Peter Lang, 2016.

Nolan, Lucas. "Milo: Even If You're Acquitted of Rape, Feminists Can Still Ruin Your Life." *Breitbart*, October, 7, 2016. https://www.breitbart.com/milo/2016/10/07/milo-even-if-youre-acquitted-of-rape-feminists-can-still-ruin-your-life/.

Noori, Maragaret. "Waasechibiiwaabikoonsing Nd'anami'aami, 'Praying through a Wired Window': Using Technology to Teach Anishinaabemowin." *Studies in American Indian Literatures* 23, no. 2 (2011): 3–24. https://doi.org/10.5250/studamerindilite.23.2.0003.

Nunberg, Geoffrey. "Farewell to the Information Age." In *The Future of the Book*, edited by Geoffrey Nunberg, 103–33. Berkeley: University of California Press, 1996.

Odland, Claire, and Nancy Feldman. "Shipibo Textile Practices 1952–2010." Presented at "Textiles and Settlement: From Plains Space to Cyber Space," Textile Society of America 12th Biennial Symposium, Lincoln, Nebraska, October 6–9, 2010. http://digitalcommons.unl.edu/tsaconf/42/.

Oldenziel, Ruth. *Making Technology Masculine: Men, Women, and Modern Machines in America, 1870–1945.* Amsterdam: Amsterdam University Press, 1999.

Olwell, Victoria. "The Body Types: Corporeal Documents and Body Politics, circa 1900." In *Literary Secretaries/Secretarial Culture*, edited by Leah Price and Pamela Thurschwell, 50. Aldershot, UK: Ashgate, 2005.

Packer, Jeremy. *Mobility without Mayhem: Safety, Cars, and Citizenship.* Durham, NC: Duke University Press, 2008.

Packer, Jeremy. "Rethinking Dependency: New Relations of Transportation and Communication." In *Thinking with James Carey: Essays on Communications, Transportation, History*, edited by Jeremy Packer and Craig Robertson, 79–100. New York: Peter Lang, 2006.

Palmquist, Aunchalee, Sarah M. Holdren, and Cynthia D. Fair. "'It Was All Taken Away': Lactation, Embodiment, and Resistance among Mothers Caring for Their Very-Low-Birth-Weight Infants in the Neonatal Intensive Care Unit." *Social Science and Medicine* 244 (2020): 1–8.

Parikka, Jussi. *A Geology of Media.* Minneapolis: University of Minnesota Press, 2015.

Parker, Brenda. "Gender, Cities, and Planning." In *The Oxford Handbook of Urban Planning*, edited by Rachel Weber and Randall Crane. Oxford: Oxford University Press, 2012.

Parks, Lisa. *Cultures in Orbit.* Durham, NC: Duke University Press, 2003.

Parks, Lisa. *Rethinking Media Coverage: Vertical Mediation and the War on Terror.* New York: Routledge, 2018.

Parks, Lisa, and Nicole Starosielski. *Signal Traffic: Critical Studies of Media Infrastructures.* Champaign: University of Illinois Press, 2015.

Patterson, Orlando. *Freedom.* New York: Basic Books, 1991.

Peiss, Kathy. *Hope in a Jar: The Making of America's Beauty Culture*. Philadelphia: University of Pennsylvania Press, 2011.

Petchesky, Rosalind. "Fetal Images: The Power of Visual Culture in the Politics of Reproduction." *Feminist Studies* 13, no. 2 (1987): 263–92.

Peters, Benjamin. *How Not to Network a Nation: The Uneasy History of the Soviet Internet*. Cambridge, MA: MIT Press, 2016.

Peters, John Durham. *The Marvelous Clouds: Toward a Philosophy of Elemental Media*. Chicago: University of Chicago Press, 2015.

Peters, John Durham. "McLuhan's Grammatical Theology." *Canadian Journal of Communication* 36 (2011): 227–42.

Peters, John Durham. "Proliferation and Obsolescence of the Historical Record in the Digital Era." In *Cultures of Obsolescence: History, Materiality, and the Digital Age*, edited by Babette Tischleder and Sarah Waserman. London: Palgrave, 2015.

Peters, John Durham. "Reading over McLuhan's Shoulder." *Canadian Journal of Communication* 44, no. 4 (2019): 489–501.

Peters, John Durham. "Technology and Ideology: The Case of the Telegraph Revisited." In *Thinking with James Carey: Essays on Communications, Transportation, History*, edited by Jeremy Packer and Craig Robertson, 137–56. New York: Peter Lang, 2006.

Plotnick, Rachel. *Power Button: A History of Pleasure, Panic, and the Politics of Pushing*. Cambridge, MA: MIT Press, 2018.

Preciado, Paul B. *Pornotopia: An Essay on Playboy's Architecture and Biopolitics*. Cambridge, MA: MIT Press, 2014.

Prescod-Roberts, Margaret. *Black Women: Bringing It All Back Home*. Glouster, UK: Falling Wall, 1980.

Quinn, Zoe. *Crash Override: How Gamergate (Nearly) Destroyed My Life and How We Can Win the Fight against Online Hate*. New York: Perseus, 2017.

Raffel, Dawn. *The Strange Case of Dr. Couney: How a Mysterious European Showman Saved Thousands of American Babies*. New York: Blue Rider, 2018.

RAND. *Specifications for the RAND Abstract and Index System*. Santa Monica, CA: RAND Computation Center, 1975.

Randolph, Peter. *Sketches of Slave Life; and From Slave Cabin to the Pulpit*. Edited by Katherine Clay Bassard. Morgantown: West Virginia University Press, 2016.

Reedy, Elizabeth A. "Historical Perspectives: Infant Incubators Turned 'Weaklings' into 'Fighters.'" *American Journal of Nursing* 103, no. 9 (2003): 64AA.

Rhee, Jennifer. *The Robotic Imaginary: The Hum and the Price of Dehumanized Labor*. Minneapolis: University of Minnesota Press, 2018.

Roberts, John. *The Intangibilities of Form: Skill and Deskilling in Art after the Readymade*. London: Verso, 1997.

Robertson, Craig. *The Filing Cabinet: A Vertical History of Information*. Minneapolis: University of Minnesota Press, 2021.

Robertson, Craig. "Granular Certainty, the Vertical Filing Cabinet, and the Transformation of Files." *Administory: Journal of the History of Public Administration* 4 (2020).

Robertson, Craig. "Learning to File: Reconfiguring Information and Information Work in the Early Twentieth Century." *Technology and Culture* 58, no. 3 (2017): 965–75.

Rodino-Colocino, Michelle, Laruen J. DeCarvalho, and Aaron Heresco. "Neo-orthodox Masculinities on *Man Caves*." *Television and New Media* 19, no. 7 (2018): 626–45.

Rolin, Kristina. "Is 'Science as Social' a Feminist Insight?" *Social Epistemology* 16, no. 3 (2002): 233–49.

Romanis, Elizabeth Chloe. "Artificial Womb Technology and the Frontiers of Human Reproduction: Conceptual Differences and Potential Implications." *Journal of Medical Ethics* 44 (2018): 751–55.

Rosner, Daniela K. *Critical Fabulations: Reworking the Methods and Margins of Design*. Cambridge, MA: MIT Press, 2018.

Rottenberg, Catherine. *The Rise of Neoliberal Feminism*. Oxford: Oxford University Press, 2018.

Russill, Chris. "Is the Earth a Medium?—Situating the Planetary in Media Theory." *Ctrl-Z: New Media Philosophy*, no. 7 (2017). http://www.ctrl-z.net.au/articles/issue-7/russill-is-the-earth-a-medium/.

Salter, Anastasia, and Bridget Blodgett. *Toxic Geek Masculinity in Media*. New York: Palgrave Macmillan, 2017.

Santos, Boaventura de Sousa. *The End of the Cognitive Empire: The Coming of Age of Epistemologies of the South*. Durham, NC: Duke University Press, 2018.

Schrader, Stuart. "Reading Jane Jacobs in the Era of #BlackLivesMatter." *Harvard Design Magazine*, no. 42 (2016). http://www.harvarddesignmagazine.org/issues/42/reading-jane-jacobs-in-the-era-of-blacklivesmatter.

Schwartz, Ruth Cowan. *More Work for Mother: The Ironies of Household Technology from the Open Hearth to the Microwave*. New York: Basic Books, 1983.

Scott, Linda. "Critical Approaches to Advertising: What Is Still Valid." *Advertising and Society* 17, no. 1–2 (2016).

Sennett, Richard. *The Craftsman*. New Haven, CT: Yale University Press, 2008.

Shade, Leslie R., and Barbara Crow. "Canadian Feminist Perspectives on Digital Technology." *TOPIA* 11 (spring 2004): 161–76.

Shannon, Claude E., and Warren Weaver. *The Mathematical Theory of Communication*. Urbana: University of Illinois Press, 1949.

Sharma, Sarah. "Exit and the Extensions of Man." *Transmediale*, August 5, 2017. https://transmediale.de/content/exit-and-the-extensions-of-man.

Sharma, Sarah. "Going to Work in Mommy's Basement." *Boston Review, Once and Future Feminist*, June 9, 2018, 86–94.

Sharma, Sarah. *In the Meantime: Temporality and Cultural Politics*. Durham, NC: Duke University Press, 2014.

Sharma, Sarah. "It Changes Space and Time! Introducing Power-Chronography." In *Communication Matters: Materialist Approaches to Media, Mobility and Networks*, edited by Jeremy Packer and Stephen Wiley. London: Routledge, 2012.

Sharma, Sarah. "A Manifesto for the Broken Machine." *Camera Obscura* 34, no. 2.104 (2020): 171–79.

Sharma, Sarah. "Many McLuhans or None at All." *Canadian Journal of Communication* 44, no. 4 (2019): 483–88.

Sharma, Sarah, and Armond Towns. "Ceasing Fire and Seizing Time: LA Gang Tours and the White Control of Mobility." *Transfers* 6, no. 1 (2016): 26–44.

Sheller, Mimi, and John Urry. "The New Mobilities Paradigm." *Environment and Planning A* 38 (2006): 207–26.

Shipbo Shamans. *Woven Songs of the Amazon: Songs of the Amazon; Healing Icaros of the Shipibo Shamans*. Fast Horse, 2006, compact disc.

Sidewalk Labs. "Street Design Principles v.1." https://eukalypton.com/en/2019/04/30/street-design-principles-v-1/.

Silverman, William A. "Incubator-Baby Side Shows." *Pediatrics* 64, no. 2 (1979): 127–41.

Simon, Bart. "Geek Chic: Machine Aesthetics, Digital Gaming, and the Cultural Politics of the Case Mod." *Games and Culture* 2, no. 3 (2007): 175–93.

Slack, Jennifer Daryl, and J. Macgregor Wise. *Culture and Technology: A Primer*. New York: Peter Lang, 2005.

Small, Andrew, and Laura Bliss. "The Race to Code the Curb." *City Lab*, April 2, 2019. https://www.citylab.com/transportation/2019/04/smart-cities-maps-curb-data-coord-sidewalk-tech-street-design/586177/.

Small, Takara. "How Smart Home Systems and Tech Have Created a New Form of Abuse." *Refinery29*, January 9, 2019. https://www.refinery29.com/en-ca/2019/01/220847/domestic-abuse-violence-harassment-smart-home-monitoring.

Smallwood, Stephanie E. *Saltwater Slavery*. Cambridge, MA: Harvard University Press, 2008.

Smith, Noah. "The Giants of the Video Game Industry Have Thrived in the Pandemic. Can the Success Continue?" *Washington Post*, May 12, 2020. https://www.washingtonpost.com/video-games/2020/05/12/video-game-industry-coronavirus/.

Smith-Windsor, Jaimie. "The Cyborg Mother: A Breached Boundary." *Ctheory.net*, April 2004. https://journals.uvic.ca/index.php/ctheory/article/view/14547.

Smyth, Stephen. "Open Curbs: The First Open Data, Multi-city Platform to Unlock Curbs." *Coord*, April 2, 2019. https://www.coord.co/post/open-curbs-the-first-open-data-multi-city-platform-to-unlock-curbs.

Sofia, Zoë. "Container Technologies." *Hypatia* 15, no. 2 (2000): 181–201.

Spencer, Susette A. "Henry Box Brown, an International Fugitive: Slavery, Resistance, and Imperialism." In *Black Geographies and the Politics of Place*, edited by Katherine McKittrick and Clyde Woods, 115–36. Toronto: Between the Lines, 2007.

Spigel, Lynn. "Designing the Smart House: Posthuman Domesticity and Conspicuous Production." *European Journal of Cultural Studies* 8, no. 4 (2005): 403–26.

Spigel, Lynn. *Make Room for TV: Television and the Family Ideal in Postwar America*. Chicago: University of Chicago Press, 1992.

Spillers, Hortense. *Black, White, and in Color: Essays on American Literature and Culture*. Chicago: University of Chicago Press, 2003.

Spivak, Gayatri Chakravorty. "Echo." *New Literary House* 24, no. 1 (1993): 17–43.

Stamps, Judith. *Unthinking Modernity: Innis, McLuhan, and the Frankfurt School*. Montreal: McGill-Queen's University Press, 2001.

Starosielski, Nicole. *The Undersea Network*. Durham, NC: Duke University Press, 2015.

St. Charles Manufacturing Co. *Your Kitchen and You*. New York: St. Charles Kitchens, 1950.

Sterne, Jonathan. "The mp3 as Cultural Artifact." *New Media and Society* 8, no. 5 (2006): 825–42.

Sterne, Jonathan. "The Theology of Sound: A Critique of Orality." *Canadian Journal of Communication* 36, no. 2 (2011): 207–25.

Sterne, Jonathan. "Transportation and Communication: Together as You've Always Wanted Them." In *Thinking with James Carey: Essays on Communications, Transportation, History*, edited by Jeremy Packer and Craig Robertson, 117–36. New York: Peter Lang, 2006.

Stover, Lauren. "Make Them Fit, Please!" *New York Times*, April 22, 2014. https://www.nytimes.com/2014/04/24/fashion/foot-surgeries-so-women-can-wear-designer-shoes-in-comfort.html.

Strasser, Susan. *Never Done: A History of American Housework*. New York: Macmillan, 2000.

Strate, Lance, and Edward Wachtel. *The Legacy of McLuhan*. Cresskill, NJ: Hampton, 2005.

Sturman, Susan. "On Black-Boxing Gender: Some Social Questions for Bruno Latour." *Social Epistemology* 20, no. 2 (2006): 181–84.

Tanaka, Yuko. *The Power of the Weave: The Hidden Meanings of Cloth*. Tokyo: International House of Japan, 2013.

Taylor, Astra. *The People's Platform: Taking Back Power and Culture in the Digital Age*. New York: Metropolitan, 2014.

Taylor, Nicholas, and Gerald Voorhees, eds. *Masculinities in Play*. New York: Palgrave Macmillan, 2018.

Taylor, T. L. *Watch Me Play: Twitch and the Rise of Game Live Streaming*. Princeton, NJ: Princeton University Press, 2018.

The Last Whole Earth Catalog. Menlo Park, CA: Portola Institute, 1971.

Theall, Donald. *The Virtual Marshall McLuhan*. Montreal: McGill-Queen's University Press, 2001.

Thomas, Destiny. "'Safe Streets' Are Not Safe for Black Lives." *CityLab*, June 8, 2020. https://www.bloomberg.com/news/articles/2020-06-08/-safe-streets-are-not-safe-for-black-lives.

Tobin, Sam. *Portable Play in Everyday Life: The Nintendo DS*. New York: Palgrave, 2013.

Tollefson, Hannah, and Darrin Barney. "More Liquid Than Liquid: Solid-Phase Bitumen and Its Forms." *Grey Room* 77 (2019): 38–57.

Towns, Armond. "The (Black) Elephant in the Room: McLuhan and the Racial." *Canadian Journal of Communication* 44, no. 4 (2019): 545–54.

Towns, Armond. "Black 'Matter' Lives." *Women's Studies in Communication* 41, no. 4 (2018): 349–58.

Towns, Armond. "The 'Lumpenproletariat's Redemption': Black Radical Potentiality and LA Gang Tours." *Souls* 19, no. 1 (2017): 39–58.

Towns, Armond. "Rebels of the Underground: Media, Orality, and the Routes of Black Emancipation." *Communication and Critical/Cultural Studies* 13, no. 2 (2016): 184–97.

Towns, Armond. "Toward a Black Media Philosophy." *Cultural Studies* 34, no. 6 (2020): 851–73.

Turner, Fred. *From Counterculture to Cyberculture*. Chicago: University of Chicago Press, 2006.

Ullman, Ellen. *Life in Code: A Personal History of Technology*. New York: Farrar, Straus and Giroux, 2017.

van Dooren, Thom. *The Wake of Crows*. New York: Columbia University Press, 2019.

Van Dijck, José, and Thomas Poell. "Understanding Social Media Logic." *Media and Communication* 1, no. 1 (2013): 2–14.

Vincent, Susan. "Preserving Domesticity: Reading Tupperware in Women's Changing Domestic, Social and Economic Roles." *Canadian Review of Sociology* 40, no. 3 (2003): 171–96.

Virilio, Paul. *Ground Zero*. London: Verso, 2002.

Vismann, Cornelia. *Files: Law and Media Technology*. Stanford, CA: Stanford University Press, 2008.

Visvanathan, Shiv. "The Language of Khadi." *India International Centre Quarterly* 30, no. 2 (2011): 24–37.

Viveiro de Castro, Eduardo. "The Relative Native: Essays on Indigenous Conceptual Worlds." *HAU: Journal of Ethnographic Theory* 3, no. 3 (2013): 473–502.

von Oertzen, Christine. "Machineries of Data Power: Manual versus Mechanical Census Compilation in Nineteenth Century Europe." *OSIRIS* 32, no. 1 (2017): 129–50.

Waitoa, Joanne, Regina Scheyvens, and Te Rina Warren. "E-Whanaungatanga: The Role of Social Media in Māori Political Empowerment." *AlterNative: An International Journal of Indigenous Peoples* 11, no. 1 (March 2015): 45–58.

Wajcman, Judy. *Feminism Confronts Technology*. University Park, PA: Penn State Press, 1991.
Wajcman, Judy. *Technofeminism*. Cambridge, UK: Polity, 2004.
Wali, Alaka, J. Claire Odland, Luisa Elvira Belaunde, Nancy Gardner Feldman, Daniel Morales Chocano, Ana Mujica-Baquerizo, and Ronald L. Weber. "The Shipibo-Conibo: Culture and Collections in Context." *Fieldiana Anthropology* 45, no. 1 (November 2016): 1–100.
Walker, Alissa. "The Case against Sidewalks." *Curbed*, February 7, 2018. https://www.curbed.com/2018/2/7/16980682/city-sidewalk-repair-future-walking-neighborhood.
Wallace, Eugenia. *Filing Methods*. New York: Ronald Press, 1924.
Ward, John O. "Witchcraft and Sorcery in the Later Roman Empire and the Early Middle Ages: An Anthropological Comment." In *Witchcraft, Woman and Society*, edited by Brian P. Levack, 117. New York: Garland, 1992.
Ware, Willis H. RAND *and the Information Revolution: A History in Essays and Vignettes*. Santa Monica, CA: RAND Corporation, 2008.
Warner, Harold, and Kenneth Mace. "Effects of Platform Fashion Shoes on Brake Response Time." *Applied Ergonomics* 5, no. 3 (1974): 143.
Watson-Smyth, Kate. "Secret History Of: Tupperware." *The Independent*, October 8, 2010. https://www.independent.co.uk/property/interiors/secret-history-of-tupperware-2100910.html.
Wemigwans, Jennifer. *A Digital Bundle: Protecting and Promoting Indigenous Knowledge*. Regina, AB: University of Regina Press, 2018.
Westrope, Andrew. "Coord Turns Street Photos into Curb Data for Six Cities." *Government Technology*, April 3, 2019. https://www.govtech.com/biz/Coord-Turns-Street-Photos-Into-Curb-Data-for-Six-Cities.html.
Whitehouse, Michael. "Platform Shoe Syndrome." *British Medical Journal* 27 (April 1974): 225.
Whitzman, Carolyn. "Taking Back Planning: Promoting Women's Safety in Public Places—the Toronto Experience." *Journal of Architectural and Planning Research* 9, no. 2 (1992): 169–79.
Wiener, Anna. *Uncanny Valley: A Memoir*. New York: MCD Press, 2020.
Williams, Robin B. Historic Pavement [website], 2016. http://www.historicpavement.com/.
Wilson, Barbara. "The Archive of Eating." *New York Times Magazine*, October 29, 2015. http://www.nytimes.com/2015/11/01/magazine/the-archive-of-eating.html.
Witteborn, Saskia. "The Digital Force in Forced Migration: Imagined Affordances and Gendered Practices." *Popular Communication* 16, no. 1 (2018): 21–31.
Wolfinger, Kirk, dir. *Moonshot: The Inside Story of the Apollo Project*. PBS, 1994.
Wynter, Sylvia. "The Ceremony Must Be Found: After Humanism." *Boundary* 2 12/13 (1984): 19–70.

Yates, JoAnne. *Control through Communication: The Rise of System in American Management*. Baltimore, MD: Johns Hopkins University Press, 1993.

Young, Liam C. "The McLuhan-Innis Field." *Canadian Journal of Communications* 44, no. 4 (2019): 527–44.

Young, Liam C. "Salt, Fragments from the History of a Medium." *Theory, Culture and Society* 37, no. 6 (2020): 135–58.

Zakim, Michael. "Producing Capitalism: The Clerk at Work." In *Capitalism Takes Command*, edited by Michael Zakim and Gary Kornblith, 242–47. Chicago: University of Chicago Press, 2012.

Zandy, Janet. *Hands: Physical Labor, Class, and Cultural Work*. New Brunswick, NJ: Rutgers University Press, 2004.

Žižek, Slavoj. *Welcome to the Desert of the Real*. London: Verso, 2002.

Zuboff, Shoshana. *The Age of Surveillance Capitalism: The Fight for a Human Future at the New Frontier of Power*. New York: Public Affairs, 2019.

Zuboff, Shoshana. *In the Age of the Smart Machine: The Future of Work and Power*. New York: Basic Books, 1988.

Zundel, Mike. "High Heels as a Mediating Technology of Organization." In *The Oxford Handbook of Media, Technology and Organization Studies*, edited by Timon Beyes, Robin Holt, and Claus Pias. Oxford: Oxford University Press, 2019.

Contributors

NASMA AHMED is a technologist and community organizer who works within the intersections of social justice, technology, and policy. She is currently director of the Digital Justice Lab, an organization that focuses on building a more just and equitable digital future. Nasma was the Ford-Mozilla Open Web Fellow in 2017–18, focusing on organizational digital security and building better literacy around privacy with youth.

MOREHSHIN ALLAHYARI is an Iranian media artist, activist, and educator based in Brooklyn, New York. Her work questions current political, sociocultural, and gender norms, with a particular emphasis on exploring the relationship between technology and art activism. Allahyari's artworks include 3D-printed objects, video, experimental animation, web art, and publications. She is most noted for her projects *Material Speculation: ISIS* (2016), 3D-printed sculptural reconstructions of ancient artifacts destroyed by ISIS (2015–16), and *The 3D Additivist Manifesto and Cookbook* (2015–16).

SARAH BANET-WEISER is professor of Media, Gender and Communication at the Annenberg School for Communication at the University of Pennsylvania and the Annenberg School for Communication and Journalism at the University of Southern California. Her research interests include gender in the media, identity, citizenship, and cultural politics, consumer culture and popular media, race and the media, and intersectional feminism. She is the author of *Empowered: Popular Feminism and Popular Misogyny* (Duke University Press, 2018). Banet-Weiser is the recipient of the International Communication Association's Outstanding Book Award for *Authentic™: The Politics of Ambivalence in a Brand Culture* (2012). She is currently working on a book titled *Believability: Gender, Race and the Labor of Being Believed*.

WENDY HUI KYONG CHUN is Simon Fraser University's Canada 150 Research Chair in New Media in the School of Communication and Director of the Digital Democracies Institute. She is author of *Control and Freedom: Power and Paranoia in the Age of Fiber Optics* (2006), *Programmed Visions: Software and Memory* (2011), *Updating to Remain the Same: Habitual New Media* (2016), and *Discriminating Data*

(2021). She has been professor and chair of the Department of Modern Culture and Media at Brown University, where she worked for almost two decades and where she's currently a visiting professor. She has also been a visiting scholar at the Annenberg School at the University of Pennsylvania, and member of the Institute for Advanced Study (Princeton), and she has held fellowships from the Guggenheim, ACLS, American Academy of Berlin, and Radcliffe Institute for Advanced Study at Harvard.

BROOKE ERIN DUFFY is an associate professor in the Department of Communication at Cornell University. Her research interests include digital and social media industries; gender, identity, and inequality; and the impact of new technologies on creative work and labor. She is the author of *(Not) Getting Paid to Do What You Love: Gender, Social Media, and Aspirational Work* (2017); *Remake, Remodel: Women's Magazines in the Digital Age* (2013); and the forthcoming *Platforms & Cultural Production*, with Thomas Poell and David Nieborg (2022).

GANAELE LANGLOIS is associate professor in the Department of Communication Studies at York University and associate director of the Infoscape Lab. Her research revolves around media theory, digital cultures, philosophy of technology, and critical theory. She is the author of *Meaning in the Age of Social Media* (2014).

SARA MARTEL is an independent scholar and training psychotherapy student in Toronto, Ontario. Her work explores the intersections of media, culture, health, and illness. She is particularly passionate about understanding the experiential and technocultural dimensions of end-of-life, grief, and mourning.

SHANNON MATTERN is professor at the New School for Social Research. Her writing and teaching focus on media architectures and infrastructures and spatial epistemologies. She has written books about libraries, maps, and the history of urban intelligence, and she writes a column for *Places Journal*.

CAIT MCKINNEY is assistant professor in the School of Communication at Simon Fraser University. McKinney is author of *Information Activism: A Queer History of Lesbian Media Technologies* (Duke University Press, 2020). McKinney's research looks at the politics of information in queer and feminist social movements, particularly digital technologies, archiving practices, and queer media histories.

JEREMY PACKER is professor in the Institute for Communication, Culture, Information and Technology and in the Faculty of Information at the University of Toronto. He is the author or editor of seven books, including *Killer Apps: War Media Machine* (Duke University Press, 2020), a historically informed critique of the military rise of automation and AI co-authored with Joshua Reeves, and the forthcoming *The*

Prison House of the Circuit: A Media Genealogy, a multi-authored historical monograph detailing the rise of digital media governance.

CRAIG ROBERTSON is an associate professor at Northeastern University. He is the author of numerous articles and book chapters on the history of information and bureaucracy. Robertson has edited two books on media history and is the author of *The Filing Cabinet: A Vertical History of Information* and *The Passport in America*.

SARAH SHARMA is an associate professor and director of the Institute for Communication, Culture, Information and Technology at the University of Toronto. She was director of the McLuhan Centre for Culture and Technology between 2017 and 2022. She is the author of *In the Meantime: Temporality and Cultural Politics* (Duke University Press, 2014). Sarah is currently working on a new monograph about technology and the gendered politics of exit.

LADAN SIAD is a Black queer trans designer and creative technologist working at the intersections of art, design, and technology to tell narratives about the world that is possible when radical visionary change flourishes. Ladan is a natural-born collaborator and has used their skills to teach and help in many community-based projects. Siad is a self-taught and community-supported multidisciplinary creative quilting together global Black genres into a visual and audio tapestry of home everywhere. Ladan will be attending OCAD in the Digital Futures Program (MDes). Ladan holds a BA in criminology and psychology from York University.

RIANKA SINGH is an assistant professor in the department of Communication and Media Studies at York University. Rianka's research focuses on the intersection of feminist media studies, platform studies, and feminist geography. Her work has been published in *First Monday, Feminist Media Studies*, and *ADA*.

NICHOLAS TAYLOR is an associate professor in the Department of Communication at North Carolina State University. His work applies feminist and posthumanist perspectives to qualitative research on play-based media. He is the lead editor on *Masculinities in Play*, the first volume on the intersections of masculinities and games. Ongoing interests include the gendered politics of gaming's physical contexts (including man caves and gaming tournaments), and the media practices of artists who work with LEGO.

ARMOND R. TOWNS is an associate professor of Communication and Media Studies at Carleton University. His areas of study include, but are not limited to, Black studies, media theory and history, cultural studies, post- and decolonial studies, the philosophy and science of race, feminist and queer geography, and political economy. Towns is the author of *On Black Media Philosophy* (2022).

JENNIFER WEMIGWANS is a new media producer/helper, writer, and scholar specializing in the convergence between education, Indigenous knowledge, and new media technologies. Her work with diverse Indigenous Knowledge projects across Turtle Island breaks new ground in conceptualizing media studies and actively contributing to Indigenous resurgence. Dr. Wemigwans is an assistant professor in the Adult Education and Community Development program at the Ontario Institute for Studies in Education, University of Toronto.

Index

Note: Page numbers followed by *f* indicate figures.

Ahmed, Sarah, 94n10, 97n25
Alphabet, 37, 48
Amazon (corporation), 47–48, 185–86, 202, 204
Amazon (region), 70, 82; cosmologies of, 72; ecosystem of, 71, 80
Anthropocene, 81–82
architecture, 26, 38; temporal, 139
automation, 140n20, 203; 3D, 194; of gestation, 95n16
ayahuasca, 71, 80

Birch, Samuel, 23–25, 33
Black feminist studies, 25–26, 28, 30, 32–33
Black geographies, 29–30, 32, 225
Black Lives Matter, 48–49, 223; Global Network, 33, 230
blackness, 15, 28, 180, 182, 185, 190; gender and, 25–26, 30, 33
Black women, 12, 29, 31, 102, 115
Book of Negroes (Birch), 23–25, 33
Braidotti, Rosi, 97n22, 202
Brent, Linda, 26, 31–32
Brown, Henry "Box," 26, 30–32
Browne, Simone, 189, 202

Campt, Tina, 15, 182, 188
capitalism, 8, 82, 133, 167–68; consumer, 98, 107; corporate, 123, 136, 173, 184; discourses of the body in, 4; end of, 229; gender and, 121; happiness and, 94; surveillance, 46

care, 197–99
childbirth, 92n1; natural, 87
class, 1, 5, 7, 10, 56; dynamics, 40; politics of, 107; technology and, 229
Collison, Robert, 146–49, 151, 157
colonialism, 205; digital, 200–202
commodification, 27, 30–33, 76, 107
communication, 13, 27, 29–30, 32, 70; *kené* and, 72–73, 82; McLuhan and, 3; platform as, 164; sidewalks as, 40, 43; television as, 37; theory, 111; Western perspective on, 72; wires and, 52
computing, 57, 145, 148–51, 153–57, 159, 196; gender and, 14, 143, 150; processes, 147; slavery and, 228
containers, 98, 100, 102–103, 105, 107, 109–16. *See also* Tupperware
containment, 98, 100, 102–103, 107, 110–11, 113–17, 139n4, 231; media of, 14. *See also* Tupperware
cords, 6, 52, 56, 58–59, 89. *See also* wires
COVID-19, 54–55; pandemic, 43, 45, 49, 55, 223; lockdown, 41
Cowan, Ruth Schwartz, 97n21, 105, 109
curb cuts, 43, 45
curbs, 37, 45–46, 48

dexterity, 127, 131–32, 134, 137, 150
digital platforms, 15, 163–65; popular feminism and, 171–73, 231

efficiency, 115, 133, 136, 152; filing cabinets and, 120, 123, 125, 127, 132, 136, 231; of gaming consoles, 57, 60; gender and, 14, 119, 129, 131, 139; Tupperware and, 104
Ehrenfeucht, Renia, 40–42
electricity, 51–52, 68, 160, 203, 231
electronic sports (esports), 53, 57–58
Emre, Merve, 95n16, 96n18
Ernst, Wolfgang, 102, 109
Experiments in Art and Technology (E.A.T.), 152–54

Federici, Silvia, 166–67
femininity, 167, 196; domestic, 104; platform shoes and, 171–72; white middle-class, 107
feminism, 1, 6, 9, 16, 166, 203, 231; Black, 26; digital platforms and, 15, 163, 165, 173; opposition to, 66, 67n21; popular, 171–73. *See also* 3D printing: feminist theory of; planning: feminist
feminist media studies, 1, 3–4, 7–8, 10–11, 17
feminist technology studies, 121, 180
file clerks, 14, 119, 121, 125, 134
filing cabinets, 13–14, 119–33, 135f, 136–39, 140n11, 225, 231; feminism and, 6

gallows, 165–68
games, 12–13, 55, 66; Dungeons and Dragons, 152; networked, 62; video, 16, 53, 55
gaming, 52, 55, 60, 62, 194; bunkers, 59, 61f, 63; cabinets, 59, 63f, 64f; consoles, 13 (*see also* PlayStation 4; Xbox); hearths, 59, 63; setups, 57–58, 63, 65–66. *See also* electronic sports (esports); wires
gender, 3–7, 24, 55–56, 143, 167, 180, 188, 199; Black, 24–25, 31; binaries, 103; blackness and, 25–26, 30, 33; efficiency and, 14, 119; information sensibilities and, 145, 160, 231; media technology and, 12; politics, 13, 53,

65–66; roles, 100; sidewalks and, 40; technology and, 1, 10, 16–17, 26, 121, 202, 229; violence and, 43; work and, 120, 134, 137
Gitelman, Lisa, 122, 132, 156

hand hugging, 89, 93n8, 94n10
Haraway, Donna, 180–82, 202
housewives, 57, 98, 105, 107, 115, 151
humanness, 15, 27, 33–34, 181, 230

imperialism, 9, 26, 211
incubators, 6, 13–14, 87, 90–92, 93nn3–4, 93–94nn6–10, 95nn12–13, 95–97nn15–19
index cards, 6, 13–14, 133, 140n11, 143, 146
indexing, 143, 146–49, 151–53, 155–56, 159; systems, 123
indigeneity, 78, 190
Indigenous Knowledge (IK), 16, 208–10, 212–15, 217–20, 222–23
Indigenous media, 78, 82, 222; arts, 214, 217
information, 12, 52, 140n12, 146–47, 154–55, 157–58, 214, 219; age, 203; filing and, 120–21, 123, 131–33, 137, 139, 231; retrieval, 14, 148, 154–59; systems, 103, 143, 159; technology, 14–15, 121, 156, 200; transportation technologies and, 27–28; women and, 16. *See also* labor: information
information management, 14, 104, 143, 148–51, 154, 156, 159–60; cultures of, 161n26
information sensibilities, 145, 148, 151, 154–56, 159
Innis, Harold Adams, 8–9, 26–27, 69, 166

Jacobs, Jane, 5, 43, 45, 48
Jafa, Arthur, 15, 182, 187

kené, 71–76, 79–82
Kittler, Friedrich, 2, 102
Knitting Needle Computer, 14, 143, 146, 148–49, 155, 157–59, 225

labor, 190; computational, 155; containers and, 114; domestic, 14, 55, 59, 103, 110, 115; feminized, 59, 66, 103, 113; gendered, 6, 14, 114, 121, 131, 141n30, 143, 148, 152; information, 120, 131–32; management of, 122, 125; manual, 17, 127, 129, 132; market, 98; maternal, 95n16, 97n19; migration and, 189; preterm, 90; reproductive technologies and, 97n21; slavery and, 168; technological, 145; women's, 105, 115, 120, 131, 134, 150
Lewis, Sophie, 92n1, 95n16
Loukaitou-Sideris, Anastasia, 40–42

McKittrick, Katherine, 12, 29–33
Masayevsa, Victor, 211, 215
masculinity, 57, 66, 137, 154, 204
materiality, 168; of the filing cabinet, 139, 231; of information, 121; of infrastructure, 29; of sidewalks, 38; of technology, 120; of Tupperware, 107
Mattern, Shannon, 12, 140n12, 143
mechanization, 107, 120, 131, 148; of women, 172
media logics, 6; internet, 16, 208
media materialism, 121, 139
media studies, 1–3, 68, 171, 209, 218–20; decolonizing, 78, 211. *See also* feminist media studies
media technologies, 6–7, 12, 14, 24, 107, 121
media theory, 27, 30, 33, 78, 103, 109–10, 203, 210; feminist, 11; Innis's, 8; McLuhan's, 1–7, 12–13, 17, 24, 26, 163; materiality of information and, 121
#MeToo movement, 15, 163, 166, 172
Microsoft, 48; Access Computer database, 154, 156, 161n33; consoles, 53
Middle Passage, 24–25, 27–28
misfiling, 120, 125, 133–34, 136
mobility, 31, 33, 45, 104; Black, 12, 24; corporeal, 37; social, 74; upward, 136; white control of, 28
mothering, 90, 97nn19–20; attached, 96n18

multiculturalism, 76, 230
Musk, Elon, 3–4, 10, 186

Nakamura, Lisa, 148, 150
neoliberalism, 97n20; gendered, 163
neonatal intensive care unit (NICU), 92, 92n2, 93nn4–5, 93n8, 94n10, 96–97nn18–21

pace, 2, 6, 27, 52, 110
patriarchy, 7–10, 14, 17
pattern, 2, 6, 10, 27, 52, 56, 110–13; designers, 150
pedestrians, 37–38, 40, 43–44, 48
Peters, John Durham, 4, 102, 111, 116
planning, 45; feminist, 40, 46; neoliberal, 46; sidewalk, 37; urban, 39, 50n36
platforms, 56, 164–69, 173, 198, 225; digital, 15, 163–65, 171–73, 231; gaming, 60, 65; media, 11, 15, 163; sidewalks as, 40, 43, 45, 48; social media, 116–17. *See also* gallows; slave auction blocks
platform shoes, 6, 164–65, 169–73
PlayStation 4, 56, 58
power, 2, 8–9, 14, 97n22, 100, 112, 143, 187, 211, 214; analysis of, 180–81, 183, 188; cars and, 36–37; colonial, 69, 82; containment as mode of, 103; culture and, 11–12; of gaming rigs, 57, 60; gender and, 54–56; media and, 6, 68, 78; platforms and, 164, 168; platform shoes and, 171–73; structures of, 116; of the tech industry, 184; technological, 185–86; the technological and, 1, 17, 189, 205, 230; technology and, 5, 7–10; transportation technologies and, 33; white male, 13; wires and, 51–54, 56, 65; women's social, 167
power dynamics, 6, 44, 121; inequitable, 2, 13, 17; of technology, 4, 183, 199
power relations, 4, 28; colonial, 200; containment and, 103, 114–15; filing cabinets and, 121; gendered, 166; platforms and, 165; wires and, 65
pregnancy, 92n1, 96n18

Index | 261

race, 1, 5, 7, 24, 30, 107, 180–81, 186, 188, 202, 229; jokes about, 143; technology and, 8, 10; wires and, 56
racial violence, 28–30
racism, 5, 7, 9, 43, 180
refusal, 15, 182–83, 188, 210
representation, 7–9, 17, 183–86, 189, 193; gender, 137; *kené* and, 72, 80
reproduction, 14, 90–91, 95–96nn16–18; high-risk, 92n1, 95n13; of slaves, 25; social, 55, 94n10
reproductive loss, 91, 92n1, 93n4
reproductive technologies, 31, 97n22
roads, 12, 26–27, 29, 33
Russill, Chris, 113, 116

scale, 2, 6–7, 10, 27, 110–11; of containment, 113
scientific management, 122, 127, 156; of the kitchen, 104
sexism, 5, 9, 119
sexual harassment, 42–43, 166
sexuality, 1, 5, 7, 10, 121; file clerks and, 134; politics of, 107; women's, 167, 171–72
shared streets, 37, 40
Sharma, Sarah, 66, 95n16, 97n19, 105, 121, 139
Shipibo-Conibo: people, 70–71; textiles, 13, 70, 74. *See also kené*
Sidewalk Labs, 37, 40, 44–48
sidewalks, 12–13, 36–49, 230; feminism and, 6. *See also* curbs; pedestrians
Simon, Bart, 57, 62
slave auction blocks, 165, 168–69
slavery, 23–26, 28–31, 228–29
smart cities, 40, 43
social reproduction, 55; technologies of, 94n10
Sofia, Zoë, 103, 111–13
space, 8–9, 30, 69, 112, 189; Black people and, 26, 29, 32; containers and, 103, 109–10; domestic, 57, 65; filing cabinets and, 121, 123, 125; games and, 55; online 210, 212–13, 220; organization of, 12; personal, 54; platforms and, 165; of reproduction, 90; right to, 13, 78; sex in, 186; Shipibo textiles and, 80; sidewalks and, 37, 40–41, 43, 45; subjectivity and, 65; transportation and, 24; travel, 102; Tupperware and, 103–104; virtual reality (VR) and, 215, 217
space-biased media, 26–27, 166
Spillers, Hortense, 12, 24–25, 30, 32
Spivak, Gayatri, 226–29, 232n12
Sterne, Jonathan, 4, 29–30
storage, 52, 102, 104, 115, 121, 123, 129; cabinets, 140n11; critique of, 139n4; file, 139n3; information, 146, 155, 159; systems, 116. *See also* containers; index cards
surveillance, 48, 62, 165, 182; cameras, 38, 48; capitalism, 46; contractors, 49; home, 9

tactility, 154, 159, 161n24, 209
tech industry, 52, 153; culture, 9; women in, 10
technological, the, 1, 7, 9, 17, 95n15, 180; intersectionality and, 188–89; power and, 185, 189, 205, 230; prison abolitionists and, 190
techno-logics, 5–11; feminist, 17, 230; gendered, 13–14
technology, 2, 17, 100, 140n20, 190, 197–98, 229; art and, 205; audio, 57; blackness and, 26, 30, 182, 184–85, 187, 191; colonization and, 220; companies, 40, 48, 189; computing and, 155, 159; containment as, 114–15, 117; digital, 201; digital bundles and, 213; feminism and, 3, 8–10, 16, 102, 180, 189, 196, 203; filing cabinet as, 14, 121; file storage, 139n3; gender and, 10, 16, 26, 121; information, 14–15, 155–56; intersectionality and, 188; labor and, 129; materiality of, 120; media and, 199, 231; office, 136; platforms as, 167, 169; platform shoe as, 173; power and, 4–5, 7–8, 11; power analysis of, 15; push-button, 132; sex and, 172; as tool, 180–81, 183, 186–87, 189, 207; Tupper-

ware as, 98, 104, 107, 109; women of color and, 202. *See also* 3D printers; 3D printing; incubators; media technologies; reproductive technologies
television, 9, 37, 43, 59; electricity and, 51; emasculating influence of, 57; sets, 58, 89
textile, 13, 69–70, 73–77, 79–81, 150
textile, 68–69, 131, 149; feminism and, 6; Indigenous, 13, 70, 75, 77; Shipibo-Conibo, 13, 70–71, 74–82; women and, 150. See also *kené*
3D printing, 16, 192–93, 195–97, 203–204; feminist theory of, 15
3D printers, 6, 16, 193, 197, 201, 204, 225
Towns, Armond, 4, 12, 160n4
transportation, 28–29, 37, 43, 45, 52; media theory of, 12, 24–27, 29; public, 191, 231; slavery and, 30–31, 33
transportation technologies, 2, 12, 23–28, 30–33
Tupperware, 6, 13–14, 98–113, 115–16, 139n4. *See also* containment

Underground Railroad, 12, 225
Understanding Media: The Extensions of Man (McLuhan), 2, 6, 11–12, 14–16, 36, 51–52, 66, 163, 203, 226, 228

virtual reality (VR), 214–18, 223
visibility, 125, 165–69, 231; platform shoes and, 171–73; as trap, 183; wires and, 56
Viveiro de Castro, Eduardo, 72, 78, 80

Western media, 78, 80, 222
witch hunts, 166–68, 174n18
whiteness, 136, 182, 184, 188
Whitzman, Carolyn, 46, 48
Whole Earth Catalog, 152–54, 157
wires, 29, 51–53, 57, 225; gaming consoles and, 13, 53–55, 58–60, 62–63, 65–66; management of, 13, 56, 58–60, 62; NICU babies and, 89–91, 93n5. *See also* electricity; gaming; Xbox
witch hunts, 166–68, 174n18
women, 15–16; Black, 12, 29, 31, 102, 115, 230; clerical workers, 137; of color, 189, 196, 200, 202; computers and, 160; dominant media and, 69; ectogenetic gestation and, 92n1; fab labs and, 195–96; filing and, 119–20, 129, 131–32, 134, 136; Haraway and white, 180; indexing and, 151, 161n26; intersectionality and, 188; *kené* and, 71; lactating, 145; in McLuhan's work, 5, 164; reproduction and, 95n16, 96n18; reproductive technologies and, 97n21; sex in space and, 186; Shipibo, 74–76; shoes and, 171–73 (*see also* platform shoes); sidewalks and, 42–43, 48; slave auctions and, 169; smart home technologies and, 114; technology and, 10–11, 16, 190, 196, 202; textile workers, 150; Tupperware and, 105, 107; witch hunts and, 166–68, 174n18
women's work, 107, 109, 129, 131, 149, 151, 154
Wynter, Sylvia, 15, 181–82

Xbox 360, 53, 58; Game Pass, 55

www.ingramcontent.com/pod-product-compliance
Lightning Source LLC
Chambersburg PA
CBHW050213240426
43671CB00013B/2315